The Beatles and Philosophy

T0151183

Popular Culture and Philosophy®
Series Editor: George A. Reisch
(Series Editor for this volume was William Irwin)

VOLUME 1
Seinfeld and Philosophy: A Book about Everything and Nothing (2000)
Edited by William Irwin

VOLUME 2
The Simpsons and Philosophy: The D'oh! of Homer (2001) Edited by William Irwin, Mark T. Conard, and Aeon J. Skoble

VOLUME 3
The Matrix and Philosophy: Welcome to the Desert of the Real (2002) Edited by William Irwin

VOLUME 4
Buffy the Vampire Slayer and Philosophy: Fear and Trembling in Sunnydale (2003) Edited by James B. South

VOLUME 5
The Lord of the Rings and Philosophy: One Book to Rule Them All (2003) Edited by Gregory Bassham and Eric Bronson

VOLUME 6
Baseball and Philosophy: Thinking Outside the Batter's Box (2004) Edited by Eric Bronson

VOLUME 7
The Sopranos and Philosophy: I Kill Therefore I Am (2004) Edited by Richard Greene and Peter Vernezze

VOLUME 8
Woody Allen and Philosophy: You Mean My Whole Fallacy Is Wrong? (2004) Edited by Mark T. Conard and Aeon J. Skoble

VOLUME 9
Harry Potter and Philosophy: If Aristotle Ran Hogwarts (2004) Edited by David Baggett and Shawn E. Klein

VOLUME 10
Mel Gibson's Passion and Philosophy: The Cross, the Questions, the Controversy (2004) Edited by Jorge J.E. Gracia

VOLUME 11
More Matrix and Philosophy: Revolutions and Reloaded Decoded (2005) Edited by William Irwin

VOLUME 12
Star Wars and Philosophy: More Powerful than You Can Possibly Imagine (2005) Edited by Jason T. Eberl and Kevin S. Decker

VOLUME 13
Superheroes and Philosophy: Truth, Justice, and the Socratic Way (2005) Edited by Tom Morris and Matt Morris

VOLUME 14
The Atkins Diet and Philosophy: Chewing the Fat with Kant and Nietzsche (2005) Edited by Lisa Heldke, Kerri Mommer, and Cynthia Pineo

VOLUME 15
The Chronicles of Narnia and Philosophy: The Lion, the Witch, and the Worldview (2005) Edited by Gregory Bassham and Jerry L. Walls

VOLUME 16
Hip Hop and Philosophy: Rhyme 2 Reason (2005) Edited by Derrick Darby and Tommie Shelby

VOLUME 17
Bob Dylan and Philosophy: It's Alright Ma (I'm Only Thinking) (2006) Edited by Peter Vernezze and Carl J. Porter

VOLUME 18
Harley-Davidson and Philosophy: Full-Throttle Aristotle (2006) Edited by Bernard E. Rollin, Carolyn M. Gray, Kerri Mommer, and Cynthia Pineo

VOLUME 19
Monty Python and Philosophy: Nudge Nudge, Think Think! (2006) Edited by Gary L. Hardcastle and George A Reisch

VOLUME 20
Poker and Philosophy: Pocket Rockets and Philosopher Kings (2006) Edited by Eric Bronson

VOLUME 21
U2 and Philosophy: How to Decipher an Atomic Band (2006) Edited by Mark A. Wrathall

VOLUME 22
The Undead and Philosophy: Chicken Soup for the Soulless (2006) Edited by Richard Greene and K. Silem Mohammad

VOLUME 23
James Bond and Philosophy: Questions Are Forever (2006) Edited by Jacob M. Held and James B. South

VOLUME 24
Bullshit and Philosophy: Guaranteed to Get Perfect Results Every Time (2006) Edited by Gary L. Hardcastle and George A. Reisch

VOLUME 25
The Beatles and Philosophy: Nothing You Can Think that Can't Be Thunk (2006) Edited by Michael Baur and Steven Baur

IN PREPARATION:

South Park and Philosophy (2007) Edited by Richard Hanley

Hitchcock and Philosophy (2007) Edited by David Baggett and William Drumin

The Grateful Dead and Philosophy (2007) Edited by Steven Gimbel

Popular Culture and Philosophy®

The Beatles and Philosophy

Nothing You Can Think that Can't Be Thunk

Edited by

MICHAEL BAUR

and

STEVEN BAUR

OPEN COURT
Chicago and La Salle, Illinois

Volume 25 in the series, Popular Culture and Philosophy®

To order books from Open Court, call 1-800-815-2280, or visit our website at www.opencourtbooks.com.

Open Court Publishing Company is a division of Carus Publishing Company.

Library of Congress Cataloging-in-Publication Data

The Beatles and philosophy : nothing you can think that can't be thunk / edited by Michael Baur and Steven Baur.
     p. cm. — (Popular culture and philosophy ; 25)
     Summary: "A collection of essays explores philosophical aspects of the Beatles' music, lyrics, and political activities. Topics addressed include: skepticism and epistemology, the philosophy of love, altered consciousness and drug culture, and Marxism and social philosophy" — Provided by publisher.
  Includes bibliographical references and index.
  ISBN-13: 978-0-8126-9606-6 (trade pbk. : alk. paper)
  ISBN-10: 0-8126-9606-9 (trade pbk. : alk. paper)
  1. Beatles. 2. Music and philosophy. I. Baur, Michael. II. Baur, Steven, 1966-
ML421.B4B4134 2006
782.42166092'2—dc22
                                   2006028299

Contents

Hey Dude! Take a Beatles Song and Make It Philosophical   ix

I
Nothing Is Real: The Beatles on Knowledge and Reality   1

1. That Is I Think I Disagree: Skepticism and Epistemology in the Beatles
   DAVID DETMER   3

2. And the Time Will Come When You See We're All One: The Beatles and Idealistic Monism
   MICHAEL BAUR   13

II
The Love You Make: The Beatles and the Philosophy of Love   25

3. All You Need Is Love: Hegel, Love, and Community
   JACOB M. HELD   27

4. All My Loving: Paul McCartney's Philosophy of Love
   ROBERT ARP   37

III
Dear Prudence, Justice, and Virtue: The Beatles and Moral Philosophy   47

5. Getting Better: The Beatles and Virtue Ethics
   JAMES S. SPIEGEL   49

6. She's a Woman: The Beatles and the Feminist Ethic
of Care
PEGGY J. BOWERS   59

IV
Why Don't We Do It in the Marketplace?
The Beatles and Social Philosophy   71

7. You Say that You've Got Everything You Want:
The Beatles and the Critique of Consumer Culture
SCOTT CALEF   73

8. You Say You Want a Revolution: The Beatles and Marx
STEVEN BAUR   87

V
Think for Yourself: The Beatles and
Existential Philosophy   107

9. Nothing's Gonna Change My World: The Beatles and
the Struggle Against Inauthenticity
ERIN KEALEY   109

10. George on Being and Somethingness
MICHAEL H. HOFFHEIMER and JOSEPH A. HOFFHEIMER   125

VI
They All Want to Change Your Head:
The Beatles and Consciousness-Raising   137

11. Realizing It's All Within Yourself: The Beatles as Surrogate
Gurus of Eastern Philosophy
RONALD LEE ZIGLER   139

12. I'd Love to Turn You On: The Beatles and the Ethics of
Altered States
JERE O'NEILL SURBER   151

VII

We Can Think It Out: The Beatles on the Practice of Philosophy   163

13. But I Can Show You a Better Time: The Beatles and
    the Practice of Philosophy
    JAMES B. SOUTH   165

14. Take a Sad Song and Make It Better: The Beatles and
    Postmodern Thought
    JAMES CROOKS   175

VIII

Zarathustra's Silver Hammer: The Beatles and Nietzsche   187

15. Fixing Metaphysical Holes: The Beatles, Nietzsche, and
    the Problem of Incompleteness
    RICK MAYOCK   189

16. The Beatles as Nietzsche's Music-Playing Socrates
    PAUL SWIFT   203

IX

Number Nine, Number Nine, Number Nine: The Play of Language and the Play of Differences in the Beatles   217

17. And of Course Henry the Horse Dances the Waltz:
    Lennon's Lyrical Language Games
    ALEXANDER R. EODICE   219

18. Four Play With a Difference
    RICHARD FALKENSTEIN and JOHN ZEIS   229

Revolvers: Beatle Album Discography   245

Not a Second Time: Beatles Covers   261

Evil All—It's Siluap! Those Hidden Clues   275

The Fools on the Hill   285

ABCD, Can I Bring Some Philosophers to Tea?   291

Hey Dude! Take a Beatles Song and Make it Philosophical

The Beatles did not regard themselves as philosophers, which—apart from being a good career choice—raises serious questions about whether it really makes sense to write a philosophical book about them. The Fab Four of the 1960s were not the Philosophical Four, and the Fab Four of Philosophy (Plato, Aristotle, Kant, and Hegel) never played in a rock band together.

At first glance, allowing philosophers to talk about the Beatles is about as wise as allowing the Blue Meanies to take over Pepperland. So why do it? But then again, why not? There's a humorous old anecdote (well, at least it's humorous to philosophers) about a businessman who—frustrated with a philosopher's reluctance to give simple and straightforward answers—finally asked, "Why do you philosophers always answer questions with more questions?" And the philosopher's reply (no doubt designed to confound the businessman even more) was to answer with yet another question: "Why not?" The implicit lesson of this anecdote applies also to the present book about the Beatles and philosophy. If it is possible to ask, "Why write a book about the Beatles and philosophy?" then it is equally possible to ask "Why not?" And there is no good reason to think that the burden of proof should automatically be placed on the person being asked to explain "Why a book about the Beatles and philosophy?," rather than on the person being asked, "Why not?"

It can be argued, furthermore, that any attempt to show that it is impossible to think philosophically about the Beatles would be self-undermining (an argument designed to show that an opponent's claims are self-undermining is what philosophers call a "retorsion argument"). A retorsion argument can be used against anyone claiming that the work of the Beatles is not suitable content for philosophy, and for the following reason. As soon as one has raised the question of whether or not the music of the Beatles is suitable content for philosophy, one has already begun to philosophize. That's because the question of what counts or does not count as fitting content for "philosophical enquiry" is itself a *philosophical* question: one cannot address the question without thinking philosophically about it. And since the very question already causes us to think philosophically about whether or not the Beatles are a suitable topic for philosophical discussion, we already have preliminary proof that one *can* think philosophically about the Beatles (even if one's original aim was to show that the Beatles do *not* provide suitable content for philosophical discussion).

According to the retorsion argument suggested above, as soon as one has begun to wonder whether it's possible to think philosophically about the Beatles, one has already begun to think philosophically about the Beatles (no matter how minimal this philosophical content may be). Of course, this retorsion argument says very little about the specific philosophical content of the Beatles' work. Specific ideas and developed theories about the Beatles and philosophy can be found in the eighteen chapters that make up the remainder of this book. But even this brief introduction on the *possibility* of thinking philosophically about the Beatles has had a positive result. For as we have seen, the very question about whether it is possible to think philosophically about the Beatles has already induced us to start thinking philosophically: almost without notice, the Magical Mystery Tour has come to take us away. Enjoy the ride!

Acknowledgments for Permissions

The Editors acknowledge permission from Sony/ATV Music Publishing to use the following songs in this volume.

The Word. Copyright 1965 (Renewed) Sony/ATV Tunes LLC. All rights administered by Sony/ATV Music Publishing, 8 Music Square West, Nashville, TN 37203. All rights reserved. Used by permission.

Nowhere Man. Copyright 1965 (Renewed) Sony/ATV Tunes LLC. All rights administered by Sony/ATV Music Publishing, 8 Music Square West, Nashville, TN 37203. All rights reserved. Used by permission.

I Am the Walrus. Copyright 1967 Sony/ATV Tunes LLC. All rights administered by Sony/ATV Music Publishing, 8 Music Square West, Nashville, TN 37203. All rights reserved. Used by permission.

Tomorrow Never Knows. Copyright 1966 Sony/ATV Tunes LLC. All rights administered by Sony/ATV Music Publishing 8 Music Square West Nashville, TN 37203. All rights reserved. Used by permission.

Strawberry Fields Forever. Copyright 1967 (Renewed) Sony/ATV Songs LLC. All rights administered by Sony/ATV Music Publishing, 8 Music Square West, Nashville, TN 37203. All rights reserved. Used by permission.

She Said She Said. Copyright 1966 (Renewed) Sony/ATV Songs LLC. All rights administered by Sony/ATV Music Publishing, 8 Music Square West, Nashville, TN 37203. All rights reserved. Used by permission.

Across the Universe. Copyright 1970 (Renewed) Sony/ATV Tunes LLC. All rights administered by Sony/ATV Music Publishing, 8 Music Square West, Nashville, TN 37203. All rights reserved. Used by permission.

I

Nothing Is Real

The Beatles
on Knowledge
and Reality

1

That Is I Think I Disagree: Skepticism and Epistemology in the Beatles

DAVID DETMER

The Beatles' early songs, like most pop songs of their time, dealt mainly in superficial clichés about love and romance. But as the Beatles matured their lyrical content deepened considerably. Inspired in part by the turbulent cultural changes of the 1960s and also by the spirit of experimentation exemplified by the best of their songwriting peers (most notably Bob Dylan), they began by the mid-sixties to write songs about fundamental political, social, and philosophical ideas. Many of these songs are at least in part about knowledge. They discuss the nature and value of knowledge, and consider the ways in which knowledge might be attained. These concerns are central to epistemology, one of the main branches of philosophy.

While it would be an exaggeration to say that the Beatles present in their songs a clear, coherent, fully worked-out theory of knowledge—they were musicians, after all, and not philosophers—two points recur frequently and consistently throughout those of their songs that touch on epistemological concerns. The first point is simply that it matters greatly what one believes. More specifically, it is important to believe what is really true, and to reject lies, delusions, and other falsehoods. Though such a claim may appear rather obvious and trivial, it is in fact controversial and widely rejected. Many people take the position that it is perfectly fine to believe whatever one wants, and to embrace certain beliefs because, for example, they are comforting or allow one to get along well with others, without concerning oneself much with the issue of their truth.[1] But the Beatles firmly reject such a strategy. In "Within You, Without You," for instance, they harshly condemn those who take refuge by hiding themselves behind a "wall of illusion," and who consequently never see the truth. The Beatles suggest that those who live this way experience lives devoid of value and meaning. And then it is "far too late" when they die, having never grappled with the most important questions in their lives.

The second recurring point is that the quest for truth is as difficult as it is valuable. Things are often not as they seem, and widely-held beliefs are frequently mistaken. Nor are experts, gurus, or others who claim to offer special knowledge or insight generally reliable. Accordingly, it is appropriate for the seeker after truth to develop a cautious and skeptical attitude. The Beatles do not go so far as to affirm skepticism in its strict, global sense—the thesis that knowledge is impossible to achieve.[2] Instead they endorse a more limited or moderate kind of skepticism. A skeptic in this sense is someone with a disbelieving, questioning disposition—a person who demands compelling evidence before believing a claim or theory. Since such evidence is often lacking, a skeptic in this moderate sense, while not denying that we are justified in some of our knowledge claims, tends to withhold assent from many beliefs that are widely held by others. Let's look at some of the Beatles' reasons for recommending such a stance.

---

[1] Walter Truett Anderson defends "a constructivist world-view," which he says "is present" whenever "a person chooses to live within a belief system for the simple comfort it brings" (*Reality Isn't What It Used to Be* [San Francisco: Harper and Row, 1990], p. 268). A classic statement of a qualified version of this thesis is William James's famous lecture, "The Will to Believe," in his *The Will to Believe and Other Essays in Popular Philosophy* (New York: Dover, 1956), pp. 1–31. There's no shortage of introductory philosophy students who defend a similar position without the slightest prompting.

[2] It's fortunate that they do not, since there are many compelling reasons to reject such a thesis. In the first place, one cannot claim, without contradicting oneself, to know that global skepticism is true. After all, if knowledge is unattainable, no one can know the skeptical thesis itself to be true. Nor, for the same reason, can any of the reasons advanced in support of such skepticism be known to be true. Finally, global skepticism asks us to accept the rather implausible claim that we don't really know things that we seem clearly to know, such as that giraffes are taller than ants, that there are more than four people alive in the world right now, and that it's impossible for a human being to eat five hundred thousand television sets in a single sitting. To reject the claim that we can know these things one would need reasons for doing so that are even more obvious, evident, and compelling than is that claim itself. It is unlikely that such reasons can be found.

The Limitations of the Senses

One of the most important and influential theories of knowledge is called "empiricism." Empiricism holds that all knowledge comes from sense experience. On this view, the only way we can learn truths about the world is by consulting the evidence given to us by our senses of sight, hearing, smell, taste, and touch.

The Beatles do not challenge the claim that we sometimes can acquire knowledge in this way. For example, in "Savoy Truffle," the subject of the song (reported to be George Harrison's friend, the guitarist Eric Clapton), enjoys eating chocolates, blissfully unaware of their damaging effects on his teeth. Eventually, however, when cavities become evident," he learns through painful experience that he has eaten too many chocolates, is now developing tooth decay, and will likely need to have his teeth pulled out.

But the Beatles also note two limitations of empiricism. One is that sense experience is sometimes illusory. In "I'm a Loser," for example, we are told the story of a man who deceives others. Though he is sad and sees himself as a loser, he plays the clown, hiding his sadness behind a cheerful mask. Repeatedly he warns us of the often illusory nature of appearances. Indeed, many things are not what they appear to be. Our senses sometimes deceive us.

The other limitation of empiricism is that the information provided by the senses, even when it is not inaccurate or deceptive, may well be incomplete. Perhaps there are truths to be learned that cannot be accessed by means of the senses. The limitation of sight, then, is simply that there is "nothing you can see that isn't shown."[3]

To compensate for these limitations, it's advisable to check perceptions against one another to try to determine whether or not the perceptual information one is receiving is coherent. It's also important to bring other resources, such as thought or reason, to bear on the accuracy of the testimony of the senses. If you "see" a hippopotamus sitting contentedly on the wing of the jet aircraft you're flying in, you can probably figure out lots of reasons why it is highly unlikely that you're seeing things

---

[3] In "Baby, You're a Rich Man" we are told that we can see "nothing that doesn't show."

accurately. Finally, it's important to supplement the data of
sense experience with those of experience more broadly con-
strued (for example, moral and aesthetic experience—you don't
literally "see" or hear the cruelty or injustice of an action, or the
poignance of a sad story) and of thought.

The Danger of Self-Deception

Another reason to adopt moderate skepticism concerns the very
real danger that we might be deceiving ourselves in our beliefs,
even when we think our beliefs are based on sound evidence.
One way in which this can happen is well captured by a lyric
from "Nowhere Man." We are told that the Nowhere Man is
blind because he "just sees what he wants to see." To some
degree or another, probably all of us suffer from this problem,
a point that the Beatles note by saying of the Nowhere Man,
"isn't he a bit like you and me?" People tend to notice those
cases in their perceptual environment that conform to their
beliefs, and simply not to notice cases that stand as evidence
against those beliefs. This perceptual bias is called "the fallacy
of positive instances." It is one of the psychological mechanisms
by which ethnic, racial, and other kinds of ugly prejudices are
reinforced. For example, many older adults in the 1960s held
bigoted views regarding young long-haired males who admired
the music of the Beatles. The older bigots tended to lump the
younger Beatles fans together, branding them as "hippies" and
regarding them as ignorant, drug-addicted idlers. Those who
held such views could easily sustain them by simple means of
selective perception. They took note of those individuals (and
there were many) who fit the stereotype; but when confronted
with long-haired Beatles fans who were hard-working, well-
educated, and responsible (and who showed no evidence of
being drug users), they seldom thought, "say, there's a coun-
terexample to my theory."

Such self-deception is further facilitated by the fact that much
of the evidence in our perceptual field is vague or ambiguous
and stands in need of interpretation. Thus, not only do we
notice the clear cases that support our views while neglecting
those clear instances that undermine them (the fallacy of positive instances), so do we also interpret unclear cases so that they
reinforce our favorite views (this might be called "subjective val-

idation.") Thus, if our theory is that people of Italian descent, uniquely, are gangsters, we will interpret the unclear conduct of Italians in such a way as to implicate them in racketeering while interpreting the similarly unclear conduct of other persons in an entirely different manner.

To give one final example of these psychological mechanisms by which we "just see what we want to see," consider belief in the predictive accuracy of astrological horoscopes. Such belief is typically sustained both by noticing the successful predictions and failing to notice the unsuccessful ones (the fallacy of positive instances) and by retroactively interpreting the vague predictions in such a way as to render them successful (subjective validation).

To counteract this tendency, it's useful to make a habit of asking oneself what would count as evidence against one's views, and then to seek out such evidence. Also, when performing a test of one's convictions (such as that predictions in horoscopes are uncannily accurate), it is helpful to formulate ahead of time just what sort of result will count for, and what against, those convictions.

Against Following the Crowd

But how can we overcome these personal biases and limitations in the area of belief? One popular strategy is that of following the crowd, of abandoning one's own judgment in favor of thinking and believing as others do.

One of the many problems with this approach is suggested by these lines from "Strawberry Fields Forever": "No one I think is in my tree. I mean it must be high or low." John Lennon reports that what he "was trying to say in that line is 'Nobody seems to be as hip as me, therefore I must be crazy or a genius.'"[4] Thus, in the song Lennon expresses his feelings of alienation, of not fitting in, of being an outsider to "normal" society. While such outsiders might, as he acknowledges, be "lower" than the rest of society (those who are mentally ill, or extraordinarily stupid or ignorant, are likely to hold beliefs that are less

---

[4] John Lennon, interviewed in David Sheff, *All We Are Saying: The Last Major Interview with John Lennon and Yoko Ono* (New York: St. Martin's Griffin, 2000), p. 157.

in tune with the truth than are those of most people), they might also be higher. And it is not only those who are intellectually gifted, but also those who are merely unusually scrupulous and skeptical, in the modest sense that the Beatles recommend, who can surpass the general public in terms of the accuracy and truthfulness of their beliefs. It would be a grave mistake for such individuals to renounce their own convictions in favor of those of the masses. Indeed, why should any of us set our sights so low? When one is trying to develop any skill, playing basketball, for example, one's aim is not to play as the average person does, but rather to play well, as well as one possibly can. One emulates great players, not the average player one encounters at the local playground. Similarly, our aim in the realm of ideas should be to think well, rather than merely to meet the uninspiring standard set by the majority. True, in comparison to the arduous task of thinking for yourself, the strategy of letting others think for you is simple—"Living is easy with eyes closed." But the result, alas, is that you end up "misunderstanding all you see."

Trouble with Gurus

If following the crowd is not a good idea, perhaps following leaders—experts, gurus, those who are on a "higher" plane—will work better. The Beatles tried this strategy, but found it wanting. The most famous instance was their brief flirtation with the Maharishi Mahesh Yogi. The Beatles, following Harrison's lead, had traveled to India to study with him. Lennon quickly became disillusioned, and suspected the Maharishi of being a fraud. He subsequently wrote "Sexy Sadie" about him, explaining, "I copped out and wouldn't write 'Maharishi, what have you done, you made a fool of everyone.'"[5]

Lennon's skeptical cast of mind is revealed in his account of the Beatles' departure from the Maharishi's ashram. When the Maharishi asked why the Beatles were leaving, Lennon replied, "'Well if you're so cosmic, you'll know why'. He was always intimating, and there were all his right hand men intimating that he

---

[5] Lennon, interviewed in Jann S. Wenner, *Lennon Remembers* (New York: Verso, 2000), p. 27. For those unfamiliar with the song, the actual lyric is, "Sexy Sadie, what have you done, you made a fool of everyone."

did miracles. He said, 'I don't know why, you must tell me.' And I just kept saying 'You know why'—and he gave me a look like, 'I'll kill you, bastard.' He gave me such a look, and I knew then when he looked at me, because I'd called his bluff."[6]

Lennon had a similar falling out with the psychologist Arthur Janov, whose famous "primal scream therapy" he had undergone in about 1970. When asked, ten years later, whether he still took that therapy, Lennon replied, "Are you kidding? No, I'm not that stupid" (*All We Are Saying*, p. 124). But then he offered a somewhat gentler response: "At first I was bitter about Maharishi being human and bitter about Janov being human. Well, I'm not bitter anymore. They're human and I'm only thinking what a dummy I was, you know" (*All We Are Saying*, p. 128).

So one problem with the strategy of following leaders is that the "leaders" are as human and fallible as we are. While some of them are as knowledgeable and honest as they are advertised to be, others are utterly ordinary, and still others are incompetents or charlatans. Thus, the strategy of turning to experts for relief from the burden of deciding what to believe is rendered pointless, since that burden is not simply removed but rather replaced by a different one, that of trying to figure out which purported expert is genuinely reliable. Thus, if your reason for subordinating your own judgment about X to that of an expert on the subject is that you want to believe what's true about X, it's only reasonable to do so if you are more competent to determine both that a given purported expert really is knowledgeable about X and that he or she can be counted on to communicate with you honestly about the subject than you are to evaluate the evidence and arguments concerning X yourself. To be sure, this

---

[6] *Lennon Remembers.*, pp. 27–28. According to Paul Horn, an American flutist who was a witness to these events, John was "always sceptical about anything until it had been proven to him" (Steve Turner, *A Hard Day's Write* [New York: HarperPerennial, 1994], p. 167. Indeed, a little more than a year later the founder of the Hare Krishna movement, Swami Bhaktivedanta, visited Lennon and his wife, Yoko Ono, at their home. He urged them to join his group, and warned them against receiving mantras from the Maharishi and other rivals of his, since such mantras, not having passed through "the proper channel" may "not really be spiritual." John challenged the Swami: "How would you know anyway?" The swami responded that he was "a member of an authorized line of disciple succession." But John's skepticism remained undiminished: "Who says who's actually in the line of descent? I mean, it's just like royalty" (Jon Wiener, *Come Together: John Lennon in His Time* [Urbana: University of Illinois Press, 1991], p. 101).

tough standard is often met, and accordingly it probably is rational for most of us to rely on experts in certain limited areas of our lives. I, for example, know so little about automobile mechanics and dentistry that I would undoubtedly make a mess of things if I were to try to figure out myself what is the cause when something goes wrong with my car or my teeth. It makes more sense for me to use whatever resources I might be able to command in figuring out which of the local mechanics and dentists are especially good, and then relying (skeptically and critically, of course) on their judgments about these matters. But when it comes to questions that I really care about, it is better to investigate them personally, provided that I am competent to do so.

"Think for Yourself": It's Your Life

But the most compelling reasons for engaging in independent, critical thought have little to do with concerns about the reliability of experts. Consider these comments of Lennon's, from an interview he gave shortly before his death: "Don't follow leaders . . . leaders is what we don't need . . . we can have people that we admire . . . We can have examples . . . But leaders is what we don't need . . ." (*All We Are Saying*, p. 19) "The idea of leadership is a false god . . . Following is not what it's about . . ." (*All We Are Saying*, p. 37). "It's quite possible to do anything, but not if you put in on the leaders . . . Don't expect Carter or Reagan or John Lennon or Yoko Ono or Bob Dylan or Jesus Christ to come and do it for you. You have to do it yourself" (*All We Are Saying*, p. 131). Notice that his point is not that all "leaders" are bad people, but rather that there's something wrong, in principle, with following leaders: "You have to do it yourself." What might he mean by that?

While it might be fine for me to let someone else extract my wisdom teeth for me or fix my car for me, it would be a disaster for me to let someone else decide for me how I should live, or determine my values and priorities for me, or develop my worldview for me. These things I must do for myself, not necessarily because no one else could possibly do it better, but rather because I wouldn't be living my life if I let someone else do these things for me. Thinking for oneself about such fundamental issues is a necessary part of maturing into an independent, autonomous person.

This I take also to be the fundamental message of Lennon's much misunderstood solo song, "God." The highlight of this composition is its litany of things, concepts, and people for which Lennon professes his disbelief. The list includes magic, I-Ching, Bible, Tarot, Hitler, Jesus, Kennedy, Buddha, mantra, Gita, yoga, kings, Elvis, Zimmerman [Bob Dylan's original last name], and Beatles. He concludes, "I just believe in me, Yoko and me, and that's reality."

Some interpret this song as an arrogant, cynical statement that all of the entities singled out for disbelief are fraudulent or worthless, and that only Lennon and Ono, whose greatness out-shines all of them, are genuinely worthy of belief. But I think Lennon's point is merely that you have to live your own life and think for yourself. At best, perhaps you can find a partner will-ing to join his or her life with yours (hence the "Yoko and me" line). As for the others, they can provide ideas to weigh and to consider, and some of them may even provide inspiration. But there's no evading your own responsibility for choosing how to live your own life. I'm sure that the author of this song would have no objection to your adding, if you were to sing the song, "I don't believe in Lennon, I just believe in me."

We'd All Love to See the Plan: The Ethics of Belief

Independent, critical thought is crucially important for one's development as a mature, autonomous person. But it should also be noted that the goal of such thinking is truth, and not, for example, the achievement of one's own personal popularity or comfort. One reason why this is so is that other people are much more likely to be harmed by my false beliefs than by my true ones. If I am a brain surgeon, I am more likely to help my patients if I operate on the basis of true information about the brain than if I carry around with me many fundamental miscon-ceptions; if you wish to listen to "A Day in the Life," and seek my help in finding it, your desire will be satisfied more quickly if I have a correct understanding of the Beatles' discography and direct you to *Sgt. Pepper's Lonely Hearts Club Band* than you will if I send you in search of *Rubber Soul;* if you are a person of a race or ethnicity other than mine, you will be better off in your dealings with me if I do not subscribe to ignorant prejudices and stereotypes regarding matters of race and ethnicity than if I do; and so on indefinitely. Consequently, insofar as I have an ethical duty to help those I can, or at least not to hurt them, a good case can be made that I have a duty to strive to believe what is true and to avoid believing falsehoods. Accordingly, I have a duty to examine evidence and arguments carefully before endorsing any claim, and to withhold my assent from claims that fail to pass muster. In short, I have an ethical duty to adopt a moderately skeptical stance. As the Beatles put it in "Revolution," "You say you've got a real solution. Well, you know, we'd all love to see the plan."

2

And the Time Will Come When You See We're All One: The Beatles and Idealistic Monism

MICHAEL BAUR

This book brings together philosophy and the Beatles, or—more precisely—it considers the work of the Beatles from a philosophical point of view. But this is not meant to imply that the Beatles *intended* to be philosophical, or that the *content* of their work is overtly philosophical in any obvious sense. In fact, there are good reasons to think of the Beatles' attitudes—and the attitudes conveyed indirectly through their work—as rather anti-philosophical.

Paul McCartney once remarked—no doubt with tongue planted firmly in cheek—that "Love Me Do" was the Beatles' greatest "philosophical song."[1] And correspondingly, John Lennon was well-known for his deliberate insertion of nonsense lyrics into Beatles songs, for the sole purpose of confounding those who thought that they could find deeper meaning in the work of the Beatles. Referring to his song, "Glass Onion," Lennon remarked: "I was just having a laugh, because there had been so much gobbledeegook written about *Sgt. Pepper*. People were saying, 'Play it backwards while standing on your head, and you'll get a secret message. . . .' So this was just my way of saying, 'You are all full of shit'" (*Beatlesongs*, p. 225).

But in spite of their lack of interest in traditional philosophy and their explicit disavowals about the deeper meaning of their songs, there are also good reasons to approach and interpret the

---

[1] Quoted in William J. Dowlding, ed., *Beatlesongs* (New York: Simon and Schuster, 1989), p. 33.

Beatles and their work from a philosophical point of view. In his *Playboy* interview from September of 1980, John praised Paul for the philosophical significance of the song, "The End," which appeared on the *Abbey Road* album: "That's Paul again. . . . He had a line in it—'The love you take is equal to the love you make'—which is a very cosmic, philosophical line. Which again proves that if [Paul] wants to, he can think" (*Beatlesongs*, p. 292). And in a similar vein, Paul revealed in an interview that Beatles songs are *meant* to be interpreted from different per-spectives and on different levels: "You put your own meaning at your own level to our songs, and that's what's great about them" (*Beatlesongs*, p. 143). Of course, there are many things that are "great" about Beatles songs; but one of the great things—certainly for those who want to be thoughtful and reflective about popular culture—is that they can be interpreted philosophically and thus appreciated in light of philosophical ideas and theories. One such theory is what might be called "idealistic monism."

In general, monism is the philosophical view that all reality is a single, unified whole and that all existing things are modes or expressions of a single, underlying essence or substance. Idealistic monism is a specific version of monism. According to idealistic monism, all existing things are modes or expressions of a single essence or substance which is essentially mental or spiritual in nature (thus idealistic monism is opposed to materi-alistic monism, according to which all existing things are modes or expressions of some underlying material substance). Many Beatles songs and musical gestures reflect a commitment to a form of idealistic monism—even if this commitment is not explicitly stated by the Beatles themselves.

By interpreting the Beatles in light of idealistic monism, we may learn a lesson not only about the Beatles, but also—more generally—about the relationship between philosophy and pop-ular culture. For philosophy can shed light on popular culture by articulating some of the more interesting and thought-pro-voking ideas often hidden or embedded within popular culture; and conversely, popular culture can facilitate the practice of phi-losophy by providing a medium through which some of philos-ophy's more relevant and intuitive claims might be illustrated. A good model for bringing together philosophy and popular culture in this way is furnished by Hegel's distinction between "observing" and "observed" consciousness.[2]

"Observing consciousness" is the consciousness of the philosophically-minded observer who "looks on" as a particular way of life or particular form of ordinary consciousness ("observed consciousness") goes about its affairs in an unreflective way. Often, this ordinary, observed consciousness lacks the theoretical perspective or conceptual framework for giving an adequate, accurate account of itself, and so the philosophical, "observing consciousness" may be in a position to assist ordinary consciousness in giving an account of itself. That is, the philosophical observer may be in a position to provide the conceptual tools or theoretical framework that ordinary (observed) consciousness needs, but otherwise lacks, for explaining its own beliefs and commitments.

A small child (like observed consciousness) may benefit from the conceptual tools available to a parent (observing consciousness), but not yet available to the child himself. The child may crave the loving attention of his parents; but even though he wants such attention, the child may not know how to *explain* that he wants this attention. And so instead of asking nicely for the desired attention, the child may throw a temper tantrum. On a certain level, the child undoubtedly *knows* what he wants, for he will glow with delight just as soon as he receives the desired attention; but he does not know how to *explain* what he wants, and so he might need the help of others (such as parents) who possess a different vocabulary, in order to give an adequate explanation of what he wants.

In a similar vein, those who produce the artifacts of popular culture (like the Beatles and other musicians) may know a thing or two about philosophically relevant ideas; but they may lack the relevant philosophical tools for *explaining* such ideas in a clear and compelling way. To make the same point in terms used by the Beatles themselves: ordinary, non-philosophical consciousness may very well "want to tell you" since it is brimming with "things to say," but it may be at a loss for the right words until it gets a little help from its friends (philosophy).

---

[2] For more on this distinction, see Hegel's "Introduction" to the *Phenomenology of Spirit* (New York: Oxford University Press, 1977), pp. 46–57.

Much of the Beatles' work can be understood as concerning itself with the claims of "idealistic monism." The Beatles did not espouse idealism or monism in any well-developed, explicitly philosophical way, but they said enough in their works to make clear that they were concerned with the sorts of questions and quandaries that "idealistic monism" is designed to address. Idealistic monism is the view that all existing things are modes or expressions of single essence or substance which is essentially mental or spiritual in nature. Now idealistic monism can be understood as both a metaphysical theory (a theory about *being*, or about what exists in reality) as well as an epistemological theory (a theory about *knowledge*, or about how we might *know* what exists in reality). Of course, metaphysical theories often imply certain epistemological views, and (conversely) epistemological theories often imply certain metaphysical views. Thus if one is (metaphysically) a materialist (that is, if one holds that the only thing that exists in reality is matter, or material things), then one cannot consistently hold (in the realm of epistemology) that immaterial operations are involved in our knowing.

In their work, the Beatles make clear that they would reject the epistemological position which, in philosophical circles, has been (pejoratively) labeled "naive realism." According to "naive realism," we can know reality as it is in itself simply by allowing ourselves to be acted upon, or passively affected, by reality as it exists on its own, independent of our knowing it. For the naive realist, our knowledge of reality is immediate, direct, and involves no mediating activity by us as knowers. Rejecting such naive realism, the Beatles tell us in their 1966 song, "Rain," that reality does *not* present itself to us in such a simple, straightforward way. Instead, what seems to present itself to us as reality is "just a state of mind." And in "Strawberry Fields Forever" (1967), John famously sings that "nothing is real." The Beatles thus reject naive realism and (as far as epistemology is concerned) appear to adopt some form of idealism (according to which "the real" is essentially mental or spiritual in nature). But what kind of idealism do they adopt?

It is clear that the form of idealism espoused by the Beatles is not an entirely skeptical or subjectivistic form of idealism. For if the Beatles subscribed to an entirely skeptical or subjectivistic form of idealism (according to which we could not know anything beyond our own subjective states of mind), then the

Beatles could not claim to know anything about reality that is worthy of, and capable of, being communicated to others. But again and again in their songs, the Beatles make clear that they have something of value to convey to us. Indeed, the same two songs which seem to espouse an unqualified idealism ("Rain" and "Strawberry Fields Forever") both also make clear that the Beatles take themselves to possess a kind of knowledge or insight that can be, and indeed *ought* to be, shared with others. Thus the protagonist in "Rain" plaintively addresses the listener by singing, "I can show you," and "Can you hear me?" In a similar vein, the protagonist of "Strawberry Fields Forever," while denying that anything is real in the naive realist's sense, nevertheless invites the listener to share meaningfully in his experience of reality: "Let me take you down." The point is that at least *something* is real and that something is worthy of being known and communicated to others (for if this were not the case, the Beatles would not have written songs in the first place); but our access to this reality is not as simple and straightforward as the naive realist would have us believe.

But now how is it possible to reject naive realism (and adopt some form of idealism), while nevertheless believing in the existence of some kind of reality that can be truly known and communicated to others? For the Beatles—as for many philosophers—the solution to this problem can be found if one's acceptance of (epistemological) idealism is accompanied by an acceptance of (metaphysical) monism; in short, if one accepts the philosophical position of idealistic monism. The American philosopher, Josiah Royce (1855–1916), espoused a form of idealistic monism, and—most helpfully for our purposes here—argued that epistemological idealism and metaphysical monism, properly understood, mutually imply and mutually support one another.

In *The World and the Individual*, Royce argues that anyone who adopts a realistic (non-idealistic) position in epistemology is implicitly committed to a non-monistic position in metaphysics.[3] For the realist, in order to be a realist, must hold that there exist (at least) two beings that are wholly independent and

---

[3] See especially Josiah Royce, Lecture III of *The World and the Individual* (New York: MacMillan, 1899).

indifferent to one another. These two independently-existing beings are: the being constituted by one's own thoughts and ideas (the "mind"), and the being constituted by (at least one) entity outside of one's own thoughts and ideas (the "external world"). The realist must think of these two beings as wholly independent and indifferent to one another, such that a change in one implies no change in the other. Thus the realist holds that a change in one's thoughts and ideas (or mind) implies no necessary change in the external object (or world); and conversely, that a change in the external object (or world) implies no necessary change in one's thoughts and ideas (or mind). Royce concludes that the realist cannot be a monist, since the realist must hold that there exist at least two real beings or substances that are wholly independent and indifferent to one another. Indeed, Royce argues that the realist's (epistemological) denial that there is an underlying unity or connection between mind and world is just a particular application of the realist's (anti-monistic, metaphysical) denial that all things are fundamentally interrelated and part of a single, underlying reality. Whether it is acknowledged or not, the realist is inevitably committed to the problematic anti-monistic view (lamented in "Within You, Without You") that there is fundamentally a "space between us all."

Royce argues, however, that just as the consistent espousal of realism entails the rejection of monism, so too the consistent espousal of idealism (and rejection of realism) entails the acceptance of monism. Thus for Royce, the term "idealistic monism" is redundant: the consistent idealist must be a monist, and the consistent monist must be an idealist. Our knowing, and the reality that is known, are not independent and indifferent to one another. Rather, a change in one necessarily implies a change in the other, for "mind" and "world" are not two independently-existing entities, but rather only modes or expressions of a single, underlying reality which is essentially mental or spiritual in nature. The underlying unity or connection between mind and world is just a particular instance of the underlying unity or connection of all things that exist.

Like Royce, the Beatles consistently espoused the view that all things are fundamentally interrelated and part of a single, underlying reality. This commitment to metaphysical monism is evident in a number of songs that deal—on one level or another—with the unity and interrelatedness of all things

("Tomorrow Never Knows," "Within You Without You," "The Inner Light," "All You Need Is Love," "All Together Now"); but it is also evident in the Beatles' obsession with writing and producing songs that could be appealing and catchy, while revolving around only one chord ("If I Needed Someone," "Paperback Writer," "The Word," and "Tomorrow Never Knows").

Even the Beatles' early experimentation with LSD can be understood in connection with their commitment to idealistic monism (though this is certainly not to suggest that those who are seriously committed to idealistic monism must also experiment with hallucinogenic drugs!). For if idealistic monism is correct, then presumably there must be some way in which the underlying unity of mind and world, and of all things in general, can be *experienced* by us. It was this desire to *experience* or to achieve *awareness* of the underlying unity of all things that—at least in part—helps to explain and contextualize the Beatles' experimentation with drugs. Having been influenced by a book called *The Psychedelic Experience: A Manual Based on the Tibetan Book of the Dead* (by Timothy Leary and Richard Alpert), the Beatles came to believe that one can achieve an awareness of the unity of all things by taking LSD and undergoing the process of "depersonalization" and "ego-loss" that accompanies drug-induced altered states. By annihilating or extinguishing one's individual selfhood through drug-induced states, they thought, one can achieve what Carl Jung and (later) Timothy Leary called "ocean consciousness": the sense that "all things are one, and that consciousness of one's individuality is merely an illusion." Thus the Beatles' tune, "The Inner Light," suggests that on a certain level we can know and experience all that is, if we would only give up our individuality and stop *trying* to know and experience all that is:

> The farther one travels
> The less one knows. . . .
> Arrive without traveling
> See all without knowing
> Do all without doing.

And in a similar vein, the song "Tomorrow Never Knows" advises the listener to "Turn off your mind" and "surrender to the void."

There's a serious problem, however, if one's desire to experience the unity of all things leads one to seek the annihilation or extinguishment of one's individuality or selfhood. The problem is that there can be no experience of anything whatsoever, if there no longer exists an individual self that is "there" to have the experience. If the individual self really is annihilated or extinguished, then—even if there is an underlying unity that binds all things together—there cannot be any *experience* or *awareness* of that unity. The underlying unity of all things will remain a blind unity, unknown to any conscious self.

Any attempt to bring about the experience or awareness of the unity of all things—if such an attempt is premised on the extinguishment or annihilation of the individual self—is necessarily self-defeating. It's no surprise that the Beatles themselves seem to have grappled with this very problem. They did so most directly in their 1966 song, "She Said, She Said," which was inspired by a conversation that John Lennon had with Peter Fonda. During a party in Los Angeles in August of 1965, Fonda reportedly told Lennon that a recent acid trip had made him lose his individual selfhood so successfully that he was able to know what it's like not to exist as an individual self, or (as the song goes) "what it's like to be dead." Lennon's response to Fonda's absurd claim could hardly be more direct and severe: "No, no, no, you're wrong. . . ."

But if one cannot experience or achieve awareness of the unity of all things through self-annihilation or self-extinguishment, then how is such an experience or awareness possible (assuming that it is possible at all)? The difficulty seems to become even more intractable when one considers that consciousness or awareness is (as many philosophers have observed) always *intentional*; that is to say, consciousness is always *about something* or always *directed at something*.[4] Thus every conscious act and every conscious representation (whether it be a belief, desire, or feeling) is always *about something* other than consciousness itself, and this "something" is the "intentional object" of consciousness. Even if the intentional object does not have any independent existence apart from con-

---

[4] The two philosophers who are most famous for emphasizing the *intentional* nature of consciousness are Franz Brentano (1838–1917) and Edmund Husserl (1859–1938).

sciousness itself, it is nevertheless still the case that consciousness—as intentional—is directed at something that is not the same as consciousness itself. For instance, a conscious fear—even if it's a delusional or misguided fear—is never a fear about consciousness itself, but always about something *other* than consciousness). It's this character of 'being intentional' that distinguishes psychic or conscious happenings from happenings that are merely physical or natural; for merely physical or natural happenings lack the 'directedness' or 'aboutness' that necessarily characterizes all mental or conscious happenings. It is an account of its intentionality that consciousness is always "called on and on," beyond itself alone and across the universe of all possible intentional objects.

Because of the intentional character of consciousness, consciousness always involves consciousness of something *other* than consciousness itself. And so here's the difficulty: on the one hand, there can be no experience or no awareness of the unity of all things, if the conscious, individual self is annihilated or extinguished; on the other hand, the conscious, individual self (just so long as it is conscious of anything at all) is always conscious of what is *other* than consciousness itself. And so instead of being aware of the unity of all things, the conscious individual self—to the extent that it is conscious at all—always seems to be aware of something that is *other* than consciousness itself, and thus always seems to be aware that there is a *difference* between itself and the object of its consciousness. But if consciousness—by virtue of being intentional—always involves consciousness of the *difference* between itself and its object, then it would seem that it is systematically impossible to achieve *consciousness* of the *unity* of all things. For built in to the very nature of consciousness is an awareness of the *difference* or *non-unity* between things (in this case, between consciousness and its intentional object). As long as consciousness is intentional, there must be a *difference* or *non-unity* between consciousness itself and its intended object; as soon as that difference or division is extinguished, then consciousness itself is extinguished. In short, it seems that *consciousness* of the *unity* of all things can never be achieved by anyone.

The German idealist philosopher, Friedrich Schelling (1775–1854) accepted the view that consciousness is always intentional; but he also argued that one could achieve consciousness or awareness of the unity of all things—even without the use of hallucinogenic drugs. But how is such consciousness possible? The key, Schelling held, was to see that one's awareness of things *other* than consciousness (rocks, minerals, plants, and other things in the non-conscious, natural world) was at some fundamental level nothing other than an awareness of the underlying substance or essence that constituted one's own consciousness. In other words, the key was to see that the forces at work in constituting things in the natural world (that is, the world that is *other than* or *different from* one's own consciousness) are the same as the forces at work in constituting one's own individual consciousness. It's just that in the natural world, these forces are at work unconsciously and without any apparent aim or purpose; and in one's individual consciousness, these forces are at work consciously and with a sense of purpose. So when an individual, conscious self is aware of something *other* than itself, Schelling argued, it is really (indirectly) aware of its own selfhood, only this selfhood appears to the conscious self under the guise of unconscious nature. In being aware of what is apparently separate from itself (for example, in being aware of chemicals seeking to bond with other chemicals or in being aware of animals seeking the company of other animals), the conscious self is really only aware of its own self, but in disguised, unconscious form. With this insight, Schelling was able to accept that consciousness is always intentional (always *about* something other than consciousness itself), but also hold that it is possible to achieve an awareness of the unity of consciousness and the unconscious world, and thus an awareness of the unity of all things in general.

In their own way, the Beatles seem to have appreciated this insight; and their own work displays many affinities with Schelling's brand of "idealistic monism." For like Schelling, the Beatles seem to have sensed that what—on one level—appears to be merely unintended, unconscious, and lacking in purpose, is—on another level—actually no different from what is conscious, intended, and purpose-driven. The Beatles often incorporated mere coincidences, accidents, and outright mistakes into their finished work, thus implying that what is merely accidental, purposeless, and unconscious, is really the same as what is intended, purposeful, and conscious (albeit in disguised form). An early example of this is the sound of guitar feedback which the Beatles decided to include at the beginning of their recording of "I Feel Fine." Another example pertains to the song, "Hey Bulldog," which was originally meant to be called, "Hey Bullfrog." But during one of their recording sessions, Paul began to make barking noises in order to make John laugh; the barking noises were picked up by the recording equipment and then integrated into the song itself, which was then re-named "Hey Bulldog."

With time, the Beatles indeed became very sophisticated and deliberate about creating opportunities for the occurrence of accidents and coincidences, which could then be integrated into their finished work. For example, members of the orchestra employed on "A Day in the Life" were instructed to wear party masks and other strange outfits during the recording of the song (the conductor himself donned a bright red, artificial, clown-style nose). The intention was to create a fresh, uncontrolled context within which the conductor and orchestra members could react to each other in new and unexpected ways.

George's composition of "While My Guitar Gently Weeps" was motivated by a similar belief in the fundamental unity of all things (including the conscious and the unconscious, the intended and the unintended). Inspired by the *I Ching* (which also teaches about the fundamental unity of all things), George deliberately decided to write a song based on a seemingly random, unintended occurrence. While visiting his parents' home in Lancashire, he picked a book off the shelf with the intention of composing a song organized around the first words he encountered. Those randomly-chosen words were "gently weeps," which then formed the basis of George's famous composition.

A final—and perhaps better-known—example of the Beatles' intentional use of the accidental or the unintended, is to be seen in their regular experimentation with backwards loopings. By using backwards loopings in their recordings, the Beatles deliberately chose to undertake the creative process of music-composition blindly—or in certain a sense, unconsciously—so as to generate new and unpredictable results, and then—only later—to integrate those results into their finished work *as if* they were originally intended. Though they did not explicitly reflect on the philosophical implications of this practice of backwards looping, the implicit lesson of this practice is the same as the lesson to be found in idealistic monism. The lesson is that what is blind, unconscious, unintended, or without purpose is—after all—not essentially different from what is deliberate, conscious, intended, and purpose-driven. The former (unconscious) kind of entity is really only an undeveloped, inchoate, and disguised form of the latter (conscious) kind. Our becoming aware of the unity of the conscious and the unconscious, and thus our becoming aware of the underlying unity of all things, does not require the extinguishment of the individual self, and does not require that we deny the intentional nature of consciousness. It requires only that we learn to see in all things—including things that are apparently blind, unconscious, and purposeless—a glimmering of our own strivings and purposes as conscious beings. Once we have learned to appreciate all things in this way, then—like the Beatles—we can grow confident in espousing the thesis of idealistic monism: "the Time Will Come When You See We're All One."

II

The Love You Make

The Beatles
and the Philosophy
of Love

3

All You Need Is Love: Hegel, Love, and Community

JACOB M. HELD

Love is a common theme in the Beatles' songs. Think about how many of their songs have "love" in the title or as the main theme. In their early songs, love is often expressed as simple juvenile crushes; after all it's only love. However, their understanding of love matures along with their music. In their later songs, they sing of love in a more meaningful or profound way, namely, as the bond between friends or humanity in general.

This type of love is not the simple desire to hold somebody's hand; it is togetherness, oneness, or unity. In "I am the Walrus," the opening lyric is suggestive of this type of bond: "I am he as you are he as you are me and we are all together" ("I am the Walrus"). Likewise, when the Beatles sing that, "all you need is love," it's love as unity and togetherness, not the infatuation of young sweethearts. This notion of unity suggests a commonality between all human beings, one that unites us at a basic level. We are identical in virtue of being equally interdependent human beings, and this commonality unites us; we are all together.

For the Beatles, love is not just an emotion. Rather, it's the ideal way of relating to others. In fact, it's the necessary way we must relate to each other in order to fully develop as human beings. Through their mature understanding of love, the Beatles are expressing the notion that our well-being is predicated on the development of healthy relationships with others. We are communal beings and can only get by with a little help from our friends. We are essentially other-regarding.

The Beatles are working with the notion of love as mutually respectful interdependence. Love is a relation between people where each person depends on the other in a non-parasitic helpful way. That is, we can't be solely self-serving and self-interested and still be loving people. Pursuing our own interests to the detriment of others would also be to our own detriment insofar as it would prevent us from adopting a perspective that enables us to respect others and develop as members of a community. This is a contentious claim. The reaction to the Beatles themselves is proof of this. Their songs and messages are at times dismissed as failed "hippie" ideals or naive youthful dreams. A loving perspective sometimes is seen to be idealistic in the pejorative sense. This cynicism is rooted in a widespread understanding of human nature.

In the majority of the Anglo-American social and political tradition, people are considered to be essentially self-interested pleasure seekers. This belief is directly opposed to the ideal of love and maintains that people are not communal by nature but rather self-interested and adversarial, namely, self-regarding. Each person is out for their own self-interest regardless of the effects their actions may have on others, and this is a desirable state of affairs. I, me, mine is the attitude of self-interest and disregard. But this notion paints a very lonely and isolated picture of existence.

In "Eleanor Rigby" we are asked: Where do all the lonely people come from? If I might offer a suggestion: the lonely people are those who are identified solely with their own self-interests. They have only enough room in their lives for themselves. These people lack the ability to make connections to others. Others, for them, are either obstacles to their greed or a means to its satisfaction. They cannot relate to others in a selfless and loving way. Although pervasive, this attitude is troublesome. The inability to view others as anything but restrictions on unrestrained avarice prevents people from being where they belong, namely, within a community.

Nobody envies Eleanor Rigby, in fact, we pity her. We can't bear the thought of such loneliness since we feel at a visceral level the need to be related and connected to other people. We have a fundamental need for unity, love, and community. But this need can only be satisfied in a community of accepting individuals. There are social and political structural requirements that must be met before our relationships can exemplify the ideal. Contemporary society promotes isolation through the ideals of greed, self-interest, and materialism. Eleanor Rigby is just one casualty.

But there is an alternative. Georg Hegel looks for the basis of love in recognition and interpersonal relations. He then outlines the structural requirements society must meet before it can support these types of relationships. In fact, his theory has provided the framework for much work in this field, and interestingly enough, it is strikingly similar to the sentiments of the mature Beatles.

Come Together: Hegel, Love, and Recognition

Imagine the Beatles to be representative of an ideal, other-regarding social world in which each person is bettered through his relations to others. Each member is augmented through his role in the band; this role allows him to become the best possible person he can be. Ringo is a better person for being a Beatle, as are George, John, and Paul. In fact, we can make the claim that each one would not be who he is if he were not a Beatle and who he is is desirable. The key element to this illustration is the fact that each member cannot solely pursue his own self-interest and he is in a better position for it. Each member is able to achieve greatness but together as a unity. Likewise, through the co-operative efforts of the members the band is also able to achieve greatness.

This example paints a picture quite different from contemporary society, which is rooted in self-interest where the state, or community, is seen to be nothing more than the result of a social contract whose sole purpose is to promote each person's self-interests by shielding them from a war of all against all.[1] In this self-regarding society, we all strive to better ourselves even when it is to the detriment of others. But others are not the only ones who suffer. Ultimately, a self-regarding perspective is to our own detriment since it isolates us. In isolation we can't develop many aspects of ourselves. If the Beatles had adopted a solely self-regarding attitude, each member demanding that

---

[1] This is a reference to Thomas Hobbes's classic social contractarian view but it applies equally well to other classic liberals such as J.S. Mill and John Rawls who similarly believe the goal of the state and community to simply be the satisfaction of each individuals self-interest.

the others serve his interests alone, it is doubtful they would have enjoyed the success they did. Each member and the band would have suffered. Hegel made a similar point roughly two hundred years ago.

Hegel believed that an ethical community is a unity where each member is bettered in virtue of her membership. Granted we may not be able to do what we please when we please, but we can also achieve a level of development or maturity impossible to reach on our own. Likewise, the community is able to become its best through the cooperative efforts of its members. And as with all social and political theories, its roots are in a theory of human nature.

Hegel's theory of human nature is phrased in terms of intersubjectivity or relatedness. Hegel states that human beings require other human beings in order to be truly and fully human and it is the state's duty to provide institutions that promote proper interpersonal relationships and thus self-realization. His (in)famous master-slave dialectic illustrates the importance of intersubjectivity through his concept of recognition.

For Hegel, mutual recognition is the ideal form of relatedness; an equal, respectful, interdependence. The master-slave dialectic, on the other hand, is an account of failed recognition, namely, inappropriate interpersonal relations that subvert self-realization. It's useful to look at insofar as it illustrates the detriment of adopting a self-regarding perspective.

In Hegel's illustration, the master and slave both desire the recognition of the other; they want to be acknowledged. But in this scenario neither can be accommodated. Let's consider a hypothetical confrontation between Ringo and Paul. Ringo demands that his input be recognized, he wants to have a greater creative role in the band. But Paul views Ringo as inessential, a mere drummer. Each is expressing a need to be known and respected as a free and rational person, and the satisfaction of this need is necessary in order for him to be fulfilled as an individual. But their current approach is bound to fail. Why?

When they first come into contact with each other their relationship isn't determined. Originally, they are just two bandmates butting heads. However, each in his desire to express himself attempts to assert his will over the other. Ringo wants his way. Paul wants his way. And neither is willing to compromise. This is self-interest run amok. The other appears as a mere object for the satisfaction of one's own desire. Ringo plays the drums for Paul's band and Paul plays the bass for Ringo's, and that is it. That is, although essentially other-regarding—they need each other—the master and slave (Paul and Ringo) encounter each other as self-regarding beings intent on satisfying their own self-interests irrespective of the will or needs of the other. They view their relation to each other not as beneficial but as either a means or an obstacle to their own gratification. Ringo stands in the way of Paul's creative vision and vice versa. A struggle ensues.

Hegel refers to this as a life or death struggle, but in the case of Paul and Ringo it won't go this far, one could just quit. If during this struggle, however, one were to actually die or quit, the process would be futile. That is, if Ringo or Paul were to quit the band, then the struggle would be fruitless and even detrimental to both. Nobody would be recognized and neither Ringo nor Paul's creative vision would come to life, so neither would be realized. So there must be a way other than death to resolve the problem. Hegel sees an alternative: one of the participants can give in to the will of the other. Whoever chooses to give in will be the slave; the dominant personality will be the master.[2] Let's say Paul wins and Ringo agrees to take a limited role in the band.

This solution, although preferable to death, is not satisfactory. Even though the master is victorious his desire will never be sated. The master has demanded recognition and this is not something that can be coerced. The master is only truly recognized when he is freely recognized by an equal, someone whom he respects. Perhaps Paul could respect John or George and thus value their input, but if he has absolutely no respect for Ringo, he will view Ringo's input as worthless. How can he esteem Ringo's judgment if he views Ringo as a lesser member of the group? Likewise, the slave fails to achieve recognition since his position as a lesser being clearly denies him respect. Ringo can't esteem himself as a fully contributing member if he willingly takes a limited role in the band. The crux of the problem is that

---

[2] For Hegel's discussion of the lord and bondsman see: G.W.F. Hegel, *The Phenomenology of Spirit*, §§ 178–196.

although each participant is essentially an other-regarding being, their behavior is self-regarding and therefore prevents the possibility of ever reaching a state of mutual recognition. And if they never reach this state, then they will never be fully realized as the social beings they essentially are.[3]

There has to be a way to work together that allows each party to participate equally and fully. "Life is very short, and there's no time for fussing and fighting" ("We Can Work it Out"). This line clearly expresses the lesson of the struggle depicted above: conflicts of interest can be resolved through compromise when each party recognizes that they need the other party and compromise is ultimately more beneficial than any alternative, even having one's own way. To behave as the master is to be one of the "people who gain the world but lose their soul" ("Within You, Without You"). You may get what you want but you lose the ability to become who you ought to be.

Hegel maintained that as social beings we must pursue interpersonal relationships that foster community, not ones that deny our essential connectedness such as self-interest, desire, and greed. Money can't by you love and love is a necessary component to a happy and healthy life.

Got to Get You into My Life

In common usage, "love" has become trivialized. Most times it means nothing more than infatuation, desire, or shallow prepackaged romance reminiscent of Hugh Grant and Julia Roberts movies. But love as a concept is much more. According to Hegel, Love is the ideal form of recognition; recognition without a conflict of wills.[4] "True validation, or actual love, occurs only among living beings that are alike in power and thus living beings for each other; from neither side does one encounter a dead being."[5] A union between two such people is impossible if one holds back. Love "is a mutual giving and taking. . . . The

---

[3] For thorough and clear discussions of the master-slave dialectic and recognition in Hegel see: Robert R. Williams, *Recognition: Fichte and Hegel on the Other* (Albany: State University of New York Press, 1992), Part Three; H.S. Harris, *Hegel's Ladder I: The Pilgrimage of Reason*, Chapter Eight.

[4] Robert R. Williams, *Recognition: Fichte and Hegel on the Other*, p. 85.

[5] G.W.F. Hegel, *Hegels Theologische Jugendschriften* (Tübingen: Minerva GmbH, 1966) p. 379.

lover who takes is not thereby made richer than the other; he is enriched indeed, but only so much as the other is."[6] In the end, the love you take is, in fact, equal to the love you make.

Love is a union; it's a bond between people. It doesn't have to be romantic or passionate. But it is also not a luxury. Love is not something that only the lucky find. Rather, love is a way of being connected to others that is necessary for our development as human beings. I *got* to get you into my life. In fact, love as relatedness is a precondition to mental health, and it begins with our perspective of the world and the way we view our relations to other people. But why is love so important? In terms of social and political philosophy, this all boils down to the nature of freedom.

My Independence Seems to Vanish in the Haze: Hegelian Freedom

Hegel maintains that freedom is not simply freedom from obstacles; it is not arbitrariness or whim. That is, freedom is not simply the ability to do what you want when you want. He denies arbitrariness the status of freedom since through arbitrariness our will is determined by contingency.[7] If we allow our desires to dictate our actions, then we allow contingent (irrational) nature to determine our will. Thus, we become dependent on desire to give our will content. If we don't give our content to ourselves, then we are not in control of ourselves. Consider an addiction to heroin or Savoy truffles. Even if one had unlimited resources with which to satisfy one's cravings this would not be freedom in any real sense of the word. Instead, we would say that the addict was a slave to her desires. Hegel is working with a distinction between freedom as license and freedom as self realization. This distinction is classically expressed as the distinction between negative and positive freedom.

The distinction between negative and positive liberty is most commonly attributed to Isaiah Berlin.[8] According to Berlin, neg-

---

[6] G.W.F. Hegel, *Early Theological Writings* (Philadelphia: University of Pennsylvania Press, 1996), pp. 306–07.

[7] See G.W.F. Hegel, "The Difference between Fichte and Schelling's Systems of Philosophy."

[8] Isaiah Berlin, *Four Essays on Liberty* (Oxford: Oxford University Press, 1969).

ative liberty "is involved in the answer to the question 'What is the area within which the subject—a person or group of persons—is or should be left to do or be what he is able to do or be, without interference by other beings?'"[9] The phrase, "without interference by other beings," is suggestive of the self-regarding nature of negative liberty. Under this conception of freedom one is as free as one's realm of non-interference is great. Negative liberty is oftentimes described as "liberty from"; liberty from obstacles, encroachment, and ultimately other people. The way in which the Beatles view the taxman is helpful. He encroaches on our freedom by taxing our feet, street, and seat. He restricts our freedom insofar as he prevents us from doing what we want, when, and how we want.

However, negative liberty is only one side of the coin. The other half is positive liberty. Berlin describes positive liberty as the answer to the question "What, or who, is the source of control or interference that can determine someone to do, or be, this rather than that?" He states that positive libertarians are not concerned so much with having free reign within a realm of non-interference but a desire for self-determination and self-realization. Positive libertarians wish to promote the realization of one's essence, nature, or true self. He characterizes positive liberty as "liberty to," namely liberty to become who one potentially, or ought, to be. The taxman in this case may not be so bad. He might provide streets, schools, and other resources that promote self-realization.

Hegel is a positive libertarian. He finds true freedom in our connection to others, their demands against us, and ours against them. If you got to be free, then you got to come together. The actualization of the self can only be achieved in a social context. Education or culture, *Bildung*, for Hegel plays a central role in this process. Through culture and education one is trained to pursue one's personal ends or whims but within a given context or ethical framework. Culture provides the opportunity to free us from the bonds of natural drives and desires while helping us mature and grow. The Beatles were on to something when they expressed the fact that our relations to

---

[9] Isaiah Berlin, "Two Concepts of Liberty," in David Miller, ed., *Liberty* (Oxford: Oxford University Press, 1991), p. 34.

others are necessary, not just to satisfy our wants and needs, but to fulfill a greater purpose, our development as human beings. We truly do only get by with a little help from our friends. We do need somebody to love, that is, to recognize and bond with. Our relationships and duties to others provide a context for our behavior. This context liberates us from the dominance of our desires and gives meaning and purpose to our life. For Hegel and the Beatles, community provides a context in which we can realize ourselves.

And in the End . . .

Although the discussion above has been limited mostly to a discussion of the nature of Hegelian love, recognition, and self-realization, love as a concept is more than merely descriptive of ideal relationships. Love is also prescriptive. Love demands of us that we relate to others in a way befitting our nature as other-regarding. All human relations are, ultimately, to be regulated by this ideal form of relatedness, namely, mutually respectful interdependence. This idea has had a long history. After Hegel, it was adopted by Marx, and later Erich Fromm. Most recently it has been adopted by Axel Honneth. These thinkers elaborate the nature of relatedness, its role in our development, and the best means in which society can promote proper relationships and therefore our freedom, that is, self-realization. There is far too much involved in this tradition to discuss any of it in depth at this point, but I would like to conclude with one final point.

The prescriptive nature of love, or recognition, demands that relationships in all areas of life adopt a respectful attitude. Honneth recognizes three specific spheres of recognition: love, rights, and solidarity. Respectively, these demand mutual recognition in personal, legal, and social relationships.[10] Fromm demands recognition in economic life, decrying the shallow materialism of late capitalism and the way in which it distorts interpersonal relations. Both of these thinkers represent aspects of the tradition of philosophy represented by Hegel (and the Beatles): the demand for recognition and our need for love. But

---

[10] Axel Honneth, *The Struggle for Recognition: The Moral Grammar of Social Conflicts* (Cambridge, Massachusetts: MIT Press, 1995).

4

All My Loving: Paul McCartney's Philosophy of Love

ROBERT ARP

Recently, while sitting in the waiting room for my regular six-month checkup at the dentist's office, I noticed a copy of *The Beatles Anthology* lying on top of the coffee table in front of me. "A big book with lots of pictures," I thought, "just the thing to look through to get my mind off the dentist's probing and poking around in my mouth." I randomly opened the book to page 357, where the four mop-tops are lying on the ground, face up, looking at the camera. Next to each of them is a quotation, and Paul McCartney's reads:

> I'm Really glad that most of the songs dealt with love, peace, and understanding. There's hardly any one of them that says: 'Go on, kids, tell them all to sod off. Leave your parents.' It's all very 'All you need is love' or John's 'Give peace a chance'. There was a good spirit behind it all, which I'm very proud of. Anyway . . . it were a grand thing, the Beatles.[1]

Reading this quotation got me to thinking about the influence of the Beatles upon Rock music, culture, and various ideologies of the 1960s. I also began to think about the Sixties as the "Decade of Free Love," whether the music of the Beatles contributed to this label, and whether this label accurately depicts the 1960s. Finally, I wondered about Paul McCartney's idea of *love* as he was writing his songs. From Paul's perspective, is love an erotic passion that you find in sexual relationships of "shagging" and

---

[1] *The Beatles Anthology* (San Francisco: Chronicle Books, 2000), p. 357.

the like? Is love associated with a general care and concern for human beings, or is it reserved for close and intimate friendships? Is it a kind of cosmic force that binds the world together and "makes the world go around," so to speak? Or, is it just a name that we give to certain physiological changes like "butterflies" in our stomachs and blood rushing to various parts of our bodies?

I'll Send All My Loving . . . But What Does Love Mean?

Paul was dating actress Jane Asher when he wrote the lyrics to "All My Loving" and, in fact, this was the first song he ever wrote where he had the words before the music.[2] But what exactly does he mean by the word *love*? Paul did indeed have a certain conception of love in mind when he wrote the lyrics to this early Beatles song, but his conception of love changed as he matured through the years. Let's look at conceptions of love envisioned by some figures in the history of Western philosophy.

When we think of love, we automatically associate it with some kind of a passionate emotion where one desires something with a great deal of intensity. This association has a long history in Western philosophy that begins with the ancient Greeks who had a conception of love understood as *eros*. In Greek mythology, Eros was a god who had a great power over mortals, causing them to do crazy things like lie, steal, and murder. In his *Theogony*, Hesiod (eighth century B.C.E.) characterizes Eros as the enemy of reason, and this erotic conception of love continued to be influential in the Golden Age of Greek philosophers who envisioned human beings as having a rational, controlled, prudent part of their soul that must keep this erotic, irrational, animalistic part of their soul in check. The irrational part of the soul that is shared with animals and that normally gets people into trouble has to do with sex, and so eros came to be associated with sexual desire. That's why today we associate "erotic" desire with sex and sexual relationships.[3] In *The*

---

[2] Interview with Paul and Linda McCartney, *Playboy* (December 1984). Internet article: www.geocities. com/~beatleboy1/dbpm.int1.html.

[3] See *Hesiod's Theogeny*, translated by Norman Brown (New York: Liberal Arts Press, 1953), pp. 56–59, lines 120–22; also, Bruce Thornton, *Eros: The Myth of Ancient Greek Sexuality* (Boulder: Westview, 1997).

Beatles Anthology Paul tells us that, during the 1960s, there was a "big period" of "amazing sexual freedom" and "free," erotic love that he and the Beatles helped to foster (pp. 201, 356).

In contrast to the irrational and animalistic "eros," the Greeks had another conception of love understood as an appreciation of another's beauty or goodness that they called *philia*. This "philial" form of love is present in Plato's (427–347 B.C.E.) writings, especially in his dialogue entitled *Symposium*, where he ultimately conceives of love as a contact with a universal "Form" of Beauty that all beautiful things in this world share in. The idea behind Plato's conception of love is that one will be led from the changeable and imperfect beautiful (and not-so-beautiful) things of this world to the unchanging and perfect universal Form of Beauty, and such a form will be satisfying to the mind, rather than the body. In fact, this kind of satisfaction can be found in philosophy, an English word that comes from two Greek words meaning *love of wisdom*, where one desires and pursues the nature of Beauty and other universal concepts.[4]

As contrasted with erotic love, in which sexual or bodily desires are met, philial love is concerned with a desire for the beauty that underlies persons, places, and things *for beauty's sake*. We find this idea today in the term *Platonic relationship*, where two people have a relationship that does not involve sex, but involves more lofty, intellectual-type pursuits. Think of Paul and Linda discussing animal rights and world peace, or pursuing their artistic interests through photography and song-writing together.

Aristotle (384–322 B.C.E.) was Plato's student, and disagreed with Plato that philial love should be concerned solely with the form of Beauty that transcends beautiful things. Love is not some universal Form of the Beautiful found through beautiful things. Rather, love entails an appreciation of the good qualities of another, as well as an interaction between lover and beloved. Love is best understood as a relationship of friendship between two people in which mutual awareness of each other's good is kept in mind. According to Aristotle, there are three levels of friendship.

---

[4] Plato, *Symposium* (Oxford: Oxford University Press, 1994), lines 196B, 201B, 210D.

1. Friendships of Utility are those relationships where mutual benefit is to be gained from each other's services, as in a business relationship. For example, Paul had this kind of relationship with the executives at Apple Records—they promoted, Paul wrote and played, and they all made lots of money.

2. Friendships of Pleasure are those relationships where pleasure is to be gained from engaging in mutually enjoyable experiences. Paul obviously had this kind of relationship with the rest of the Beatles playing music on stage for people.

3. Friendships of Virtue are the best and most noble friendships, and are found between those who are most wise, virtuous, and good. In this kind of friendship, as Aristotle so poetically puts it, the "two bodies share one soul" in that the two lovers have the common desire for one another's good—a good that is concerned with the most true, noble, and virtuous in life. It might not have been full-fledged, but I think that Paul had a kind of Friendship of Virtue with Linda.[5]

In contrast to Aristotle's idea of love as filial friendship, with its emphasis upon the emotions of human beings and human relationships, the ancient Greek philosopher Empedocles (492–424 B.C.E.) envisions Love and its opposite, Strife, as cosmic principles at work in the cycle of the universe. Love is the source of all that's generative, unified, harmonious, and good; while Strife is the source of all that is destructive, disunified, chaotic, and evil. The cosmos is held in tension between the forces of Love and Strife, and at various times either Love is dominant, or Strife is dominant.[6] There are two important points to be drawn from the Empedoclean conception of love. The first is that love is not just something that affects human relationships—love literally "makes the world go around" as a cosmological principle! The second important point is that love is a

---

[5] Aristotle, *Nicomachean Ethics*, in *The Complete Works of Aristotle* (Princeton: Princeton University Press, 1984), Books VIII and IX.

[6] Empedocles, *Fragments*. In *The First Philosophers of Greece* (London: Kegan Paul, 1898), pp. 157–234.

binding force that affects all human beings as the source of what is harmonious, peaceful, just, and good. Paul certainly thought that love and hate could "take on lives of their own" so to speak, leading people to peace, harmony, and respect or war, chaos, and violence. This's why he could agree with Lennon that love "seems like the underlying theme to the universe" (*Beatles Anthology*, p. 193).

The ancient Greek Stoics—whose founder was Zeno of Citium (344–262 B.C.E.)—had a conception of love as a kind of universal respect for all of humankind. Love requires that one should be detached enough from this world and its pleasures to appreciate the beauty and goodness of all of humanity, thus bringing about a universal harmony and peace, which is the ultimate goal of a happy life. Stoic love treats all humans as "Citizens of the World," as opposed to being concerned only with your own family or the citizens in your specific community.[7] The Stoic conception of love is similar to Immanuel Kant's (1724–1804 C.E.) call for general respect for persons as "ends in themselves." For both the Stoics and Kant, this kind of universal sisterly or brotherly love is something that needs to be fostered if peace, both within a community or between communities, is ever to be achieved.[8] Think of Paul's remark at the beginning of this chapter where he tells us that most of the Beatles' songs dealt with "All you need is love" or "Give peace a chance."

Kant was a Christian who was influenced by a Greek and Christian idea of love known as *agape* (pronounced "a-ga-pay") that emphasizes not only affection between humans and a god, but also universal care among all members of the human community. The Christian conception of agape is rooted in Biblical passages such as: "You shall love the Lord your God with all your heart, and with all your soul, and with all your might" (Deuteronomy 6:5); "love your neighbor as yourself" (Leviticus

---

[7] See A.A. Long, *Epictetus: A Stoic and Socratic Guide to Life* (Oxford: Oxford University Press, 2002); also Martha Nussbaum, *The Therapy of Desire* (Princeton: Princeton University Press, 1994).

[8] See Immanuel Kant, *Groundwork for the Metaphysics of Morals*, edited by Alan Wood and Jerome Schneewind (New Haven: Yale University Press, 2001), Third Section, Ak. 438; Immanuel Kant, *Perpetual Peace, and Other Essays on Politics, History, and Morals* (Indianapolis: Hackett, 1983); James Bohman and Matthias Lutz-Bachmann, eds., *Perpetual Peace: Essays on Kant's Cosmopolitan Ideal* (Cambridge, Massachusetts: MIT Press).

19:18; also Matthew 22:37); and "love your enemies" (Matthew 5:44–45). Also, sisterly or brotherly love among all members of humanity is reflective of God's love (Psalms 91:14; 1 John 4:16), and will be the way in which to bring about peace and harmony in communities (1 Corinthians; 1 John 4:16–20; James 2:9).

Paul's Philosophy of Love

Which of these ideas best mesh with Paul's own philosophy of love? I don't think that Paul was *consciously* or explicitly work-ing from any of the ideas of love I just mentioned—either while writing lyrics or while living his life. I don't know for sure whether Paul actually studied any of the thinkers in the history of Western philosophy or their ideas of love, let alone whether he was using a particular thinker's conception of love as a model for his lyrics or way of life. Yet none of us lives in an intellectual vacuum. Ideas are communicated within a culture or between cultures, and we all are influenced by ideas that have come before us.

Paul's early songs were reflective of a philosophy of love that emphasized the erotic dimension. This makes sense since when we are young—lacking maturity, exploring our bodies, gaining experiences, and appeasing our raging hormones—our idea of love is usually closely associated with passionate sexual desire. Many historians, writers, and commentators have noted that the 1960s were a decade of free love, with the idea that this "free-dom" was associated with erotic, sexual forms of expression.[9] Pictures and video of hippies having sex in the mud at Woodstock immediately come to mind. In many ways, the sex-ual expression of the Sixties was a reaction to the sexual *repres-sion* of the 1950s and earlier generations, as illustrated nicely in the movie *Pleasantville*. Mark Hertsgaard notes that The Beatles were "seen as symbols of the 1960s counterculture" in terms of advocating freer forms of sexual expression, fun, spiritual explo-ration, and mind-expanding drugs.[10]

---

[9] See Francis Wheen, *The Sixties* (London: Century, 1982); Edward Grey, *The Sixties* (Hove: Wayland, 1989); Bob Larson, *Hippies, Hindus, and Rock & Roll* (Carol Stream: Creation Press, 1972); Michael Brake, *The Sociology of Youth and Youth Subcultures: Sex and Drugs and Rock 'n' Roll* (London: Routledge, 1980).

[10] Mark Hertgaard, *A Day in the Life* (New York: Delacorte, 1995), pp. 123, 125. Also see

With respect to erotic "free" love, Paul tells us that during the 1960s there was a "big period" of "amazing sexual freedom" that *he* and the Beatles helped to foster (*Beatles Anthology*, pp. 201, 356). Paul himself did a lot of "shagging," and while in Hamburg the rest of The Beatles and he "got a fairly swift baptism by fire into the sex scene. There was a lot of it about and we were off the leash" (pp. 52–53). In an interview about getting to know the future Linda McCartney, he claims: "At a certain age you start to think, 'I've got to get serious, I can't just be a *playboy* (italics added) all my life'," alluding to the erotic lifestyle he had been living.[11]

A few of Paul's earlier songs reflect this erotic form of love as well. In "I Saw Her Standing There," the original lyric, "never been a beauty queen," was replaced by a phrase Paul preferred for its sexual innuendo (*Playboy* interview). In "Hold Me Tight," Paul expresses an intense demand for purely physical closeness. And in "From Me to You," the references to bodily sensations and physical contact can only be interpreted as concerned with erotic love.

As Paul matured in the 1960s, he realized that he wanted to settle down into a long-lasting relationship with a woman who could be his friend, and who could reciprocate a deeper, long-lasting kind of love than is found in erotic escapades. Thus, he tells us that whenever he thought about getting serious, "Linda came into my mind" (*Wingspan*, p. 10). Meeting Linda motivated Paul's shift from the erotic to the philial conceptions of love. The question now becomes, what form of philial love, Platonic or Aristotelian, did Paul advocate in his life and lyrics during this period?

According to Plato's idea of love, there is a universally recognizable form of Beauty that all people can come to see as reflected in beautiful things, and such beautiful things bring us closer to that Beauty. In fact, some beautiful thing makes us *want* to be in contact with Beauty itself. I think that, in some way, Paul was aware of this notion of the Beautiful, and wrote his love songs knowing that what he had to say about Linda—

Robert Pielke, *So You Say You Want a Revolution: Rock Music in American Culture* (Chicago: Nelson-Hall, 1988), p. 170.

[11] Mark Lewisohn, *Wingspan: Paul McCartney's Band on the Run* (London: Little, Brown, 2002), p. 10.

or Jane Asher, or his first love, for that matter—would resonate with anyone who took the time to recognize the beauty reflected in another person or in some relationship. Paul's love songs continue to be purchased and played all over the world. In 2002, Michael Karwowski noted that The Beatles had sold over six hundred million records worldwide, and that Paul's "Yesterday" had been played six million times, while "Michelle" had been played four million times on American radio alone.[12] Such astronomical record sales and radio requests suggest that humans do recognize and long for glimpses of Beauty itself that beautiful things like Paul's love songs hint at. Or, at least, that Paul's longing for beauty in these songs resonated with his audience. Paul has "filled the world with silly love songs" and there's nothing wrong with that.

Perhaps the specific form of philial relationship Paul and Linda had was one that Aristotle speaks of as a Friendship of Pleasure, in which lover and beloved are bound together by common pleasurable interests. Paul tells us that once they started spending more time together during the recording of the *White Album*, "we realized we had many things in common: Rock and Roll, nature, art, photography, painting" (*Wingspan*, p. 10). Thus, Paul writes in "Two of Us" that they send postcards and write letters to each other, burn matches, and chase paper while making memories longer than the road stretching out ahead of them. Also, Linda went on to play the keyboards and sing backup for Wings after the Beatles broke up, which seems to validate what Paul had said about the two of them having rock 'n' roll in common.

Perhaps, though, Paul and Linda's relationship hinted at what Aristotle referred to as a Friendship of Virtue, where two bodies share one virtuous and noble soul, and each person in the relationship has the good of the other in mind. The love songs Paul wrote about Linda reflect his perception of their love as an everlasting ("I Will," "She's a Woman"), memory-making ("Two of Us"), reciprocal ("Maybe I'm Amazed"), and deeper kind of friendship than is found merely in mutual pleasures ("Dear Friend," "My Love"). Also, they supported one another not only

---

[12] Michael Karwowski, "Fifty Years of British Popular Culture," in *Contemporary Review* (2002) p. 283.

in rearing their children to be persons of integrity (*Wingspan*, pp. 18–24), but in their various causes throughout the 1970s, 1980s, and 1990s by raising public awareness of animal rights, the victimization of women, Greenpeace, cancer research, the vegetarian lifestyle, and the legitimate uses of marijuana (as well as *illegal* uses of marijuana, like when Paul made international news for being busted for marijuana possession on January 16th, 1980 in Tokyo!).[13]

It seems that Paul always had this kind of friendship in mind in some inchoate form throughout his life. His parents modeled this form of relationship.[14] In the song "P.S. I Love You," he promises lifelong devotion, and in "Things We Said Today" he envisions an eternal attachment. Both of these early songs have a sense that love is something more than just a one-night stand. Even though Paul had many a one-night stand throughout his early and middle career with the Beatles, there was still a sense that ultimately, after having sown many a wild oat, he would settle down with a woman who would be able to share more directly in his love of music, reciprocate TLC, share common values, and bear his children.

Like the rest of the Beatles, Paul shared Empedocles's conception of love as a cosmic and binding force that would be the way to harmony, peace, and happiness for all of humankind. Recall that for Empedocles, Love and Strife are the two forces productive of all that is good and evil in the universe. Paul sounds very Empedoclean when, while discussing the existence and nature of god, he acknowledges that there are the "two forces of Good and Evil" that have been present throughout history (*Beatles Anthology*, p. 18). In "Tomorrow Never Knows," Paul claims that "love is all and love is everyone." In "The Word," the word is love, and it is possible that this is a new take on St. John's gospel proclamation that "In the beginning was the word." In "The End," Paul writes that "in the end, the love you take is equal to the love you make," and of this line Lennon

---

[13] See "The Linda McCartney List" online at www.macca-1.org/lindamac/.

[14] See what Paul says about Linda and his parents in Barry Miles, *Paul McCartney: Many Years from Now* (New York: Holt, 1997), Chapter 1; also Chris Salewicz, *McCartney: The Biography* (London: Macdonald, 1986); Chris Welch, *Paul McCartney: The Definitive Biography* (London: Proteus, 1984); Ray Coleman, *McCartney: Yesterday and Today* (London: Boxtree, 1995).

aptly comments, "A very *cosmic* (italics added), philosophical line" (*Beatles Anthology*, p. 357). In a 1965 interview, Paul agrees with Lennon's claim that love "seems like the underlying theme to the universe" (*Beatles Anthology*, p. 193).

Finally, I think that Paul had a conception of love as the Stoic-Kantian-Christian idea of universal affection and respect for all of humankind. He contributed his time and talents to Lennon's "Give Peace a Chance" and co-wrote "All You Need Is Love" as specifically anti-war songs. Paul was well aware of the Vietnam conflict, and commented in an interview with David Frost on BBC-TV that we should "Make Love Not War" and suggested that the whole "point" of life is to "just do it to the best of your ability. Do it as best you can, you know, and try to help . . . yourself and others."[15] Paul, as well as the other Beatles, felt that love needed to extend beyond the home, local community, or country into the entire world so that harmony and peace could ultimately be achieved.[16]

It Were a Grand Thing, the Beatles

Following Linda's death, Paul found new love with Heather Mills, though unfortunately that marriage has ended in a bitter divorce. Paul has continued to write songs about love, and his music still has the most profound impact upon us, stirring our emotions and leaving us with lasting impressions. One of my personal favorites is "Maybe I'm Amazed"—in a Platonic way, it reminds me of the goodness, honesty, and integrity of my own wife, Susan. Given Paul's ideas about love, he probably would not quarrel with this quotation from Ringo: "We were honest with each other and we were honest about the music. The music was positive. It was positive in love. They did write—we all wrote—about other things, but the basic Beatles message was love" (*Beatles Anthology*, p. 356).

---

[15] BBC Interview with David Frost. Internet article: www.geocities.com/~beatleboy1/db122767.int.html.

[16] See James Blake, *All You Needed Was Love* (London: Hamlyn, 1981).

III

Dear Prudence, Justice, and Virtue

The Beatles
and Moral Philosophy

5

Getting Better: The Beatles and Virtue Ethics

JAMES S. SPIEGEL

The Beatles might not be known as moral philosophers, but their lyrics vividly illustrate one of the long-standing approaches to philosophical ethics, dating all the way back to the ancient Greeks. This is the tradition known as "virtue ethics." While other major ethics emphasize universal principles, such as Kant's categorical imperative and Mill's principle of utility, the virtue ethics perspective focuses on personal character. Rather than asking, "What principle ought I to obey?" the virtue ethicist asks, "What kind of *person* ought I to be?"

Chief among virtue ethicists is Aristotle. Although he inherited from his mentor, Plato, an emphasis on moral character, he was the first to systematically catalogue and analyze the virtues, which he did in his classic book *Nicomachean Ethics*. To this day philosophers and lay-persons alike continue to benefit from Aristotle's approach. In fact, the Beatles' lyrics (and sometimes their lives) illustrate many aspects of Aristotle's ethics, particularly his doctrine of the virtues.

Happiness Is a Contemplative Life

According to Aristotle, every human endeavor aims at some good. Medicine aims at the health of the body; education aims at the acquisition of knowledge; and carpentry aims at the construction of furniture, houses, and such. But human life cannot consist entirely in the variety of particular goods for which we toil and sweat. There must be some overarching aim or end, a good for human life generally. This, says Aristotle, is happiness or *eudaimonia,* living well in the fullest sense. But what does it mean to be happy, to live well?

Aristotle maintained that there are basically three responses to this question, at least as displayed in the ways that people actually choose to order their lives. Some pursue the life of pleasure, in which the chief aim is money. This attitude is expressed in the classic song "Money": "Money don't get everything it's true. But what it don't get I can't use. So gimme money—that's what I want."[1] But this perspective ignores something very important, as the Beatles remind us in "Can't Buy Me Love." There are things money cannot buy, and among them is genuine love.

The problem, says Aristotle, is that money "is merely useful and for the sake of something else."[2] The pursuit that brings genuine happiness must be "always desirable in itself and never for the sake of something else" (*Ethics,* line 941). So a life ordered around the acquisition of wealth is fundamentally misguided and cannot be truly happy, regardless of how vast one's riches. Indeed, there are those who "Gain the world and lose their soul. / They don't know; they can't see. / Are you one of them?" ("Within You and Without You").

Another common pursuit is honor, to be held in high esteem by others, whether that takes the form of political aspiration or, as expressed by the girl in the Beatles' "Drive My Car," fame in the entertainment industry: "Asked a girl what she wanted to be / She said, "baby can't you see?" / I wanna be famous, a star of the screen. ("Drive My Car"). Here even love is subservient to this poor girl's quest for personal fame. As absurd as this attitude appears when put in such stark terms, it's actually quite common. Many people would (and in fact do) sacrifice even their most precious relationships for the sake of their own ambition.

Of course, high reputation fails as a worthy life pursuit because it is too superficial. As Aristotle notes, it depends upon "those who bestow honor rather than on him who receives it" (*Ethics,* line 938). Something that can be so easily taken from a person is not a proper object of ultimate concern. Not only this,

---

[1] Berry Gordy, Jr. and Janie Bradford. Originally recorded by Barrett Strong (1959). Recorded by the Beatles in 1963 (*With the Beatles*).
[2] Aristotle, *Nicomachean Ethics,* in Richard McKeon, ed., *The Basic Works of Aristotle* (New York: Random House, 1941), line 939.

but high reputation has its drawbacks, and these, too, go beyond one's control. Consider Beatlemania, about which Harrison says, "At first it was fun. We enjoyed it in the early days, but then it just became tiresome." By the second American tour, he says, "we couldn't move."[3] Lennon concludes: "People think fame and money bring freedom, but they don't. We're more conscious now of the limitations it places on us rather than the freedom" (*Beatles Anthology*, p. 147). And Harrison says, "The only place we ever got any peace was when we got in the suite and locked ourselves in the bathroom. The bathroom was about the only place you could have any peace" (*Beatles Anthology*, p. 155). The Beatles had become prisoners of their own fame. Such is the pitfall of seeking happiness in something that others control. Whatever is the source of true happiness, therefore, must be self-sufficient, impervious to what others think.

The proper human good and source of real happiness, says Aristotle, is the contemplative life, the full exercise of one's rational powers aimed at the acquisition of wisdom. The life of wisdom avoids the problems plaguing the other two major life pursuits. Not only is wisdom an end in itself, it cannot be taken away against one's will.

That the contemplative life is the happy life is also based in human nature itself, Aristotle claims. For anything to be excellent—be it a shoe, a cup, or an automobile—it must fulfill its *telos*, that is, its unique function or purpose. The same is true of human beings, and our *telos* is defined by our rationality—it's what distinguishes us from plants and animals. It follows that our proper function is to act rationally. This is happiness (*eudaimonia*): the life of excellence according to the human *telos* (as opposed to, say, dancing with your date, playing in an octupus's garden, or a warm gun). It features the full and complete exercise of one's vital capacities.

The Word Is Good: Aristotelian Virtue

A particular excellence is called a virtue. When it comes to human activity, these come in two principal forms: intellectual and moral. Intellectual virtues arise through instruction. Moral

---

[3] *The Beatles Anthology* (San Francisco: Chronicle Books, 2000), p. 123.

virtues, in contrast, are developed through intentional action. A moral virtue is essentially a skill, a good habit that has been ingrained through practice. And through practice one can overcome even some vicious habits, like the bloke in "Getting Better," who used to inflict both mental and physical cruelty on his woman but is now struggling to improve his behavior.

To improve morally or change one's moral "scene" demands effort, not just sincere desire. Nor is it a simple matter of innate ability, as moral virtues do not arise in us if we just "act naturally." Rather, as is the case with other areas of human life, we become better or worse as a result of what we do. Thus, explains Aristotle, "it is from playing the lyre that both good and bad lyre-players are produced. And . . . men will be good or bad builders as a result of building well or badly" (*Ethics*, lines 952–953). So it is with virtue and vice. The more we act virtuously or viciously, the more virtuous or vicious our character becomes. ("Vicious" derives from "vice.")

But all of this raises the question: Just what *are* the virtues? And what traits, for that matter, are vicious? Generally speaking, a virtue is a good moral habit, while a vice is a bad moral habit. And virtues and vices are properly defined in terms of one another. A virtue is a midpoint between extremes, an intermediate between two vices, one involving deficiency and the other involving excess. Liberality, for instance, is the virtue of giving freely to others. It lies between the vices of meanness and prodigality. These are, respectively, stinginess with one's possessions and extravagant generosity or wastefulness.

So, says Aristotle, "the prodigal exceeds in spending and falls short in taking, while the mean man exceeds in taking and falls short in spending" (*Ethics*, line 960), like the character from *Abbey Road*, "Mean Mister Mustard," whoise grotesquely penurious lifestyle is itemized in humorous detail.

Here we have a particularly ridiculous miser, a comical Howard Hughes. Such people are much more common than those who err on the opposite extreme of prodigality. Indeed, it's hard to find people who give to the point of excess. The reason for this, Aristotle explains, is that one vice is always more dangerous than the other, which, because of our natural urge of self-preservation, tends to drive us to the opposite extreme. Thus, cowards are more common than the foolhardy, the sheepish are more common than the shameless, and, in this case, misers are more common than prodigals.

A distinctly aristocratic Aristotelian virtue is pride. This is the trait of one who thinks himself worthy of great things and who in fact is so worthy. The vices on either extreme are vanity and pettiness. The one who thinks herself worthy of great honor, but is not, is vain, while the one who is worthy but does not so regard herself is petty. Falling into the former category, it seems, is the object of this castigating lyric, mercifully disguised as "Sexy Sadie": "Sexy Sadie, how did you know / The world was waiting just for you? . . . / Ooh, how did you know?" ("Sexy Sadie"). Of course, the object of Lennon's mockery here is the Maharishi Mahesh Yogi, who turned out to be something less than the holy man the Beatles thought him to be. His main interest in the band, it turned out, was financial. Thus, he was not only vain but hypocritical.

The vice of pettiness is illustrated in a more obscure Beatles's song, penned by Harrison for the *Yellow Submarine* soundtrack. The point of the lyric is to counterbalance the hysteria and near worship of the band's music, if only by reminding fans of the obvious fact that they were only making music.

> It doesn't really matter what chords I play
> What words I say or what time of day it is,
> As it's only a Northern song. ("Only a Northern Song")

But as any rational musicologist knows, the Beatles were not just making any music. They were making some of the greatest music of the century. So to diminish the significance of this, as this song does, appears to be petty. Or is Harrison being ironic here? This might be a simple case of Beatle humor—a topic to which we shall return shortly.

Modesty is yet another moral summit between two immoral valleys. The modest person maintains proper feelings toward his or her public appearance. To be too public with one's body is to be shameless, and to go to the other extreme is bashfulness. An example of the former appears on the White Album, in the song "Why Don't We Do It in the Road?" Here we have a song that not only describes something shameless but which might itself be shameless. The Beatles themselves seemed to recognize this, as Lennon dared McCartney to sing it! Of course, Paul took the dare, and the result is the most ribald moment in the Beatles discography.[4]

On the same album appears a good example of the vice opposite shamelessness, a plea to Mia Farrow's sister, Prudence, who appears to have suffered from severe shyness during her stay in Rishikesh with the Beatles and the Maharishi. As Ringo recounts, "Prudence meditated and hibernated. We saw her twice in the two weeks I was there. Everyone would be banging on the door: 'Are you still alive?'" (*Beatles Anthology*, p. 284). Hence Lennon's plaintive refrain about Prudence's reluctance to socialize.

When it comes to the matter of anger, the moral virtue is good temper, found in the person who gets angry at the right things and to a degree that is appropriate. In contrast, the spiritless person makes too many allowances and does not show enough indignation at the appropriate things. Generally, a spiritless person lacks vitality and vigor. In circumstances where one has been wronged in some way, such a person falls short in the area of anger. The irascible person, however, is short-tempered and thus errs on the side of excess. Such people, says Aristotle, "get angry quickly and with the wrong persons and at the wrong things and more than is right" (*Ethics*, line 996).

Consider, for example, responding to a two-timing girlfriend. A proper response might be to confront her along the lines explained in "No Reply," simply recounting the observations of her infidelity. And even if the girl begs to be given another chance, the wise course might be simply to say, "No, not a second time." After all, as the old adage goes, "fool me once, shame on you; fool me twice, shame on me." But the irascible response described in "Run for Your Life," threatening to kill her if she cheats again, is excessive. Some other Lennon compositions, such as "You Can't Do That" and "I'll Cry Instead," illustrate this tendency toward overreaction and vengeance in response to lost romance. Lennon's hypocrisy here is stunning, of course, given his own numerous affairs, culminating in his leaving Cynthia for Yoko Ono.

Speaking of which, Cynthia's response to John's leaving her for Yoko seems to illustrate the vice of spiritlessness. Not only

---

[4] This song is surpassed for lewdness by some Beatle solo projects, however, with John and Yoko's *Two Virgins* album being the clear "winner" in that category.

did she demonstrate no anger at his unfaithfulness; she essentially approved it. In her book, *A Twist of Lennon,* Cynthia remarks coolly: "When I first set eyes on Yoko, I knew that she was the one for John. It was pure instinct; the chemistry was right, the mental aura that surrounded them was almost identical."[5] Cynthia proceeded to make it easy for John and Yoko by moving out of the house herself rather than kicking the couple out. She continues: "I didn't blame John and Yoko. I understood their love. I knew I couldn't fight the unity of mind and body that they had with each other" (*John Lennon,* p. 157). However casual one's view of marriage, surely such brazen behavior deserves an angry rebuke—if not a "Run for Your Life" response, at least something along the lines of "You Can't Do That"!

Perhaps the most important virtue in the Aristotelian catalogue is justice, which is essentially fairness or the moral skill of giving to each its due. Unlike the other virtues, justice is somewhat ambiguous, applying differently in various contexts. First, there is distributive justice, which concerns the proper distribution of wealth and honor among people. There is also commercial justice, which obtains in contexts of exchange, such as when people buy and sell goods. Finally, there is remedial justice, which is called for when rectifying a situation in which some harm has occurred. What unites all particular forms of justice, Aristotle notes, is *proportionality.* For every distribution, exchange, or damage of goods there is a proper ratio or equilibrium that is due. To achieve the correct proportion is just, and to violate it is unjust.

Numerous Beatles songs illustrate injustice of various kinds. Outstanding among these is Harrison's "Taxman," a pointed jibe at the British revenue system. The Beatles' gross income put them in an appalling ninety-five-percent tax bracket:

> Let me tell you how it will be.
> There's one for you, nineteen for me. . . .
> Should five percent appear too small
> Be thankful I don't take it all,
> 'Cause I'm the taxman. Yeah, I'm the taxman. ("Taxman")

---

[5] Quoted in Richard Buskin, *John Lennon: His Life and Legend* (Lincolnwood: Publications International, 1991), p. 151.

The Beatles' income was a result of their own hard work. And, with Beatlemania, they had even sacrificed their own personal freedom and peace of mind.[6] Such a steeply progressive tax system was terribly unjust, the Beatles thought, and with good reason. They would argue that true proportionality recommends a flatter tax, where everyone is taxed a certain percentage of their income. In any case, Lennon remarks, "we believe that if you earn it, you may as well keep it, unless there's a communal or Communist or real Christian society. But while we're living in this, I protest against paying the Government what I have to pay them" (*Beatles Anthology*, p. 207).

A non-monetary case of injustice is illustrated in the song "She's Leaving Home," a poignant story of a young girl who runs away from home. After discovering her note, the girl's mother: "Breaks down and cries to her husband / 'Daddy, our baby's gone! / Why would she treat us so thoughtlessly? / How could she do this to me?' ("She's Leaving Home"). The young girl has been given so much, but she repays her parents with rejection. At the least, dedicated parenting warrants a child's deep gratitude and respect. The girl's actions betray attitudes quite contrary to these and are quite disproportionate to what she owes her parents. So her running away is profoundly unjust. (Note that this analysis of the song is very different from that of Erin Kealey, elsewhere in this volume. Kealey sees the girl's leaving home as essentially a statement of personal authenticity.)

Also noteworthy in these lyrics is sympathy with the parent's perspective. The Beatles were often condemned by the older generation for leading their kids astray and undermining parental authority. While this critique may have been partly justified, "She's Leaving Home" demonstrates that the Beatles' saw both sides of the issue of youthful rebellion. Lennon later remarked that their use of the phrase "never a thought for ourselves" originated with his Aunt Mimi. She said this often as she cared for him after the departure of John's father and death of his mother. Perhaps Lennon was haunted by the recognition that he had unjustly taken for granted the sacrifices of his generous Aunt.

---

[6] As George Harrison says, "The people gave their money and they gave their screams, but the Beatles gave their nervous systems" (*The Beatles Anthology*, p. 354).

A final Aristotelian virtue is wit. If some are surprised by the notion that cracking a joke can be morally virtuous, they need only consider that amusement is a significant dimension of human social life. As usual, according to Aristotle, one can err either on the side of deficiency or excess when it comes to amusement. Those who are neither inclined to make jokes nor to appreciate the jokes of others are boorish. More broadly, the boor is insensitive to others, has a rude manner, and shows little interest in being agreeable to others. On the other hand, there is the buffoon, who is clownish to the point of being ludicrous and socially disruptive. In Aristotle's words, the buffoon "is the slave of his sense of humor, and spares neither himself nor others if he can raise a laugh, and says things none of which a man of refinement would say" (*Ethics*, line 1001). The virtue between these extremes is ready-wittedness, the moral skill of tastefully joking. A witty person knows when a joke is socially appropriate and uses humorous remarks to edify others and enhance a social situation.

The Beatles themselves displayed tremendous wit, both personally and in their lyrics. With regard to the latter, the Beatles' humor makes their songs more endearing. Sometimes their wit is simply playful, such as in "Maxwell's Silver Hammer," "Piggies," and "You Know My Name (Look up My Number)." In other cases, they use humor to reinforce a serious political point:

> You say you'll change the constitution.
> Well you know, we all want to change your head.
> You tell me it's the institution.
> Well you know, you better free your mind instead.
> But if you go carrying pictures of Chairman Mao
> You ain't gonna make it with anyone anyhow. ("Revolution")

Or, in still other instances, they use humor to mask a serious personal struggle, as in "Everybody's Got Something to Hide Except for Me and My Monkey" and "The Ballad of John and Yoko." The Beatles recommend that we not take ourselves too seriously nor lose our joy and the lightness of being that their music is determined to celebrate. The wit in their songs deftly hits the mean between boorishness and buffoonery.

It's Getting Very Near the End . . .

The Beatles illustrate numerous Aristotelian virtues, including liberality, pride, modesty, good temper, justice, and wit. As we have seen, their lyrics typically endorse particular virtues by ridiculing or mocking their respective vices, such as meanness, vanity, and injustice, though they sometimes directly illustrate the virtues themselves, like wit and good temper. And, occasionally, the Beatles' songs, or even the Beatles themselves, illustrate some vices, such as irascibility and shamelessness.

For Aristotle, the virtues constitute the sorts of traits that one must have in order to be a good person. They are particular excellences that we must display if we are to realize our unique human *telos* or end. To achieve this end is to flourish as a human being. So, if you want to be truly happy, then be good.

The virtuous life is difficult and calls for a lifetime of steady effort. As Aristotle says, "one swallow does not make a summer, nor does one day; and so too one day, or a short time, does not make a man blessed and happy" (*Ethics*, line 943). You cannot live a morally perfect life. But as you practice virtue, improving your habits and forming your character with each good choice, you will find that it's getting better all the time.

6

She's a Woman: The Beatles and the Feminist Ethic of Care

PEGGY J. BOWERS

> If you want to know more about femininity, enquire from your own experience of life, or turn to the poets.
>
> —Sigmund Freud, *Femininity*

July 6th, 1957, the date that, as every diehard Beatles fan knows, changed forever the fledgling musical form known as rock-'n'roll. James Paul McCartney, a fifteen-year-old student at Liverpool Institute Grammar School and aspiring guitarist, met John Winston Lennon, leader of the Quarry Men, at a summer fete for St. Peter's Parish Church. Soon after, the legendary Lennon-McCartney duo began inauspiciously producing rock tunes, their friendship forged in rock'n'roll, working class backgrounds, and more importantly for our purposes, the loss of each's very significant maternal relationship. Paul, whose mother had already died of breast cancer, and John, whose own mother was struck and killed by a car a year after he met Paul, were two motherless sons with an unquestionable feminine side.

With the addition of George Harrison in 1958, a schoolmate who impressed Paul with his perfectionistic musical drive on the guitar at the tender age of fourteen (practicing until his fingers bled), the triumvirate of mystical, philosophical, relationally astute and sometimes sardonic songwriters were strung into an instrument poised to create and resonate to strains of society to which the Establishment was seemingly deaf. While John added a linguistic sensitivity, George arguably gave the band a soul, leading them into Eastern mysticism, and musical forms and

instruments focused on the emotional, which ultimately legiti-
mated the group's expression of feminine (if not explicitly feminist) sensibilities.

As they evolved in the tough slums of Liverpool and
Hamburg, working multiple gigs that would often have them
performing for ten hours a day, their unique artistic vision developed amid a cultural backdrop that was far from ideal. Devin
McKinney[1] paints a bleak picture of the social and economic circumstances that marked these formative days of the Beatles as
they experimented with a variety of musical forms within an
often socially stratified and depressing environment.

Rather than expressing the anger and nihilism that bands
such as the *Sex Pistols* would popularize a generation later, Paul,
John, George, and Ringo espoused the simple belief that self-
preservation is possible only through networks of social support
and interconnection. These pronouncements of profound love
and need, perhaps best summarized by songs like "With a Little
Help from My Friends," demonstrate that rather than displaying
their scars through anti-social themes that promoted isolation,
they came to appreciate the necessities of caring. While the
Beatles did complicate the bland, naive portraiture characterized
by the bubble-gum machine of popular music, their music further presented a consistent ethical vision that was both original
and sophisticated.

What Is My Life, Without Your Love?

In her pioneering work revising the primary developmental
models stemming from the field of social psychology, Carol
Gilligan[2] is often cited as one of the central figures in the moral
philosophy known as the "feminist ethic of care." When she
examined the research of foundational figures such as Kohlberg,
she found that particular forms of logic were validated over others and that young girls were more likely to rank lower than
their male counterparts for moral reasoning. Rather than
approaching ethical problems from a highly individualized per-

[1] *The Beatles in Dream and History* (Cambridge, Massachusetts: Harvard University
Press, 2003).
[2] *In a Different Voice: Psychological Theory and Women's Development* (Cambridge,
Massachusetts: Harvard University Press, 1987).

spective, the girls had a tendency to complicate Kohlberg's questions by asking about the relational qualities of the scenarios that he provided. Because their solutions were not based in some absolute principle (for example, "stealing is wrong"), they were perceived as underdeveloped at moral reasoning.

Gilligan contended that these respondents were not lacking in their ethical development, but rather expressed an alternative ethical sensibility that existing models of moral reasoning ignored. In her critique of Sigmund Freud, Gilligan writes that dialogic connection, "rather than seeming as an illusion or taking on explosive transcendental cast, appears as a primary feature of both individual psychology and civilized life" (p. 48). This ability to understand the impact that one's actions have upon others and that social networks form the foundation of society, a sensibility that is often more developed in women, became the basis for Gilligan's critique of existing models of moral reasoning.

Although at first it may seem farfetched to think that the Beatles' music articulates a systematic feminist philosophy, both Paul and John—after having collaborated with one another almost exclusively during their early careers as Beatles—eventually entered into important collaborative relationships with female companions: Linda in the case of Paul, and Yoko in the case of John. While their music is not explicitly feminist, careful analysis reveals a powerful subtext of moral reasoning that has long been associated with the feminine style in western culture. This strain of moral philosophy seeks to subvert the assumption that moral agents approach moral questions free from social and relational context. The feminist ethic of care emerges as a challenge to masculine modes of reasoning where subjects emerge in isolation from the social forces that have, in reality, shaped them. Rather than devaluing feminine modes of reasoning as inferior, this new model seeks to use the concept of care as a way to rebuild our moral logic in a way that unveils the illusion of isolation so central to the modernist subject.

Music that is so resonant within popular culture for such a long period of time shapes perceptions, floating from context to context where it infiltrates consciousness in sometimes unknowable ways. The overt relational themes in Beatles music reveal a moral counterculture rooted in the ethic of care. What emerges is a drama where art not only imitates, but constitutes life.

Happiness Is a Warm Relationship?

In Gilligan's bifurcation between masculine and feminine modes of reasoning, she suggests that these distinctions are based largely on differing perceptions regarding interpersonal interactions. Viewing intimacy as a threat often exhibits itself in male culture as a sign of weakness—a mistake that opens the reasoning subject to the possibility of betrayal. Even in the early stages of the Beatles' career, one sees sustained attention to the importance of interdependence, or deliberate mutual reliance on one another. In songs such as "Help," one sees this dynamic as a natural part of the maturation process:

> When I was younger so much younger than today
> I never needed anybody's help in any way.
> But now these days are gone, I'm not so self-assured
> Now I find I've changed my mind and opened up the doors.

"Help" portrays the idea that one needs meaningful relationships to manage one's existence as an epiphany—a sudden recognition of self-evident facts. The satisfaction gained from contact with others extends beyond the need to fulfill bodily desire; it stems from a need to complete one's sense of self and derive the confidence to navigate one's life. As Paul echoes in "Yesterday," without his significant relationship, "Suddenly, I'm not half the man I used to be." Viewing the need for care as a natural part of the human condition, its subsequent recognition through a variety of themes became an almost fanatical mission in the following years.

Given this thematic tendency in the Beatles' music, it's not surprising that they would be drawn to musical genres such as the Delta Blues with its hyperbolic expressions of interdependency. When Paul opines in "Oh Darling" that if his lover leaves him he won't be able to get along without her, he is expressing one of the emotions most identified with the economically depressed South, fear of social isolation. In the absence of material prosperity, one is left with nothing but social networks to manage and channel emotions into socially productive ways. Even in the significant stylistic shifts such as the whimsical orchestral piece "When I'm Sixty-Four," which disconcertingly makes the connection between being needed and being fed, one can see that togetherness is more than a pleasurable act of leisure. It is central to the labor of life. In emotionally provocative songs such as "Oh Darling" where begging and pleading for love is commonplace, one sees a highly feminized form of dialogue. In a great deal of popular music, the threat of passion is expressed as a blinding force of the body, perhaps as a woman who uses her sexuality to deceive a man and ultimately hurt or betray him. For the Beatles, this passion becomes a source not of managing sexual appetite, but an avenue for comfort and self-realization.

I've Got a Feeling

The expressions of pure emotive force in the Beatles' music can be explosive. Think of songs such as "Here Comes the Sun" and "Good Day Sunshine," that portray joy as an embodied experience that creates social bonds. "Here Comes the Sun" in particular summons the warming sensations of life when George engages his significant other by observing, "little darling, the smile's returning to their faces. Little darling, it seems like years since it's been here. Here comes the sun. Here comes the sun and I say, it's alright." Notice that the heightened sense of life is experienced not only through individual thoughts and feelings, but through seeing these evidenced on the faces of others, strengthening their shared sense of belonging.

George, so famous for his weeping guitar, was overtly aware of the power of music to express raw emotion. In his autobiography[3] he notes that what attracted him to the sitar and to Indian music was its ability to evoke strong emotional experiences in a given space and time. The Beatles' flirtations with Eastern mysticism and experimentation with psychedelic drugs stemmed from a desire to seek alternative modes for understanding the nature of the self. As the band began work on the *Sgt. Pepper's* project, Allan Kozinn notes that John in particular had become heavily influenced by the *Tibetan Book of the Dead,* which teaches that each human possesses an archetypal subconscious containing a poetic language of higher truth that can be tapped using a variety of meditative methods.[4] This loss of self to some universal dynamic becomes an expression of what George would call the "the space between us all" described in "Within

---

[3] George Harrison, *I, Me, Mine* (New York: Simon and Schuster, 1980).
[4] Allan Kozinn, *The Beatles* (London: Phaidon, 1995).

You Without You." Perhaps one of the most ecstatic interpenetrations of self with some larger dynamic comes in "Hey Jude" where the subject is reminded to "let her into your heart. Then you can start to make it better."

The way the passions relate to the evolution of human societies, particularly the way that these passions are coded within aesthetic performances has interested philosophers reaching back to classical western thought. With Plato's famous assault upon the arts as fraudulent imitations of life, the passions that they produce have also been the subject of suspicion. The Beatles' forays into pure pathos are beautifully articulated by "She's Leaving Home," a narrative about a young woman leaving home unexpectedly. Allan Gibbard notes that some negative emotions dealing with loss or guilt often produce social bonds by reinforcing social norms[5] "She's Leaving Home" can be interpreted as a morality tale humanizing the pain that parents feel when their children assert their own identities, but using the Aristotelian concept of catharsis, we feel pity for the grieving couple through the vicarious performance of the narrative. Songs like this do not produce pity via the narrator expressing his own grief, but ask the audience to identify with a couple who are completely external to their own experience. This training in empathy, an important component of the ethic of care, rather than reinforcing social norms, may in fact simply raise awareness that there are those beyond ourselves—beyond narrator and audience—who exist as sympathetic entities.

Your Mother Should Know

One of the primary critiques that has pursued Gilligan's work is the argument that she reinforces essentialist boundaries by simply reaffirming the old "boys think: girls feel" dichotomy. When the Beatles seek to personify nurture and empathy, they often turn to female personae or icons, which are sometimes transformations of their own mothers, to create a meaningful representation of caring. In Paul's "Let It Be," he observes, "when I find myself in times of trouble, Mother Mary comes to me, speaking words of wisdom." Although Paul is speaking of his

---

[5] *Wise Choices, Apt Feelings: A Theory of Normative Judgment* (Oxford: Oxford University Press, 1990).

own mother, named Mary, the plausible double entendre with the Virgin Mary is palpable. Given the Christian mythology that features an often angry, judgmental, and capricious patriarchal entity moderated by a feminine presence that provides both a comfort and a shield, this personification of comfort through the image of the Mother Mary, and his own mother, is highly resonant as a cultural image. Yet not only does she shield, but she engages the narrator in dialogue that provides wisdom to manage the trials that he must face, as one might imagine an orphan longing for his mother to arise from the dead and soothe him. John's own ethereal tribute to his mother, Julia, makes her a gentle, wise, romanticized, goddess figure, with whom he longs to connect, physically and emotionally, the picture of her so beautiful it brings him peace. "Here, There, and Everywhere" sees this feminine force as ubiquitous in human culture. Recognizing that the feminist ethic is central to male maturation means boys don't just think, they feel—in part because of a relational exchange with the feminine. This exchange is not exclusively sexual, but rather, is a way to expand one's horizons. The Beatles' lyrics indicate an acute awareness that the development of the self occurs only by recognizing others.

The Real Revolution: You Can Learn how to Be in Time

The centrality of interdependence as a theme for the Beatles' work makes a powerful emotional statement about their own interpersonal orientations. Viewing relational connection as an innate social virtue, they transformed their own experiences into a roadmap to point toward this as the ultimate goal of a fulfilled life. Examining lyrics from songs such as "The Word" one can see this even further:

> Spread the word and you'll be free
> Spread the word and be like me
> Spread the word I'm thinking of
> Have you heard the word is love

The word "love" is among the most overused, ambiguous concepts in contemporary popular music. Through sheer repetition and overuse, terms like "love" become hollow signifiers in which emotional intensity is lost or absent. To make this concept meaningful, one has to infuse it with some type of moral force. Anthony Elliott argues that while John Lennon often wrote songs about togetherness, he also sought to "estrange politics from its institutionalized forms, to displace rationalism with art, to replace the call to action with the demand for fresh thinking." [6] As evidence of this consider "Revolution 1": "You tell me it's the institution, well, you know, you better free your mind instead." The ethic of care cautions against empty, generalized emotion. Caring must occur in the particular, in that small set of people and creatures for whom we can substantively, dynamically feel and act. "Love, love, love" might need to be part of our collective social identity, but at least in the Beatles' lyrics, love is embodied in the names and faces of those immediately around us, the lovers and friends, both living and dead, for whom John poignantly reminds us in "In my Life" he will always keep a place in his heart

Much of this aesthetic shift toward a new ethic of care begins with the process of narration. Stephen Benson writes that narrative is grounded in a dialogic act. [7] A key element of the Beatles' unique style of narration is an intimate relationship with the subjects of their songs—making a subject both the object of description as well as the one who is addressed. Songs such as "Get Back" demonstrate how the Beatles shift seamlessly between these various roles. Jo Jo's exploits are described in some detail in third person, then the chorus becomes an exhortation that directs him to look to his social roots for the source of his restlessness. At times, it is unclear whether "get back" is directed at Jo Jo, Loretta, or the song's generalized listener. By moving Jo Jo from being an object to being directly addressed, a narrative position formerly held by the audience, the song fosters a direct empathetic relationship, transporting the listener into Jo Jo's shoes for a moment. These narrative strategies appear in songs like "Come Together" where after being informed that the object of narration will "hold you in his armchair so you can feel his disease," the listener is directly addressed and exhorted by the familiar chorus. Through such

---

[6] *The Mourning of John Lennon* (Berkeley: University of California Press, 1999), p. 114.
[7] Stephen Benson, "For Want of a Better Term? Polyphony and the Value of Music in Bakhtin and Kundera," *Narrative* 11 (2003), pp. 292–311.

narration, listeners are transported into the songs and identify vicariously through the individuals described in the stories.

Carry that Weight

A central argument that has led to the denigration of women as moral agents in society and to the dismissal of the ethic of care as a philosophical perspective is their relegation to the private sphere. While Rousseau was advocating the perfectibility of the passions, he also argued that for a woman to "pursue goals whose aim was not the welfare of her family, was for her to lose those qualities which would make her estimable and desirable."[8] Because of this traditional consignment of women to domestic spaces they have been denied access to the public spaces where moral warrants become public policies. This quandary has led some proponents of the ethic of care to encourage not just women to seek power in public spaces, but society to re-evaluate the type of labor that women produce as socially beneficial and worthy of reward.[9] The song "Lady Madonna" addresses this issue by using the Virgin Mary as a symbol for a low-income mother whose rent money, rather than children, might need to be sent from heaven.

This song seems on one level to admire the primary image of female nurturance in the face of great economic and domestic odds. Paul has said that he wrote it as a tribute to women, understandable given the number of women he must have seen labor with several children and little money in the blue-collar neighborhood of his youth. Aside from the laudatory aspect of the song, however, it resonates to an element of morality often missing from other ethical systems of thought. Shame is arguably a relational moral quality, an emotion dependent on our perceived connection to another, and a powerful guardian of boundaries that will preserve that relationship. We feel shame under the scrutiny of another; we act in morally prescribed ways to avoid that shame. The shameful circumstances of Lady Madonna elicit Paul's justifiable admiration, but also should evoke shame in those who dismiss the crucial moral role the nurturer plays.

---

[8] Jean Grimshaw, "The Idea of a Female Ethic," in Peter Singer, ed., *A Companion to Ethics* (Oxford: Blackwell, 1991), p. 491.
[9] Virginia Held, "Care and the Extension of Markets," *Hypatia* 17 (2002), pp. 19–33.

I'm Looking through You

When the Beatles began to experiment with discordant forms of music, often their narrative lyrics pointed out the apathy in our social relationships. One of the most compelling examples is "A Day in the Life," a song punctuated by its classic atonal climaxes. Amid dissonance and confusion are fragmentary narratives that suggest a simultaneous familiarity and inability to recognize everyday objects and persons.

> He blew his mind out in a car
> He didn't notice that the lights had changed
> A crowd of people stood and stared
> They'd seen his face before.
> Nobody was really sure if he was from the House of Lords.

In "A Day in the Life," the trip jars the listener from his or her everyday complacency in the face of societal anonymity. The musical violence attempts to create rupture in the listeners' perspective—drawing them to listen and, in this case, see their ethical apathy as a concrete and definable object.

Nowhere is this attempt to manufacture an ethic of recognition more beautifully realized than in "Eleanor Rigby" with its haunting chorus, "all the lonely people, where do they all come from?" Jacqueline Warwick argues that this song challenges feminine identity by presenting Eleanor Rigby as ultimately unsympathetic: "while a woman listening to *Revolver* can negotiate many of the gendered subject positions it presents in order to make them fit her, Eleanor Rigby seems insurmountably unappealing."[10] Instead, she says, Aretha Franklin's cover ("I am Eleanor Rigby") is more appealing because the singer places herself in Rigby's position rather than relegating her to being a mere object of the narrator's curiosity—a spectacle of ineptitude.

Yet Warwick's profound desire to reinterpret the song may in fact demonstrate its effectiveness in facilitating an ethic of care. As we are told that she, "picks up the rice in the church where a wedding has been. Lives in a Dream. Waits by the window,

---

[10] Jacqueline Warwick, "'I'm Eleanor Rigby': Female Identity and *Revolver*," in Russell Reising, ed., *Every Sound There Is: The Beatles'* Revolver *and the Transformation of Rock and Roll* (Burlington: Ashgate, 2002), p. 65.

wearing the face that she keeps in a jar by the door. Who is it for?" this final question is directed back to the listener. No one, not even Father McKenzie, who scripts sermons that go both unheard and unheeded, can save Eleanor and the millions like her (or himself, for that matter) from the fate of isolation. If not even God cares, then who will? This song's familiar apathy defines its moral force. Its unapologetically stark descriptions stand as an indictment to all of us who, in the particular faces of our fellow humans, have one by one made the lonely world Eleanor Rigby inhabits. "For well you know that it's a fool who plays it cool," Paul reminds us in "Hey Jude", "by making his world a little colder." We are not supposed to feel good or empowered by Eleanor's plight because precisely this dynamic breeds relational complacency. Rigby is a powerful image not for what she reinforces, but because of the social failures that she represents.

And in the End, the Love You Take . . .

Gilligan's feminist ethic of care revises traditional notions of virtue from those dealing with the isolation of the sovereign rational subject to a system of thought that attempts to place significant value on the redeeming qualities of interdependence. Using thematic and aesthetic strategies to create shifts in the conventional perspectives of their listeners, one can find a number of parallels between the Beatles' artistic expression and this philosophical viewpoint. Examining the relationship between philosophy and popular culture often tells us more about philosophy than it does about the pop icons it is supposed to illuminate. In this case, through the musical arts, the Beatles create the contours for living out a more humane culture. By setting the listener in dialogue with figures like Rigby and Jo Jo, the Beatles set the stage for an ethic based upon recognition, rather than one of contemplation. This ethic emerges gently but insistently, yet stopping short of polemic, carefully ensconcing these encouragements in beautifully crafted aesthetic performances. Given the power that these songs have had over the years, this continued interest demonstrates the power of art to create shifts in ethical consciousness.

IV

Why Don't We Do It in the Marketplace?

The Beatles
and Social Philosophy

7

You Say that You've Got Everything You Want: The Beatles and the Critique of Consumer Culture

SCOTT CALEF

There's no doubt the Beatles enjoyed being rich; Lennon and McCartney sometimes began their joint song writing sessions by saying "Let's write a swimming pool!"[1] There was an underlying tension between their materialistic desires and creativity, however, and despite their underprivileged backgrounds they were too sensitive to ignore it for long.

After all, if you're writing swimming pools, are you really making art? Without some consumerism, there would be no Beatles—no driving ambition to make it big, no records or CDs. Nor corporation t-shirts, Coca Cola, or Yellow Submarine bath toys! Even so, the Beatles meant it when they sang that love and fun can't be bought.

It's All Too Much

On the other hand, maybe they just didn't try hard enough. According to *US News and World Report*, Americans spend more on garbage bags than ninety other countries spend on everything combined; we have twice as many shopping malls as high schools.[2] That *sounds* bad, but is it, really? What's wrong with consumer culture? And what *is* consumer culture, anyway? These are philosophical questions, and to answer them we

---

[1] Mark Hertsgaard, *A Day in the Life: The Music and Artistry of the Beatles* (New York: Delacorte, 1995), p. 123.
[2] *US News and World Report* (June 28th–July 5th, 2004), p. 59.

should look not only to the Beatles themselves, astute observers of the scene that they were, but to philosophers and social critics like Rousseau, who blamed property and commodities for many evils.

So, what's consumer culture and what's wrong with it? To begin, consumer cultures view the ownership of objects as a primary means to happiness and fulfillment. This is dangerous for many reasons. For one, a possession-centered life is dependent upon externals, and externals are rarely under our complete control. As another British band put it, "You can't always get what you want." In his most famous moral treatise, the *Nichomachean Ethics,* Aristotle admits that happiness requires external goods. Nobody, he reasoned, could be happy who was starving, repulsive, friendless, or without *Help!* However, he also argues that the happy life should be self-contained and within one's control as much as possible. John contends that "when it starts to rain, everything's the same" ("Rain"). He doesn't much care whether it rains or shines because either way the weather's fine. John can't control the climate, but he *can* control his state of mind; his contentment isn't at the mercy of forces beyond his command.

The trick seems to be, not to have everything you want, but contentedly to want what you have. What's true of the weather is true of wealth and all it can buy. Unfortunately, according to Rousseau, consumer societies foster so many wants and needs that it's difficult to satisfy them all. Rousseau looks at consumer society by comparing it with a "state of nature," a hypothetical condition supposedly existing prior to society. Before humans invented societies and merchandise he describes man "quenching his thirst at a stream, dining on acorns, finding his rest at the foot of the same tree that furnished his meal, and therewith, his needs are satisfied."[3] One answer to consumerist dependency, then, is to want and value what is free, simple, natural, and easily acquired. Forget about that new home theatre system with 5.1 digital surround sound and big-ass flat-screen TV (hmmm, on second thought, that sounds pretty good! No, no, no!). Instead "sit beside a mountain stream" and become a Child of Nature— one of Mother Nature's Sons (or Daughters)—and relax in your

---

[3] Rousseau, p. 105. All my Rousseau references in this chapter are to *The First and Second Discourses* (New York: St. Martin's Press, 1964).

field of grass with swaying daisies beneath the sun. Or, if nature's not your bag (or you're stuck in Liverpool!), the Beatles' alternative antidote to dependency is found in the self-sufficiency of unconditional love. In the end, "All You Need is Love," and since "the love you take is equal to the love you make," we aren't dependent upon uncontrollable circumstances for our needs. We're always free to love. If we do, we'll have all we need.

The problem isn't just that we become dependent upon externals, however. After all, some people are rich, lucky, or pretty good at getting what they want. But even then problems arise. Rousseau notes that soon after humans began inventing all sorts of commodities they "lost almost all their pleasantness through habit, and as they had at the same time degenerated into true needs, being deprived of them became much more cruel than possessing them was sweet; and people were unhappy to lose them without being happy to possess them" (p. 147). We quickly take our possessions for granted. We think we need them though they produce little lasting satisfaction, and to acquire them "a man must break his back" and forego leisure ("Girl"). Rousseau thus calls the growth of commodity consciousness and a spirit of acquisitiveness "the first yoke" humans imposed on themselves "without thinking" (p.147).

My Love Don't Give Me Presents

A further difficulty is that our obsession with owning things infects our relationships. Rousseau thinks our most important relationships are derived from property and mediated though our possessions. Consequently, in highly consumptive cultures values like friendship and love become commercially tainted. We begin viewing our partners as assets that we have a right to control, and when we can't, we become "possessive" and jealous. John sings that he'd rather see his girlfriend dead than with another man ("Run for Your Life").

Rousseau argues that sexual exclusivity and the family are outgrowths of private property. Where there's no property there's no division of labor, and therefore no mutual dependence. All people, both men and women, are then free, independent and self-sufficient. But once property is established, a division of labor becomes inevitable and men and women slip into separate roles. Suddenly, no longer independent, they need one another, and families are the natural outgrowth of this dependence.

We often try to "purchase" the "object" of our affection with gifts or the promise of a certain lifestyle. Although Paul claims not to care much for money, he recognizes its romantic utility; if expensive jewelry won't do the trick, he'll give everything he's got to give to hear her say "I love you too" ("Can't Buy Me Love"). In "She's Leaving Home," the parents seek to deny their daughter the opportunity to experience and live her own life through making her economically indebted to them. Since all their lives they struggled hard to get by, they think she's treating them thoughtlessly by leaving. Their love is defined by what they've sacrificed to provide. Alternatively, we may love someone, even unconsciously, as much for what they can give us as for themselves.

If we're honest, we probably accept that money *can* buy us love (if we have enough of it) and that rich people can acquire more desirable partners than poor people. John sings, "She's in love with me, and I feel fine." But is she really? She's so glad she's telling the whole world, but what's she shouting from the rooftops? Her baby buys her diamond rings and things. Would she love him as much if he were poor or lost everything? In "A Hard Day's Night" John relates how he works all day to earn enough to keep his woman in style. It sounds like drudgery, but to him, it's worth it to hear her say she's going to give him everything. But notice: he isn't getting "everything" from her unless he pays for it! And as "Drive My Car" makes plain, if you want the trophy girl, a star of the screen, you'd better be able to tell her your prospects are good.

Unfortunately, this strategy has inherent limitations. Some people have no intention of giving what they've pledged: The vain and belittling woman in "Girl" promises the world, and though her suitor is pathetic enough to believe her, in his heart he knows it's a lie. And even sincere offers may be rejected: In "I'm Down" John describes the everyday and depressing occurrence of women casting away the rings men buy them.

Tell Me What You See

Consumer cultures also embrace hierarchical modes of identification. Capitalism tempts us to equate our self-worth with our economic position and to judge others by that standard too. If "you're a rich man" you're "one of the beautiful people." Those who don't pursue—or can't successfully obtain—the things valued by consumer culture are "left behind" or made to feel left out. Three important consequences result.

- First, we become frantic in our efforts to achieve success. The Beatles mock such bourgeois industriousness in "I'm Only Sleeping": The peppy hustle of urban one-up-manship is "crazy" and a waste of energy. Eventually even the corporate drones will discover there's no need.

- Second, appearances acquire great importance. I must maintain the facade of a certain lifestyle, even if it requires living beyond my means. Although these appearances aren't restricted to conspicuous wealth, Rousseau writes that "for one's own advantage it was necessary to appear to be other than what one in fact was. To be and to seem to be became two altogether different things; and from this distinction came conspicuous ostentation, deceptive cunning, and all the vices that follow from them" (pp. 155–56). We thus become alienated from others by a wall of pretense. Other people's identities are unknown to us ("Hey Bulldog"). We become actors occupying roles, "waiting for someone to perform with." But, Paul reminds us, "you'll do" ("Hey Jude"). We're fine as we are, and there's no need to dissemble. Or, as John prefers to put it in "Everybody's Got Something to Hide Except for Me and My Monkey," there's real joy in authenticity, where the opposites—the outside (how we appear to others) and the inside (how we really are)—are unified and the masks removed.

- Third, where appearances acquire such monumental social significance, conformity is emphasized over individuality. To "belong" is to wear the fashions and drive the automobile and shop at the stores that serve to define our social position (or the one to which we aspire).

The Beatles have great fun with this in *A Hard Day's Night*. George, conscripted by some corporate "maven" of hip to assess a new clothing line for teens, pronounces them "dead grotty." The exec knowingly replies, "It's rather touching, really. Here's this kid trying to give me his utterly valueless opinion when I

know for a fact that within a month he'll be suffering from a violent inferiority complex and loss of status because he isn't wearing one of these nasty things. Of course they're grotty, you
wretched nit! That's why they were designed! But that's what
you'll want!" George, unmoved, calmly sneers "I won't."
Informed that he'd better shape up or he won't meet Susan, the
firm's resident teenager and company-created pop icon who
symbolizes him, George retorts:

GEORGE: Oh, you mean that posh bird who gets everything
wrong. . . .
EXEC: She's a trend setter. It's her profession.
GEORGE: She's a drag. A well-known drag. . . .
EXEC: Get him out! He's mocking the programmed image!

In "Only A Northern Song" George muses that it "doesn't
really matter" what we put on or how much we make or how
we style our hair.

You May Think the Band Are Not Quite Right

An aesthetic objection to consumer-inspired conformity is that
it's bad for art (as well as fashion). Skeptics should listen to
Spice Girls and *NSYNC albums between episodes of *American
Idol*. The market homogenizes artistic endeavor because artists
outside the mainstream are unlikely to have their work promoted. "Inevitably, financial temptations lead the manager to
exhort the artist to stick to whatever formula worked."[4]

In his famous pamphlet *What is Art?* Tolstoy argues that genuine art must be the expression of feeling, and of a unique feeling.[5] So-called art produced by a calculated effort to achieve

---

[4] Martin Lewis, in his introduction to Brian Epstein's autobiography, *A Cellar Full of
Noise,* (New York: Byron Preiss, 1998), p. 12. Although Lewis particularly praises Brian
Epstein for *not* being that sort of manager, even the Beatles sometimes looked back critically at their own work when they felt they knocked off a song just because they
needed a new single or had to fill space to complete an album. John and George were
particularly self-deprecating in this respect. John, for example, called *Being for the
Benefit of Mr. Kite* a "straight lift" and confessed, "I wasn't very proud of that. There was
no real work. I was just going through the motions because we needed a new song for
Sgt. Pepper at that moment" (Hunter Davies, *The Beatles* [New York: Norton, 1996], p.
275.)

[5] Leo Tolstoy, *What Is Art?* (London: Oxford University Press, 1938 [1898]).

anything other than expression is, for Tolstoy, an inauthentic sham. (Songs written to buy swimming pools are right out!) The paperback writer symbolizes everything wrong with "art" from this perspective. The singer is hawking an utterly derivative novel (a novel "based on a novel") which, despite its wholly unmarketable and soon-to-be-added-to thousand pages, he is all-too-willing to "change around" to please the publisher. He's writing it because he "needs a job" and pleads with the anonymous "Sir or Madam" that it could "make a million." Art, for this hack, is a matter of cranking out material that will make a profit for corporate decision makers.[6]

Come Together

As citizens center their lives around their private property and live behind a wall of appearance, their sense of solidarity with others and of genuine community is diminished. For Rousseau, this is particularly evident between the classes when the affluent become inured to the plight of the suffering masses, the Lady Madonnas of the world. He deplores "the sort of inequality that reigns among all civilized people" which allows "a handful of men to be glutted with superfluities while the starving multitude lacks necessities" (pp. 180–81).

Ironically, the more we conform by embracing consumer society's vision of the good life, the more isolated and alone we become. Mister Mustard is a selfish miser attempting to save paper by concealing it in bodily orifices so others won't know he has it; the only place he ever goes is to look at the Queen, a symbol of the state and social collective for whom he has nothing but contempt: he always shouts out obscenities. Indeed, so cut off is Mustard that he shaves in the dark, unable even to face himself in the mirror. Although an eccentric and stingy skinflint is no model of conspicuous consumption, the impulse to hoard and accumulate is closely related. He's bitter because he

---

[6] Through Apple, the Beatles made a noble attempt to provide artists of all kinds an alternative to scraping at the doors of businessmen to get their work before the public. Discussing Apple, Paul said: "We're in the happy position of not needing any more money. So for the first time, the bosses aren't in it for profit." Chris Ingram, *The Rough Guide to the Beatles* (London: Rough Guides, 2003), p. 60. Unfortunately, this fascinating experiment proved too unwieldy to sustain as differences within the band—and their financial and management inexperience—gradually became more acutely felt.

has to sleep in the park and can't afford what Pam's shop wages provide her. And yet he either can't, or won't, play the game of getting a real job and trying to fit in.

Happiness Is a Warm Gun

Mustard's obscene life is hardly unique. Consumer societies have a deeply regrettable effect on the human psyche. Rousseau believes modern people have been corrupted, and that what we think of as "human nature" (for example, that humans are intrinsically selfish, violent or greedy) is not natural at all. Humans, he insists, have "an innate repugnance to see any sensitive being suffer" (p. 95). Unfortunately, we're no longer natural. Our responses no longer derive from unforced, inborn feelings of compassion but from the artificial (and much weaker) replacements society invented after largely squelching these strong, original impulses—namely, law, morality, religion and ethical philosophy.

We naturally pity the wretched and forlorn, but society suppresses such tender sentiments. By fostering competition, selfishness, envy, jealousy, shame, resentment, pride, contempt, greed, and alienation, capitalism alters our very natures. As unhealthy emotional states are inadvertently encouraged, so are violence and destruction of the environment. We become "piggies" in "starched white shirts" without a care for "what goes on around." Clutching our utensils we feast on bacon, consuming each other to satisfy our appetites.

Act Naturally

But if we're not "piggies" by nature, what is human nature? How do we differ from other species? And more importantly for our present purposes, how does human nature tie in with consumerism?

Rousseau answers that only humans are free; non-humans act from instinct, not choice (pp. 113–14). Both feel the same urges for food, drink, rest or sex, but only humans can resist these inclinations. Freedom, then, is defined by Rousseau as the ability to oppose the promptings of nature and act contrary to them. In this sense, human nature consists in the ability to behave unnaturally. We turn from what is natural toward what is unnatural, and for us, *that's* natural! This is the origin, within the human soul, of consumerism. Because we are free we want what is unnatural, manufactured, unwholesome, fake, assembled. Although not the original sense of the term "Rubber Soul," that phrase encapsulates very nicely the idea that the human spirit is constituted through artificiality. This is a kind of perversion.

We noted above that, for Rousseau, humans have suffered a loss of pity. In "While My Guitar Gently Weeps," George makes a very similar point, and laments that love is sleeping. We haven't yet awakened to love, or perhaps, we've lost the consciousness of how to love. Nobody taught us how to unfold our love because we're being manipulated by those who profit at our shallowness; George claims we're controlled by anonymous powers by whom we've been "bought and sold." [7]   Being thus controlled, our values will take us in the wrong direction: we've been diverted, perverted and inverted. This is such a sadness that even his guitar can't keep from crying.

Nothing Is Real

Several additional criticisms of consumerism can be traced to the Beatles' infatuation with eastern spirituality—and drugs. These experiences inspired metaphysical claims that material objects are not wholly real but are a kind of illusion. A life focused on the acquisition of things is therefore a life devoted to the accumulation of what is, in the end, nothing and meaningless.

This perspective has a long and venerable history in philosophy. Plato, for example, argued that objects perceived by the senses are only partially real because they partake of both Being and Nonbeing. For Plato, what is real is permanent, unchanging, simple, and knowable to the intellect. Plato called these immutable, pure essences "Forms." [8] Numbers are a good example. Take John's favorite from the *White Album*, "Number Nine." We don't know the number nine because we see, hear, or smell

---

[7] David Quantick amusingly notes that "In creating 'While My Guitar Gently Weeps' he [George] also inadvertently invented 70s rock, which is arguably a bad thing but ensured the sale of small cigarette lighters for the next decade." *The Making of the Beatles' White Album* (Chicago: A Capella, 2002), p. 90.

[8] Some scholars (mistakenly, in my view) attribute to numbers a status which is one degree of reality below the forms, on the basis of Plato's discussion of the "divided line" in his *Republic*, lines 509d–511e.

it; it's more like an idea, although an everlasting one. And, that "the one after 909" is 910 is an "eternal" or timeless truth. It would be true even if humans had never existed to count. Mathematical truths and numbers, for Plato, are objects apprehended by means of intelligence, not perception.

Other examples of Forms are what philosophers call "universals." If John, Paul, George, and Ringo are all musicians, they must have something in common (or "universal") which *makes* them musicians. Moreover, what they have in common must also be shared by the Stones, the Yardbirds, the Who, Stu Sutcliff, and Pete Best (poor bastards!)—even Gerry and the Pacemakers! What all musicians have in common isn't something tangible like a musician, and yet, without this commonality, no musicians would exist. So, Plato would say, the Beatles are "real" insofar as they partake of the Forms (such as the Form "musician"), but unreal insofar as they are not themselves Forms. They occupy an intermediate status between the real and unreal.

Plato likens all things in the sensory world to shadows or reflections—indicative of another greater reality upon which they depend, but in themselves unsubstantial. The great task of humanity is to cultivate the philosophical realization of the truth behind the appearances. In one of Plato's greatest works, the *Symposium*, the power of love elevates the soul from affection for a particular person such as Paul (the cute one!) to knowledge of the pure and universal Form of Love.

This is also, in a nutshell, the core idea behind much of the Indian philosophy influencing the Beatles' thinking and lyrics. According to "Strawberry Fields Forever" "nothing is real" and so there's "nothing to get hung about." In "Within You Without You" George bemoans those who take refuge behind a "wall of illusion" and "never glimpse the truth." The implications for consumerism are clear. The wise individual will not waste his or her life trying to acquire things which are illusory and unreal. Commodities are not inherently bad, but *attachment* to them is spiritually counterproductive. Needless to say, in consumer culture attachment is rife. In "Another Girl," Paul equates folly with taking what one does not want. Why waste time wanting what is nothing, empty, a deception? Although "nothing is real" (that is, *no thing* is real), Plato was right about the universal reality of Love: "love is all and love is everyone" ("Tomorrow Never Knows").

Erin Flynn has suggested to me that Paul and George some-times focus on different aspects of the problem of desire. For George, and in Indian philosophy generally, desire and attach-ment are frequently viewed as problems in themselves. The dif-ference between wanting what is admirable and what is ignoble is akin to wishing one were bound by golden chains instead of iron ones. In other places, though, George seems more con-cerned with inordinate desires and overindulgence then with desire *per se*, as when he sings, "All the world is birthday cake, so take a piece, but not too much" (*It's All Too Much*). For Paul, wanting the *wrong* things (and taking what he doesn't want) is clearly the problem, not desire itself. But consumer cultures are all about fostering desires for the wrong things. Think: Big Macs, Captain Crunch, and Pepsi instead of fruits and vegetables. When was the last time you saw an advertisement for spinach or carrots on TV?

For No One

George acerbically remarked, "You can't mass produce cosmic consciousness."[9] Consumerism dulls spiritual and philosophical perception by reinforcing and strengthening the ego, making it more difficult to resist the illusion noted above. The philosophy behind "I Me Mine" is that "it is our preoccupation with our indi-vidual egos—what 'I' want, what belongs to 'me', what's 'mine'—which prevents us from being absorbed into the uni-versal consciousness, where there is no duality and no ego."[10] George struggled to renounce the self in a world that glorified him, but the challenge belongs to each of us: "*Everyone's* saying it . . . I me mine." Identification with possessions strengthens the ego, but, George says, if you keep yourself in proper perspec-tive peace of mind is possible ("Within You Without You").

All Things Must Pass

According to the Beatles, then, consumerism is unwise given the illusory nature of things and the ego- and illusion-strengthening bonds it reinforces. In addition, materialistic attachments are

---

[9] Keith Badman, *The Beatles Off the Record* (London: Omnibus, 2001), p. 364.
[10] Steve Turner, *A Hard Day's Write* (New York: HarperCollins, 1999), p. 177.

irrational given the impermanence that pervades the world. There are two sides to this. First, things don't last. Secondly, neither do we.

Both sides are poignantly illustrated in Lennon's "In My Life." Although he will never lose affection for people, things and places from his past and will often stop and think about them, some have changed forever and not for better. Some have gone. Some are dead. And, in the face of new loves and new experiences, "these memories lose their meaning." Tara Brown, the heir to the Guinness fortune immortalized in "A Day in the Life" as a "lucky man who made the grade," proved all too mortal as he "blew his mind out in a car."[11] Far too often people fail to see the truth until "it's far too late, when they pass away"; among these are "people who gain the world and lose their soul" ("Within You Without You"). The unpredictable and inevitable fact of our own deaths should place in proper perspective the mere accoutrements of our lives and our fixation with status. As John sings elsewhere, once you're gone "you don't take nothing with you but your soul—THINK!'"

I'm So Tired

Given that life is very short how do we want to spend it? According to the Beatles, an existence devoted to the endless pursuit of more and more stuff is a wearying, tedious, troublesome life. The anonymous parents in "She's Leaving Home" tell the story: To be able to say that they gave their daughter "everything money can buy" they made choices forcing them to admit that they sacrificed and struggled and never thought of themselves. Unfortunately, they didn't grasp that money can't buy fun and happiness. Not only do we exhaust ourselves working to buy things, our purchases don't begin to compensate for what we surrender to obtain them. At that point our prized possessions begin to weigh us down ("And Your Bird Can Sing").

---

[11] Hertsgaard comments: "He had everything money could buy, but found himself no more immune to death's arbitrary, dispassionate arrival than the lowliest proletarian. . . . In the moment of death, all delusion is shattered, everyone is equal. Lennon clinches the point with the wistful, mocking epitaph 'Nobody was really sure if he was from the House of Lords.' The gathered crowd knows they've 'seen his face before' but they can't place it; in the broad scheme of things, he is barely a bit player" (p. 3).

Sure, if you refuse to stay on the treadmill you might be thought a slacker, and yet, what's the point of sprinting from the bottom to the top of the slide helter skelter if it doesn't get you anywhere you really want to be? John returns the criticism that he's slovenly with an accusation of his own: "they're crazy" ("I'm Only Sleeping"). His critics are barmy, but John's "got a good reason" for taking the easy way out ("Day Tripper"). If you can relate to the haggard employee in "A Day in the Life" whose existence is an incessant round of waking up to the alarm, falling out of bed and hustling downstairs to gulp a cup of coffee for breakfast only to realize he's already late, you also have a good reason.

Getting Better

Fortunately—if Rousseau's right—we're free and can change. The Beatles' message of hope is that we needn't be swept along in a state of dull indifference; our consciousness can be raised and transformed. Starting now, we can begin "taking time for a number of things that weren't important yesterday."

8

You Say You Want a Revolution: Marx and the Beatles

STEVEN BAUR

Karl Marx is the only Western philosopher to make the cover of a Beatles album. His appearance among the luminaries gracing the cover of *Sgt. Pepper's Lonely Hearts Club Band* suggests a special affinity for the great German philosopher and social theorist, and, indeed, much of the Beatles' work demonstrates the influence of Marxist ways of thinking.

The Beatles would ultimately pursue a goal quite similar to that of Marx—to change the way people think about the world in order to create a better, more just world—a theme particularly evident in their later work. Yet Marx's ideas are relevant to a consideration of the Beatles' entire career, including their work predating the group's self-conscious political awakening. Born into the lower rungs of a highly industrialized, rigidly class-based society, the four Liverpudlians occupy the same social category as the proletarian protagonists Marx sought to enlighten, unite, and empower. Over the course of their career, they would advocate the same kind of political consciousness that Marx sought to inspire, and, like Marx, they would imagine a more communal re-ordering of society. The Beatles' career and music provide numerous examples that usefully illustrate ideas central to Marx's thinking.

Marx was a pragmatist at heart and believed that philosophy should serve to improve the human condition, rather than exist as a purely abstract pursuit detached from the issues and problems of the real world. Thus, he pursued a practical philosophy that could explain the historical development of human civilization and lead to solutions for improving it—a philosophy "not just to interpret the world, but to change it," as he put it in his *Theses on Feuerbach* (1845).

Marx maintained that material economic factors more than anything else determine the nature and history of human society and consciousness—a notion that subsequent writers have referred to as *historical materialism*. Changes in the economic *base*, to use Marx's term, propelled the development of human civilization through successive historical phases, culminating, Marx theorized, with the age of communism once the working masses wrested control over the means of production from their capitalist oppressors. For Marx, the economic base (that is, the means by which a society produces its material necessities) determines not only social structures and hierarchies, but also conditions the ideological *superstructure*—schools, the media, religion, and other institutions that shape the way people understand the world and their place in it. Thus, instead of revolting to overturn the blatant economic and social inequities, the working masses—immersed from birth in the capitalist *ideology*—are led to believe that they have a real stake in the industrial economy ("if I just work hard enough flipping these burgers, I'll own McDonald's one day") or accept their condition of subjugation simply as "just the way things are." Marx tried to displace this *false consciousness* (that is, an understanding of the world that justifies the status quo no matter how unjust) by exposing the real social inequities of the industrial capitalist age and thereby compelling the working masses to revolt.

A Hard Day's Night

Marx, dedicated materialist that he was, would insist that any discussion of the Beatles must necessarily start with a consideration of their real material circumstances. For Marx, social classes are defined by the ways in which individuals relate to a society's means of production. Widespread industrialization in the nineteenth century heightened class antagonism, as industrial technology widened the socio-economic gap between those who controlled the means of production and the wage laborers they employed, increasingly dividing society into "two great hostile camps," the *bourgeoisie* and the *proletariat*. Strongly influenced by Hegelian dialectics, Marx emphasized class antagonism, which he characterized as the very engine driving the progress of human civilization, an idea that Marx's followers labeled *dialectical materialism.* As Marx put it, "the history of all hitherto existing society is the history of class struggle," a Hegelian clash of opposing forces that inevitably leads to a higher (communist) synthesis.[1]

All four of the Beatles were entrenched on the labor side of the labor-capital divide that Marx sought to expose and rectify. Outside of becoming pop stars, none of the Beatles could have reasonably aspired to much more than the working-class existence most of their ancestors led, dominated by tedious work at a factory, mill, shipyard, or other dirty, dangerous workplace, with no real stake in the profits resulting from their toil. Marx was particularly concerned about the nature and meaning of labor in industrial societies. Replacing the pre-industrial craftsman who controlled all stages in the production of his wares, industrial technology reduced laborers to bit players in a larger mechanism designed to mass-produce commodities as efficiently as possible.

Marx used the term *alienation* (or *estrangement*) to describe the nature of labor under industrial capitalism. Unable to compete with the efficiency of industrial technology, craftsmen and independent producers are forced to sell their labor to those who own the means of production, a massive conglomeration of wealth and power Marx refers to as *capital.* Thus "bought" by capital, the laborer no longer controls the nature of his or her labor, the conditions under which he or she must work, or the compensation he or she will receive. Thus, the division of labor demanded by the industrial mode of production divorces workers from the end product, over which they have no control or ownership. Thus estranged from the products of their work, laborers can be exploited to create *surplus value*—that is, the profit margin by which the market value of the commodities exceeds the cost to produce them—which the capitalist pockets.

It is precisely this condition of alienation and a lifelong career of tedious labor with meager rewards that the Beatles sought to avoid by pursuing a career in music. As Paul McCartney put it, "We didn't all get into music for a job! We got

---

[1] Karl Marx, *The Communist Manifesto* (1848), reprinted in Robert C. Tucker, ed., *The Marx-Engels Reader*, second edition (New York: Norton, 1978), p. 473. Marx himself never used the terms "historical materialism" or "dialectical materialism."

into it to avoid a job, in truth—and to get lots of girls." Of course, the music industry is just that—an industry—but it is one of the few industries (sports and other forms of entertainment also come to mind) in which someone from the bottom of the socio-economic hierarchy can rapidly gain great wealth and social standing by virtue of an extraordinary talent or skill. This notwithstanding, the music industry, like any other large industry, was characterized by the exploitative labor-capital dichotomy that Marx exposed and critiqued. The Beatles, like countless other aspiring pop stars, started out as cheap labor dependent upon and subject to the demands of the capitalists who owned the industrial means of production, such as record labels, nightclubs and concert venues, radio stations, and sheet music presses.[2]

Those demands were substantial for the Beatles, among the hardest working lads you'd find in any industry. They were pushed relentlessly during their earliest professional stints in Hamburg, where they worked under notoriously demanding club owners. At times they were forced to play continuously for twelve hours, with their employers constantly badgering them to *mach Schau*—that is, "make show"—which, to keep the interest of the working-class roughs who frequented the seedy Reeperbahn club district, meant intense, exaggerated performances rendered at volumes loud enough to satisfy the hardiest of Hamburgers. Back in England, under the gentle persuasion and ambitious scheduling of their manager Brian Epstein—a record store owner, who, by virtue of his access to capital, assumed an ownership interest in the band—the Beatles were pushed relentlessly to maintain a grueling touring schedule.[3] On some occasions they gave as many as three shows in one night in three different cities, hauling their gear and themselves hun-

---

[2] Because the music industry seems so attractive from a labor standpoint, there is always a glut on the labor market and, as a result, a constant supply of cheap labor, comprising the countless musicians—often willing to work for free or sign grossly exploitative record and publishing contracts—in their desperate bid to "make it big" in the music industry.

[3] Epstein seems to have dealt fairly and honestly with the Beatles and used his privileged socio-economic standing to assist them. By Epstein's own account, however, he considered the artists he had under contract to be his property, as when he referred to bassist Johnny Gustafson of the Merseybeats as "a very fine property, strong musically and physically and very good-looking" (Brian Epstein, *A Cellarful of Noise* [Adelaide, Australia: Rigby Limited, 1964], p. 77).

dreds of miles, working from sundown to sunrise to deliver their famously dynamic and exhausting performances—a hard day's night, indeed!

The music industry is among those industries that produce not only commodities (such as recordings, sheet music, and concert tickets), but also "intellectual property" (the songs themselves). In essence, the whole notion of intellectual property, which came into being with copyright laws passed in the early 1900s, turned songs into a form of capital—in the Beatles' case a rather large chunk of capital. Because of the great premium in the industry on this intellectual property and the songwriter's unique ability to produce it, the music industry is exceptional in that those on the labor side of the industry, as songwriters, have access to a form of capital. Yet the industry still maintains the upper hand because musicians must depend upon record labels, music publishers, and concert venues to commodify, mass-produce, and distribute their songs, which have little economic value without access to the music industry's massive production, marketing, and distribution apparatuses. This control over the means of production has often enabled music-industry executives to wrest ownership of intellectual property from those who actually produce it through exploitative recording and publishing contracts that leave musicians with only a minority interest—if any at all—in their own songs. The Beatles themselves remain estranged from the products of their labor. The vast majority of their songs are owned by the Sony Corporation, to which they have been accruing surplus value since 1995. Meanwhile, the Beatles have no control over how their music or lyrics are used.[4]

Now the Beatles' songs—including those that openly demonstrate their proletarian affiliations and attitudes (as discussed

---

[4] The rights to the Lennon-McCartney song catalogue (ownership of this intellectual property) originally belonged to Northern Songs, a corporate entity established by Epstein and music publishing mogul Dick James, the latter of whom maintained a controlling interest over the songs. In 1969, Northern Songs was sold to the Associated Television Corporation (ATV), which in turn put its music catalogue up for auction in 1985. In a highly publicized transaction, Michael Jackson—then at the height of his success in the music industry—outbid Paul McCartney to acquire the Lennon-McCartney catalogue. Jackson's music publishing business merged with Sony in 1995, and the majority of the Beatles' songs currently belong to the Jackson-ATV-Sony conglomerate, with Sony owning the controlling interest (and therefore the right to sell the songs and their lyrics to advertisers).

below)—appear in advertisements for products appealing to such specifically bourgeois interests as luxury cars ("Help" for Lincoln-Mercury), high-end audio equipment ("Getting Better" for Phillips), life insurance ("When I'm Sixty-Four" for Allstate), business communications systems ("Come Together" for Nortel Networks), and accounting services ("Taxman" for H&R Block). Perhaps most perversely, "Revolution"—a song that brought Marxist ideas to the forefront of 1960s popular culture—appears in advertisements for Nike, a corporation that seems to be the very model of the exploitative corporate establishment that Marx sought to topple. The Beatles, estranged from their own catalogue, can do nothing about it, and Sony pockets the substantial fees for licensing the use of this intellectual property.

Still, from the Beatles' perspective this beats wage labor, and a minority interest in the final product is better than no stake at all, which is the fate of workers in most industries. For the Beatles, the unprecedented sales of their records and merchandise meant that even a minority interest brought the group massive earnings. So massive, in fact, that the Beatles raised enough capital to purchase their own means of production and established Apple Records, a company ostensibly designed to put artists ahead of profits. As Paul put it, "We're in the happy position of not really needing any more money so for the first time the bosses aren't in it for the profit."

More cynically, Peter Brown asserts in his "insider's" biography of the Beatles that the band launched Apple Records primarily to establish a tax shelter for their newfound wealth. In this case, the Beatles' efforts to dodge the taxman would place them squarely in line with bourgeois ideas concerning the distribution of industrial wealth and squarely at odds with Marx, who called for the abolition of private property altogether.[5] To be sure, the Beatles' exceptional talents and enormous success enabled them to extricate themselves from the condition of alienation and subordination experienced by laborers in most industries, and international stardom meant they no longer had to work like dogs, as they did for years, to satisfy their capitalist taskmasters.

---

[5] Peter Brown and Steven Gaines, *The Love You Make: An Insider's Story of The Beatles* (New York: Signet, 1983), p. 254.

We All Want to Change Your Head

Now becoming wealthy members of the capitalist establishment doesn't necessarily mean towing the capitalist line. Like other media, the music industry can promote ideas and beliefs that support a particular political agenda—or, to put it in Marxist terms, it produces ideology. For Marx, a society's intellectual culture is controlled by socio-economic elites and typically serves to buttress the established socio-economic hierarchy. As he put it in *The German Ideology*, written with Frederick Engels in 1846:

> The ideas of the ruling class are in every epoch the ruling ideas: i.e., the class which is the ruling *material* force of society is at the same time its ruling *intellectual* force. The class which has the means of material production, consequently also controls the intellectual production, so that the ideas of those who lack the means of mental production are on the whole subject to it.

The capitalists who own and control the means of cultural production can use culture to propagate a worldview that understands the capitalist social order, in spite of its vast inequities, as just and natural. That is, they promulgate a *dominant ideology*, a set of ideas that justifies and naturalizes the dominant class's position of dominance. In Marxist social theory, the notion of ideology is central, because without a successful ideology, subordinate groups would recognize their condition of oppression as unjust and perverse and would revolt against the capitalist classes. Instead, immersed from birth in the ideas of this dominant class, the working masses live under false consciousness, unable to conceive of the possibility of an alternative to the capitalist social order. Marx sought to foster a working-class consciousness by demonstrating that vast socio-economic disparities typical of capitalist societies, far from being just and natural, are actually unjust and perverse.

So what kind of ideology emerges from the music of the Beatles, and what kind of consciousness does it promote? From a Marxist perspective, these are the most important questions to ask of any form of culture. Twentieth-century Marxist theorists have differed widely in their assessments of mass-produced, globally distributed popular culture, a phenomenon that didn't exist in Marx's day. At one end of the spectrum, Marxist champions of popular culture emphasize its connection to the masses—"popular culture" is understood to be the "culture of the people," as opposed to the "high" culture of socio-economic elites. Such writers emphasize the role of the people in defining popular culture through fan choices, and they value popular culture for addressing the needs and desires of the masses in a manner that is readily understood. For Marxist proponents of popular culture, the very acts of singing, dancing, and exhibiting styles of dress and behavior associated with certain genres of popular music can be viewed as acts of resistance in and of themselves, whether or not they involve the articulation of any explicit social or political statement. According to this line of thinking, public displays of personal liberty, particularly those involving groups of individuals unified through dance, song, and personal style, are subversive insofar as those participating defy the modes of physical discipline and personal decorum imposed in other arenas of capitalist societies, and they do so with the collectivity of a mass movement.

On the other hand, Marxist critics of popular culture emphasize its connection to industry and commerce and charge that popular culture functions as a diversion from the realities of social and economic inequality in capitalist societies. According to this less optimistic view, popular music serves to pacify the working, exploited masses, at times even giving them the illusory sense of participating in a form of transgressive, revolutionary behavior. With the public thus duped, popular culture provides a kind of steam valve, allowing the oppressed masses to release anger in short, controlled outbursts, all the while providing capitalists a seemingly inexhaustible array of profitable commodities through which to further enhance their position of economic dominance.

To be sure, popular music is conflicted, contradictory, confounding territory. I mean, how do you account for a category that encompasses examples ranging from the Sex Pistols' anarchic caterwaul to the soothing romantic balladry of the Carpenters? And what are we to make of the fact that huge corporations invest loads of capital to broadcast (and, of course, to sell) some of the most aggressive and disruptive voices emerging from the subordinate classes? And where else do we find working-class toughs and career company men collaborating (and clashing) regularly?

As the Beatles' example demonstrates, there can be tension and compromise in the process of producing cultural products. Take the Beatles' very image, for instance. Soon after assuming management of the band, Epstein made the boys grudgingly drop their rough, leather-laden teddy-boy look (and its proletarian associations) in exchange for prim and proper uniform suits (and their bourgeois associations), yet the Beatles kept their uncouth long hair, a gesture of defiance that would become the most recognizable way for young men in the 1960s to express opposition to bourgeois norms and expectations.

The Italian Marxist thinker Antonio Gramsci emphasizes this negotiative aspect of cultural production, conceiving of popular culture as neither the unadulterated expression "of the people" nor simply as a monolithic propaganda mechanism for the dominant class, but as the very site where ideological struggles and negotiations take place. True to his Marxist roots, Gramsci acknowledges that this is not a level playing field: those who own the means of cultural production hold a great advantage in defining the ideological content of their products. Nonetheless, in the collaborative processes of cultural production, there is often room for negotiation and compromise—sometimes enough room to allow subversive ideas to make their way into the mainstream cultural mix.

The Beatles' proletarian affiliations are hardly unique among rock-'n'-roll performers. In fact, most early rockers emerged from working-class origins, and early rock-'n'-roll music, with its raw, gritty sound, appealed directly to working-class sensibilities. This notwithstanding, labor politics and working-class issues were rarely the focus of rock-'n'-roll song lyrics. On the contrary, most rock-'n'-roll music from the 1950s and early 1960s—the repertory from which the Beatles learned their craft—was emphatically *not* about labor, but rather celebrated those freedoms denied in the workplace. Whether rockin' around the clock, twisting and shouting, or shimmying in their blue suede shoes, young people in the 1950s found in rock-'n'-roll music and the culture they developed around it a distinct alternative to the real conditions of subjugation and oppression that many experienced in school, at home, or at work.

The Beatles' early hits are no exception. None of the songs released during the first two years of the band's professional recording career (1962–63) features any hint of an emergent

anti-establishment consciousness.[6] While these tunes did introduce the group's revolutionary sound, they all focus on a subject that was typical of mainstream popular music of the day:
adolescent love and courtship. The Beatles' biggest hit from
1964, "A Hard Day's Night," similarly revolves around youthful
romance, but it also represents the first instance in which the
world of work appears in the Beatles' lyrics. Furthermore, labor
is described in a way that exposes the oppressive, dehumaniz-
ing conditions that the working classes faced in the workplace,
where people are forced to work like dogs. Yet "A Hard Day's
Night" could hardly be taken as a Marxist critique of industrial
capitalism. The song doesn't call for the working dogs to unite
and overthrow the capitalist establishment, but rather presents a
protagonist who endures oppression and still manages to convince himself that he "feels alright." This inability to recognize
one's own condition of subjugation and to willingly endure
injustice is precisely what Marx meant by false consciousness.

While the lyrics to "A Hard Day's Night" may not be very progressive from a Marxist perspective, that a popular song in 1964
acknowledged labor at all was uncommon. It is the only song
from the Billboard Top 100 pop chart of 1964 that makes any
reference whatsoever to the world of work, a list that includes
such paeans to adolescent love and leisure as "Doo Wah Diddy
Diddy" (Manfred Mann), "The Shoop Shoop Song (It's In His
Kiss)" (Betty Everett), "My Boy Lollipop" (Little Millie Small),
"Glad All Over" (The Dave Clark Five), and "Fun, Fun, Fun"
(The Beach Boys).[7] It's not surprising that the Beatles should
have work on their mind in 1964, for they truly were working
like dogs all year, producing two albums, releasing three singles,
making a movie, and giving massive concert tours of North
America, Britain, Australia, and New Zealand, as well as perfor-

---

[6] Songs from this period include "Love Me Do," "Please Please Me," "I Saw Her Standing
There," "From Me to You," "She Loves You," "All My Loving," and "I Want to Hold Your
Hand."
[7] This is not to suggest there were no popular songs that acknowledged labor pre-dat-
ing the Beatles' rise to fame. Examples that come to mind include "Summertime Blues"
(Eddie Cochran, 1958), "Get a Job" (The Silhouettes, 1958), "Working for the Man" (Roy
Orbison, 1962), and "Uptown" (The Crystals, 1962). Of course, the blues and R&B reper-
tories from which rock-'n'-roll emerged are rife with social and political commentary, as
is the folk music repertory that would soon become another of the many influences
incorporated into the Beatles work.

mances in Denmark, the Netherlands, Hong Kong, Sweden, and France, not to mention numerous television and radio appearances, photo sessions, and interviews all along the way.

To meet their record company's demand that they finish a record in time for the Christmas season, their second album of 1964 had to be thrown together hastily during their British tour, requiring the Beatles to fly back to London and record on every "day off" from the tour. To meet their grueling record production schedule in the midst of their equally grueling touring schedule the Beatles resorted to using six cover tunes to fill space on the record. Thus, the demand that the Beatles ceaselessly produce ever more commodities further alienated them from their work and forced them to put out a record that bears less of their imprint than anything they had previously done (or would do in the future). Perhaps recognizing the extent to which they were being exploited to accommodate the marketing frenzy that accompanied Beatlemania, the band called the album *Beatles for Sale.*

Whether or not this gesture represents the emergence of a Marxist critical consciousness, the Beatles had an encounter that year that would certainly alter their consciousness and influence the tone and content of their subsequent work. During their 1964 North American tour, the band met Bob Dylan, the poet and folksinger who brought folk music to prominence in the early 1960s. (They also became acquainted, for the first time, with marijuana, which Dylan brought to their New York hotel room.) The folk music movement had strong, long-standing associations with anti-establishment causes, and its practitioners produced protest songs of all varieties. The rise of Dylan challenged the Beatles, competitors that they were, to write artful, socially relevant lyrics of their own rather than continuing to churn out silly love songs. The Beatles took the challenge (and the marijuana) to heart and soon became leading figures in the 1960s counterculture, a politically motivated, socially active youth movement (at least initially) determined to subvert the unwitting acquiescence of the masses to capitalist rule.

The rise of the counterculture in the mid-1960s alarmed government officials, religious authorities, business leaders, and other establishmentarians, some of whom went so far as to implicate the Beatles in a large-scale socialist plot to brainwash young people, incite a mass revolution, and bring down

Western capitalist civilization.[8] In fact, the FBI kept files on John Lennon and had him deported in 1972, forcing the cancellation of a national tour and effectively silencing this outspoken critic of the Nixon administration.

The Beatles' two albums from 1965, *Help!* and *Rubber Soul*, show the marked influence of the folk music movement, including prevalent acoustic timbres and more poetic, philosophical lyrics. The latter of the two albums also shows the group's emerging counter-cultural tendencies and experimentation with altered states of consciousness. The band's warped image on the cover of *Rubber Soul* hints at the psychedelic extremes they would approach on their next two albums. For many leaders of the counterculture, experimentation with psychedelic drugs enabled one to conceive of alternative ways of thinking and being, rather than uncritically accepting the established social order as the only possibility. As Paul exclaimed that night after being "turned on" to marijuana by Bob Dylan, "I'm thinking for the first time, really *thinking*!"[9] Not surprisingly, many of the leaders of the counterculture, from hallucinogenic drug guru Timothy Leary to folk-influenced rock musicians like the Beatles, were deeply influenced by the writings of Marx. The phrase coined by Leary that would become a slogan for the counterculture, "Tune in, turn on, and drop out," echoes Marx's demand that people begin to look critically at the state of society under capitalism ("tune in"), learn to think outside of the capitalist box and imagine other ways of living ("turn on"), and reject bourgeois notions of success and refuse to compete in the capitalist rat race ("drop out"). Marx, of course, would have insisted on a fourth step: *Revolt!* For Marx, it's not enough to just "drop out" and live on the margins of capitalist society. Anyone who can see through the dominant capitalist ideology and recognize the established socio-economic order as arbitrary and unjust (as opposed to natural and just, as they would have us believe) is morally compelled to rise up and join the revolution.

While *Help!* and *Rubber Soul* show traces of the Beatles' exposure to both folk music and mind-altering drugs, none of

---

[8] See, for instance, the series of publications issued by Rev. David A. Noebel since the late 1960s implicating the Beatles and others in a global Marxist conspiracy.

[9] Paul quoted in Brown and Gaines, *The Love You Make*, p. 144, emphasis in the original.

the songs on either album make any explicit attempt at social or political commentary. On the subsequent album, *Revolver*, evidence of the Beatles' emerging critical consciousness is more pronounced, with incisive, questioning lyrics and a range of sounds that defied convention with a vengeance. Two songs from *Revolver*, "Tomorrow Never Knows" and "I'm Only Sleeping," openly countervail against the capitalist work ethic. In the former, John advises listeners to "turn off [their] minds, relax, and float downstream," a directive similar to Leary's aforementioned dictum. The song advises listeners, as did Marx, to achieve a detached, critical awareness of the human condition, to question conventional notions of truth and right-eousness, and to consider the possibility of alternatives to the "way things are." The otherworldliness of the lyrics is under-lined by a psychedelic, trance-inducing sound collage—involv-ing sitar drones, primal drumming, randomized tape loops, backwards tracking, and other electronic and studio effects—providing an aural representation of an alternative world. Similarly, in the hazy, lazy "I'm Only Sleeping," the Beatles flatly reject the diligence and industriousness so deeply ingrained and highly valued in capitalist societies, instead rec-ommending reflective inaction as an equally worthy expendi-ture of one's time. The lyrics point up, as Marx did, the perversity of the competitive, everyone-for-themselves capital-ist economy and its attendant pressures. Thus, anyone who buys into capitalism and its oppressive demands is depicted as caught up in a mindless and exhausting rigamarole of high-velocity performance. More important, the lyrics emphasize Marx's insistence that it doesn't have to be this way, if we could just start to think outside of the capitalist box, a point empha-sized by the repetition in the backing vocals. While Marx would have approved of such an attempt to defy bourgeois norms and expectations, he would have had little patience for the slothful self-indulgence advocated in "I'm Only Sleeping." Upon hear-ing the song, Marx would have exhorted the Beatles to wake up and get involved in organized resistance.

Many identify 1967 as the year the counterculture reached the height of its social and political influence. On June 1st of that year, the Beatles kicked off the "Summer of Love" with the release of their deeply psychedelic *Sgt. Pepper's Lonely Hearts Club Band*, the album featuring Marx's visage. One of John's

While "Piggies" explicitly adopts the critical stance and verbal rhetoric of the counterculture, some conservative critics took greater issue with the opening track on *The Beatles*, McCartney's "Back in the USSR." Although conceived as a parody of Chuck Berry's 1959 classic "Back in the USA," McCartney's clever homage to the duck-walking American rock-'n'-roller was seen by some as an act of treachery, a proclamation of allegiance to the ideological and political adversaries of the capitalist West. The perception that the Beatles had adopted the Marxist political ideology of the Soviet Union was reinforced by the band's release that same year of three songs titled "Revolution"—that is the single "Revolution," released as the B side to "Hey Jude" (August 1968), and "Revolution #1" and "Revolution #9," both released on *The Beatles*. Not surprisingly, John—the Beatle most conversant with Marxist theory—was the primary creative force behind all three recordings (although Yoko had a good hand in the composition and recording of "Revolution #9"). The three tracks illustrate the extent to which Lennon was wrestling with the revolutionary philosopher's ideas around 1968. John wholeheartedly accepted Marx's diagnosis that the masses, immersed in capitalist ideology from childhood, were living in a state of false consciousness and needed to conceptualize a less individualistic and more equitable society. When Lennon sang, "we all want to change your head," he was, like Marx, trying to promote a new kind of consciousness—one that prioritized communal wellbeing over individual success.

But the three versions of "Revolution" reveal Lennon's deep ambivalence over one of the fundamental tenets of Marxist thought—the necessity of violent revolution for real historical change and social progress.[12] Remember, Marx was thoroughly committed to historical materialism—the notion the material economic factors more than anything else shape history, society, and human consciousness—so merely changing heads is not enough. It may be the necessary first step, but until the physical means of material production are wrested away from the capitalist class, through violent revolution if necessary, nothing will actually change. Lennon's own struggle with Marx's insistence on the necessity of violent struggle is evident in the vari-

---

[12] As Marx plainly put it, "Revolutions are the locomotives of history."

ous recordings of "Revolution." In the single version, Lennon quite explicitly rules out violence as a solution to social injustice ("when you talk about destruction, don't you know that you can count me out"); however, he is more equivocal in "Revolution #1," hesitatingly adding the word "in" as if to acknowledge that violent struggle may indeed be necessary to bring about social progress as Marx argued.

John described "Revolution #9" as "a drawing of a revolution . . . an unconscious picture of what I actually think will happen when it happens."[13] To be sure, this avant-garde sound collage presents a disturbing and chaotic array of sounds and noises suggestive of the violence and unpredictability of a social revo- lution. This radically cacophonous recording (for a pop record anyway) includes disjunct and seemingly random snippets of voices talking, screaming, and singing, brief instrumental pas- sages (many recorded backwards or otherwise distorted), excerpts from films and radio programs, and additional sound effects that contribute to the sonic mayhem. The recording takes up a decidedly anti-commercial stance prevalent among left- leaning artists of the era.

If, as some Marxists have charged, mass mediated popular culture is nothing more than a pleasant distraction for the masses, diverting their attention from real social issues while producing huge amounts of wealth, concentrated in the hands of relatively few industry big wigs (or mop tops for that matter), then these artists sought to use popular culture as a disruptive force, aiming not to please and distract but to disturb and agi- tate. As John put it, "The idea is not to comfort people, not to make them feel better, but to make them feel worse."[14] "Revolution #9" is an extreme case of this kind of disruptive anti-commercialism; rather than the *Beatles for Sale*, this is the Beatles trying to be unsellable (and unsettling).

Lennon, the most outspoken social activist in the Beatles and the most conversant in Marxist theory, would toe the Marxist line even more steadfastly after the breakup. His bluntly politi- cal "Working Class Hero" (1970) is the closest thing rock has to a Marxist anthem (although Lennon's "Power to the People"

---

[13] John quoted in Jann Wenner, *Lennon Remembers: The Rolling Stone Interviews* (Harmondsworth: Penguin, 1971), pp. 131–32.
[14] John quoted in Simon Frith, "John Lennon," *Marxism Today* (January 1981), p. 23.

from 1971 comes close). In a style that evokes the protest songs of the Leftist folk movement, Lennon incisively describes the phenomenon of alienated labor:

> When they've tortured and scared you for twenty odd years,
> Then they expect you to pick a career,
> When you can't really function you're so full of fear.

In the subsequent verse, Lennon reiterates Marx's assertion that the ideological superstructure reinforces the economic base by promoting false consciousness among the masses: "Keep you doped with religion and sex and TV, / And you think you're so clever and classless and free, / But you're still fucking peasants as far as I can see."

The language may be from the gutter, but the ideas are right out of Marx. In fact some of the language is right out of Marx as well. Lennon's allegation that listener's are "doped on religion" is remarkably close to Marx's famous charge that organized religion acts as an "opiate" that suppresses political consciousness and action.[15]

In "Imagine" (1971), Lennon similarly pursued the Marxist project of jolting listeners out of false consciousness to imagine the possibility of alternatives to the capitalist social order. When he asks us to imagine no possessions, Lennon gets at what Marx and Engels summed up as the essence of communist theory: the abolition of private property.[16] Furthermore, when Lennon asks us to imagine no religion, he further reiterates Marx's efforts to counter religious ideologies that divert human consciousness from unjust socio-economic realities with the promise of divine rewards in the hereafter. Like Marx, Lennon urges his audience to "live for today," that is work for change in the present, material world rather than worrying about an immaterial afterlife, the

---

[15] As Marx put it in his *Critique of Hegel's Philosophy of Right* (1843–44), "Religion is the sigh of the oppressed creature, the heart of a heartless world, just as it is the spirit of a spiritless situation. It is the opium of the people. The abolition of religion as the illusory happiness of the people is required for their real happiness. The demand to give up the illusion about its condition is the demand to give up a condition which needs illusions."

[16] To provide the exact quote, "The theory of the communists may be summed up in the single phrase: abolition of private property." Karl Marx and Friedrich Engels, *The Communist Manifesto* (New York: Washington Square Press, 1964 [1848]), p. 80.

very notion of which Marx, rationalist and materialist that he was, rejected outright.

And herein lies the paradox of popular culture from a Marxist perspective. While it is largely controlled by a corporate establishment, popular taste often compels the industry to market artists who project counter-establishment ideas and images. In the process of going mainstream, however, subversive ideas and images can lose their subversive power, as they can be co-opted, commodified, and contained within existing power structures.[17]

As we have seen, the Beatles' career exemplifies well this kind of negotiation that takes place among musicians, music industry executives, and the record-buying public in the production of popular music culture. The Beatles emerged from the lower rungs of the social and musical hierarchy and initially projected a solidly working-class image and values, but they were willing to clean up their act enough to get mainstream exposure. Their enormous success gave them the clout to exercise greater expressive freedom, which they often used to espouse anti-establishment ideas. But even so, those very ideas are owned by capitalists, and have been co-opted in ways that undermine their subversive potential and promote capitalist interests (such as to sell shoes). Furthermore, even if the industrial establishment does participate in the dissemination of anti-establishment ideology, the industry itself is regulated by government agencies that can shut down any companies or individuals seen to pose a reasonable threat, as John Lennon learned during his 1972 deportation from the United States.

Lennon himself concluded that the Beatles' efforts to affect the kind of changes that Marx imagined went largely for naught. "The people who are in control and in power and the class system and the whole bullshit bourgeois scene is exactly the same except that there is a lot of middle-class kids with long hair walking around . . . But apart from that, nothing happened except that we all dressed up. The same bastards are in control, the same

---

[17] Consider, for instance, the "Pat Boone-ification" of rock-'n'-roll shortly after it burst on the national scene in the mid-1950s. The rise of rock-'n'-roll stoked enormous anxieties concerning race and sexuality. The mainstream popular music industry countered with "whiter," "cleaner" versions of many rock-'n'-roll hits. In most cases, Pat Boone and other "safe" performers had greater success with their covers than the original usually black artists.

people are runnin' everything."[18] Here Lennon makes precisely the same distinction Marx made when he asserted "a revolution involves a change in structure; a change in style is not a revolution." For all of the critical, leftist, and subversive content in their music, the Beatles themselves never embraced Marx's belief in the necessity of violent revolution to bring about real social change. Ultimately, their pacifism clashed with Marx's materialism, which, to his mind, made revolution—a real change in the material relationships between the people and the means of production—inevitable. While they embraced and reiterated much of his social critique, they were unwilling—or too comfortable, as their more radical critics charged—to advocate the social upheaval Marx deemed necessary to bring about a more just society.

To put it in Marxist terms, the Beatles were working primarily on the level of the ideological superstructure, and I've got a feeling that Marx would have appreciated much of what they had to say; however, they eschewed what for Marx was the more important work of transforming the economic base. In fact the Beatles have, unwittingly or not, contributed much to help sustain that economic base. The Beatles themselves remain big business almost forty years after their breakup, with a seemingly endless flow of Beatle commodities hitting the market every Christmas shopping season.

Even though the Beatles' career demonstrates the extent to which capitalism can co-opt the most radical voices, one need not agree with Lennon's grim assessment of the band's social impact. The ideological work accomplished by the Beatles and other leaders of the 1960s counterculture did in fact have consequences in the material world, not only providing a compelling soundtrack for the civil rights movement and other social movements that have led to real advances towards social equity, but also moving the cultural mainstream significantly towards the left, helping to transform the dominant ideology in such a way that those advances became possible. One could also make the case that the quality of the Beatles' music demonstrates that capitalism is not entirely bankrupt. For could a completely corrupted system ever produce works like "Hey Jude," "Rain," and "A Day in the Life"?

---

[18] Wenner, *Lennon Remembers*, pp. 11–12.

V

Think for Yourself

The Beatles and Existential Philosophy

9

Nothing's Gonna Change My World: The Beatles and the Struggle Against Inauthenticity

ERIN KEALEY

Into This World We're Thrown

Beginning in 1965, the Beatles take a philosophical turn from singing the romantic songs that brought them early popular success to scripting more profound and critically acclaimed lyrics that probe the human condition. Inspired by the insightful songwriting of Bob Dylan, they start to explore such issues as getting lost in the crowd, alienation, self-deception, and the call to a better way of life.

We all have moments when we feel out of place in the world or experience a lack of direction, and the Beatles present great imagery of the isolation involved in these moments. As they try to disrupt our comfortable existence, the Beatles force us to confront some disturbing questions: Have we been deceived into believing in certain goals and accomplishments which are not our own? Are we all participating in a life that controls us because facing our own condition is just too frightening? German philosopher Martin Heidegger says yes, and a major part of his 1927 work, *Being and Time*, speaks to this position.

But, if we are not living our own lives, whose life are we living? Heidegger explains that we get snared in the everyday hustle of the shared, impersonal world of *das Man*. Throughout their musical journey, the Beatles chronicle the struggle we all have with *das Man*. Often translated as "the they," this term literally means "the anyone" in the sense that it generally contains every individual yet fails to recognize any specific person. Each of us relates to the inauthentic world of *das Man*, which is the familiar shared realm of conventional wisdom and acceptable behavior. We tend to get lost in everyday concerns, which are undefined by any particular person and indifferent to our individual circumstances. *Das Man* gives us a sense of control because it provides an established framework of answers to difficult questions and lets us think that we have a firm grasp on understanding the world around us. We gain the authority of the nameless mass in statements that begin impersonally, like "Everybody knows . . ." or "No one would . . ." Yet, in doing so, we escape the responsibility of answering these important questions for ourselves. *Das Man* dismisses, evades, and covers up the significance of the questions we ask about our existence.

Heidegger uses the term *Dasein* (literally, "there-being") to express the human condition, and it invokes the unique and powerful exploration of human existence in *Being and Time*. In philosophical discussions, this term often goes untranslated. For practical purposes here, we can understand *Dasein* as meaning "human being." Heidegger's investigation of *Dasein* has particular importance because of the question of Being for us all: What does it mean that we exist, and what is the everyday life that absorbs our identities? Heidegger explores "*Dasein* in its everydayness," beginning his investigation with the ways in which we experience the world in our everyday practical concerns. It turns out that this everyday existence is inauthentic because we depend on the easy perspectives handed to us by *das Man*. Ultimately, we can come up with our own views and create an authentic existence in the same way we disclose meaning to objects we encounter: we *dwell* with them by letting them exist and become significant for us.

We usually determine the importance of an object or event simply by how it might be used. This understanding of something's purpose often guides everyday practical concerns, but it is an inauthentic perspective because it is wrapped up in the meanings we take for granted. If we want to disclose the authentic meaning of something, we have to "let it be" and reveal its significance for ourselves. Instead of depending on the conventional views of objects we encounter, we can discover meaning in the very way we exist through meditative thinking.

Heidegger contends that we can find meaningful relationships in the experiences we gather with objects in the world without becoming slaves to conventionality. The Beatles tell us that "there will be an answer" about the meaning of existence if we choose to "let it be." This also gives us a way to approach the great opus of Beatles songs. By thinking about them in the context of our struggle against inauthentic interpretations of the world around us, the lyrics take on great significance and help us understand some difficult ideas. If we gather the lyrics closest to us, we can release the meaningfulness of the songs that we have enjoyed for so many years.

Like Heidegger, we can begin our investigation with everyday existence—that is, how we lose ourselves in familiar routines. In Heidegger's view of everyday existence, we find ourselves *thrown* into a world of concerns. As the Doors plainly illustrate in "Riders on the Storm": "Into this house we're born. / Into this world we're thrown." Basically, some aspects of our existence are inescapable, and we must accept these facts. Like the Beatles who "wake up to the sound of music" in "Let It Be," we are thrown into a given situation without any explanation. This *thrownness* is scary because it cannot be controlled. We can only really control how we react to the way we find ourselves in the world, like making the effort to hear "words of wisdom."

We also find ourselves feeling a certain way about our relationship with the world of our concerns. Heidegger believes that a human being can come to terms with this aspect of existence, and that we can ultimately create our own possibilities. From our thrownness, we are called to take the responsibility of shaping our experiences to let them be significant and not just empty, fleeting moments. However, we usually avoid this responsibility by sinking into the ready convenience of an inauthentic existence. As we hear the Beatles wrestle with inauthenticity throughout their musical journey, we can be inspired to take on our own task of living authentically by giving our own lives significance.

People Who Gain the World and Lose Their Soul: Everyday Human Existence

Everyday human existence is loud, vague, and lacks any firm ground of understanding. This seems rather bleak, but it's the average worldview that we encounter in our ordinarily busy lives. Think of a normal day, like in "Good Morning, Good Morning" (*Sgt. Pepper's Lonely Hearts Club Band*, 1967).

Discourse plays an important role for Heidegger in the way human beings work to interpret the world because it allows us to articulate and communicate the meaningfulness of existence to each other. However, considering the overwhelming focus on small talk and superficial concerns in our daily lives, we rarely participate in the valuable discourse that Heidegger esteems. Everyday idle chatter doesn't delve into the meaning of our existence. We're bombarded with superficial rather than mean-ingful interpretations—and it gets loud. This meaninglessness is accompanied by an ambiguous lack of direction, with "people running round" at the end of the workday. Instead of disclosing the significance of our existence, concerns like teatime and flirt-ing take priority in the inauthentic conventional world where everyone you see is half asleep.

We've seen that, in the very way we exist, we come to understand things by *letting them be*. However, everyday human existence tends to be inauthentic, so we usually don't make the effort to reach a meaningful understanding of objects and events. As the Beatles present in "A Day in the Life" (*Sgt. Pepper's Lonely Hearts Club Band*, 1967), we hear about dreamy news images before and after the rush of a routine familiar to so many of us: getting out of bed and trying to get to school or work on time. Instead of encountering things and trying to understand them, we get caught up in impersonal observations. Reminiscent of those passing moments spent in line at the grocery store, we scan headlines, read the latest gos-sip in catchy phrases, and learn nothing substantial about the celebrity personalities portrayed in the newest scandalous pho-tographs. This entanglement, in which we crave new experi-ences without actually understanding them, demonstrates Heidegger's view of curiosity.

By not dwelling with, or really trying to understand, the news events depicted in the writing, photograph, or film men-tioned in "A Day in the Life," the onlooking "crowd of people turned away" from understanding the situation toward the next captivating distraction. The curious crowd does not reach any authentic understanding. They remain in a superficial state of leaping from event to event, just as our eyes scan from head-line to headline on magazine covers in check-out lines. Since no one takes the time to understand what happens and who is involved, the people in the crowd develop a collective emotional ambiguity, a consequence of being wrapped up in the shared conventional world. The inauthentic response to the situation is: "And though the news was rather sad / well I just had to laugh." Further, the crowd expresses uncertain reactions by staring at the suicide victim as if "they'd seen his face before / nobody was really sure." Such *ambiguity*, in addition to the characteristic elements of *idle talk* and *curiosity*, results from the fundamentally inauthentic mode of everyday existence, which Heidegger characterizes as our *fallenness*.

Heidegger's idea of fallenness does not have any religious implications, nor is it even used as a negative characterization of everyday existence. After finding ourselves thrown into a situation, we tend to *fall* into the ready comfort of the inauthentic given world. An easy escape into the familiar events and explanations in the conventional realm allows us to avoid responsibility for establishing our own answers to questions of meaning. In fallenness, we tend to become absorbed in the tranquility of inauthenticity and lose ourselves in the busy and routine hustle of life. We experience a restlessness that adds to the facade of inauthenticity, covering up the fact that the tranquility provided is impersonal and empty. The Beatles mention "the people who hide / themselves behind a wall of illusion" in "Within You Without You" (*Sgt. Pepper's Lonely Hearts Club Band*, 1967). Everyday conventions provide us with this world of illusions, and the Beatles explain that those who are entangled in such an inauthentic mode of existence may "never glimpse the truth."

"Within You Without You" also introduces the special place that the Beatles take in the struggle against inauthenticity in order to alert us to our absorbed existence. The Beatles warn us of the consequences of accepting the shared world as our own without question. They confront us with the possibility that we may not even know that we're lost and alienated: "And the people / who gain the world and lose their soul / they don't know they can't see / are you one of them?" As we will see, the Beatles compassionately attempt to guide us toward a better life, one in which we are not alienated and actually have some ownership in our true existence. However, this authentic mode of existing will come with a great burden of responsibility.

Look at All the Lonely People: The Alienation and Self-Deception of Living Inauthentically

The tranquility of inauthenticity includes the belief that we already have answers to questions we may develop. The Beatles tell us in "Only a Northern Song" (*Yellow Submarine*, 1969) that the chords and words of the song, not to mention the time of day or their clothes and hair, are all meaningless. If we come up with questions about their music, we can be assured that "it doesn't really matter" because "it's only a Northern Song." But maybe the prearranged answers won't suffice. The Beatles also tell us: "If you think the harmony / is a little dark and out of key / you're correct, there's nobody there." At this moment, the Beatles break through the assurance of tranquility to give us an insight into our struggle with the dominant interpretations of inauthenticity. From time to time, we may get the feeling that something is amiss in the practical concerns and commotion of our everyday lives. Our lives may appear to be empty, but this appearance comes from sensing dark themes or an unusual tone. We're primarily oriented toward our world of concerns by a disposition, or what Heidegger calls *moodedness* or *state of mind*.

The Beatles demonstrate our mooded interaction with the world in "Rain" (*Paperback Writer / Rain*, 1966). Rain or shine, "everything's the same" because "it's just a state of mind." However, many people flee from their own reactions to the way moods disclose concerns: "If the rain comes they run and hide their heads." The tranquility of living inauthentically even affects responses to the times that are more comfortable, as the Beatles tell us: "When the sun shines they slip into the shade . . . and drink their lemonade." Just as there is no escape from the weather, good or bad, there is no escape from our mooded way of experiencing the world. Yet we continue to flee from confronting, and potentially understanding, our authentic existence.

In "Strawberry Fields Forever" (*Magical Mystery Tour*, 1967), the Beatles tell us "it's getting hard to be someone," because forging an authentic existence is so difficult. Yet, if we can be absorbed so easily in conventions, wouldn't it be better to live inauthentically? In other words, why should we struggle to create our own possibilities if generic and acceptable identities are so easily provided by inauthenticity? It may seem relaxed when we hear that "nothing is real and nothing to get hung about," but we sometimes find ourselves unable to grasp what's really going on around us, much less ascertain our own states of mind. "Living is easy with eyes closed," like how we function as anonymous members of the inauthentic crowd. However, we end up misunderstanding our experiences and getting confused about our circumstances: "Always, no sometimes, think it's me, but you know I know when it's a dream. / I think I know I mean a 'Yes' but it's all wrong, that is I think I disagree." Again, we see that our moods, even if ambiguous, can alert us to the fact that we are fallen and lost in an impersonal world. Heidegger's existential analysis attempts to explain why it's easy for us to live inauthentically, but falling has its consequences.

We're attracted to routines because they give us the impression that we live as part of a regular, secure existence—just like everyone else, normal. The distinction between living authentically or inauthentically is very important because it is ultimately up to us to make our own lives meaningful. If we don't choose to accept this responsibility, we can get lost and alienated in trivial tasks like Father McKenzie of "Eleanor Rigby" (*Revolver*, 1966), who darns socks that no one will see. Even the time he spends writing his sermon is wasted because he is not writing it to save anyone—he is just going through the motions. "All the lonely people" living inauthentically don't have their own place in the world, like Eleanor Rigby who "lives in a dream." The Beatles show us that getting more comfortable in our fallenness leads to a deeper sense of alienation and greater self-deception.

The conveniences of a fallen existence even include an inauthentic ego—an identity stripped down to averageness. Like Eleanor Rigby who presents to the world a "face that she keeps in a jar by the door," this identity does not authentically reach anyone. In an authentic existence, we take control of our own meaningful possibilities; in an inauthentic existence, we are swept up in trivial concerns and we deceive ourselves into accepting an alienated identity. In "I Me Mine" (*Let It Be*, 1970), the Beatles explain: "Now they're frightened of leaving it. / Ev'ryone's weaving it." We all participate in building this conventional world so we can relate to each other, but sometimes we depend on it too much and can't imagine life without it. Living inauthentically allows our lives to be structured and interpreted by a shared and indifferent selfhood. If we fall into such

an inauthentic existence, we must be called to recognize our
true potential.

As the Nowhere Man Sits in His Nowhere Land: The Call to Authenticity

What awakens us from our restless slumber of inauthenticity is
a call from within. We see in "I've Got a Feeling" (*Let It Be*, 1970)
that we can't hide from this experience, we can only deny its
importance. We are confronted with wasted years of "wandering
around / wondering how come nobody told" us about our
absorption. Yet we can immediately fall back into the generalizations and prepared answers dictated by inauthenticity in
order to cover up that "feeling deep inside." Again we get
wrapped up in the self-deception of "I Me Mine" when we flee
from the responsibilities of authentic existence. The averageness
of inauthenticity gives us all an easy escape by leveling down
the experience of the call. We use common generalizations to
minimize the impact of individuality, like the Beatles express in
the second part of "I've Got a Feeling": "Ev'rybody had a good
year. / Ev'rybody let their hair down. / Ev'rybody pulled their
socks up. / Ev'rybody put their foot down." We avoid the
responsibility of carving out our own identities by falling in line
with the impersonal selfhood of inauthenticity.

As we fall into the shared world of everyday concerns,
authentic individuality is stripped away. Rather than disclosing
what Heidegger calls our *ownmost potential*, we exist inauthentically as nameless members of the crowd. Inauthentic existence
becomes one without a home, or our own place, because the
"there" (the "*da*" of *Dasein*) is controlled by average everydayness. Such a "Nowhere Man" (*Rubber Soul*, 1965) makes no
place for himself and does not take an active role in shaping his
own possibilities. Instead, he merely sits "in his nowhere land /
making all his nowhere plans for nobody." The Beatles attempt
to reach out and warn the Nowhere Man that he is missing
opportunities in his Nowhere Land: "The world is at your command," and the Beatles try to alert him to the possibility of an
authentic existence.

The Beatles also note the similarity between the Nowhere
Man and "you and me." We all find ourselves thrown into a
world and, at times, alienated from that inner unity that would

be possible if we weren't so scattered in everyday concerns. "Nowhere Man" describes how we exist in fallenness, but the Beatles try to awaken us from this tranquil world. They rouse us with their call to authenticity by forcing us to recognize our absorption in the collective mentality of an impersonal world. They challenge us to see other people as individuals rather than part of some immense undefined mass.

The call to authenticity is unexpected and erupts into routine existence. Often characterized as a hallucinogenic account, the Beatles paint a fantastic portrait of the strength of illusions, like those provided by inauthentic existence, in "Lucy in the Sky with Diamonds" (*Sgt. Pepper's Lonely Hearts Club Band*, 1967). While we picture ourselves in the astounding world that the Beatles conjure, a "girl with kaleidoscope eyes" becomes the sudden appearance that disrupts the flow of dreamy images. She calls us from the illusions that are just "waiting to take you away." Everyday conventions entice us with social acceptance when "everyone smiles as you drift past the flowers." An inauthentic identity is as readily available to us as idling taxis: "Climb in the back with your head in the clouds / and you're gone." Just as we saw in "I Me Mine," we can lose ourselves to a mistaken conception of our own existence. But at any moment in our day as we travel around, we can find that we are submerged in a world of illusions if we see that "someone is there at the turnstile." By pointing out the girl, the Beatles afford us the opportunity to recognize that we are wrapped up in an impersonal world. If we notice the girl that stands out from the crowd, we can take the first difficult steps of breaking through the illusions of everydayness.

Yet, as the Beatles explain in "I've Just Seen a Face" (*Help!*, 1965), the pull of inauthenticity "keeps calling me back again." The struggle to maintain an authentic existence continues throughout life—a way of living every day in each decision we make. We must be ready to recognize our own potential for authenticity alongside the loud chatter of inauthentic concerns: "Had it been another day / I might have looked the other way / And I'd have never been aware." If we aren't ready to be called to our own possibilities, we might just turn away from them and go on with everyday practical concerns. Like the call to live authentically, "The Fool on the Hill" (*Magical Mystery Tour*, 1967) is "talking perfectly loud / but nobody ever hears him / or the sound he appears to make." We must be ready to be called from our noisy and ambiguous concerns in order to take ownership of our lives. This readiness introduces the importance of *reticence* for Heidegger.

Being reticent involves a deliberate choice to push aside the clamor and commotion of inauthenticity. We can choose to either continue fleeing from the burden of taking on our own authenticity or responsibly break away from our surrender to inauthenticity. If we choose to vacate the inauthentic tranquility in which we find ourselves, we can emerge into a new mode of existence where we can take "the time for a number of things / that weren't important yesterday." This recognition in "Fixing a Hole" (*Sgt. Pepper's Lonely Hearts Club Band*, 1967) comes with the effort of "fixing a hole where the rain gets in." By shaping the world of our concerns instead of depending on the Nowhere Land of accepted conventions, we can have a place to go that is our own.

Listen to the Color of Your Dreams: The Task of Living Authentically

One of the most difficult things in recognizing a call to authentic existence is coming to terms with an appropriate participation in the inauthentic world. Heidegger doesn't think that we can bask in some illuminating authenticity detached from the public world. As the Beatles inform Prudence Farrow in "Dear Prudence" (*The Beatles [White Album]*, 1968), we cannot escape interactions with the conventional world. Instead of meditating for too long, Prudence needs to open her eyes and come out to play. We have to participate in a shared world because we look around at the places we find ourselves thrown into and discover that we are part of everything. We exist in the world with others, and being thrown with a past introduces historical conventions that cannot be denied. If we answer the call to live authentically, we can begin to *project* our own possibilities. Projection is a *throwing forward* where we begin to take control of the shape of our own lives—not apart from the conventional world, but alongside it. We each can choose to direct ourselves toward actualizing our individual potential.

In addition to projecting our own possibilities, we must also face and take responsibility for our own past. We can authentically bring the past into our present states of mind, and the Beatles demonstrate this in "Penny Lane" (*Magical Mystery Tour*, 1967) where memories of bygone occasions seem to fill the senses. The setting of past memories comes alive in the present. The Beatles introduce us to characters who are then brought together in a notably peculiar situation, much like how we need to integrate our past with our own present circumstances. We often escape the responsibility of appropriating our past by sinking into the ease of conventional viewpoints.

Longing for "Yesterday" (*Help!*, 1965) demonstrates an inauthentic mode of viewing the past. Inauthenticity gives us "a place to hide away" when we are suddenly confronted with our historical past. But why do we flee authentic existence in this way? "Help!" (*Help!*, 1965) describes the insecurity we can feel when we take on the burden of authentically appropriating our past. At the prospect of losing the familiar grounding of our inauthentic youthful independence, the Beatles respond: "Now these days are gone, I'm not so self-assured. / Now I find I've changed my mind and opened up the doors." Authentic existence allows us to open up our own possibilities, but it turns out to be quite a burden as we lose the conventions that provide such an easy grounding in life.

The call to authenticity introduces a confrontation with an uncanny lack of meaning in our lives. What are we *letting be* in the moments we experience uncanniness? That we are lost in the empty concerns of the Nowhere Land, perpetuated by the indifferent mentality of the crowd. Indeed, we find ourselves without a "home" of our own because we are trapped in an inauthentic and impersonal world. Heidegger's term for uncanniness is *Unheimlichkeit*, which is literally the sense of "unhomeliness" we feel when we recognize "Something inside that was always denied / for so many years" like the girl in "She's Leaving Home" (*Sgt. Pepper's Lonely Hearts Club Band*, 1967). She leaves the given inauthentic world upheld by her parents in order to embark on her own life. Her parents mourn the loss of their daughter, but she leaves "Quietly turning the backdoor key / stepping outside she is free." They can't understand why she has left their comfortable home where they have struggled to provide her with contentment and security. We experience uncanniness when we are confronted by our intimate familiarity with an inauthentic existence—when we sense our self-deception. Still holding on to their inauthentic existence, the girl's parents awake that Wednesday morning to find themselves isolated with no voice in their daughter's actions. However, she has taken the first steps toward recognizing her own possibilities and controlling her own future.

We always have possibilities, even if we are falling and our own possibilities are suppressed by absorption in inauthenticity. Because our existence unfolds throughout life, we are never finished existing while we are alive. In addition to dealing with our past and present, we must also take responsibility for our given future, which includes dying. Inauthenticity evades any meaningful confrontation with death by making it an event that can be considered objectively. Trivializing death makes it more comfortable and less likely that we will experience our own individuality. One of the ways to trivialize death and make it an acceptable occurrence is the familiar response to witnessing the deaths of others. In an inauthentic existence, we can say that the loss of someone is a shame, but we move on with our lives and avoid the anxiety of facing our own individual finitude.

The Beatles suggest that we should accept the givens of our existence in "Tomorrow Never Knows" (*Revolver*, 1966). They wisely mention that "ignorance and hate mourn the dead . . . But listen to the color of your dreams, / it is not leaving." We may cover up our possibilities and trivialize uncomfortable aspects of our lives, but they remain a part of us. Falling into inauthenticity may lure us into believing our finitude is not a practical concern: "Turn off your mind, relax and float down stream, / it is not dying . . . Lay down all thoughts, surrender to the void, / it is shining." The inauthentic world of the crowd will continue to shine even after individuals die, so it's easy to evade the confrontation with our own deaths if we are lost in this shared world. Ultimately, the Beatles hope that we "may see the meaning of within, / it is being."

Our existence is bound by a beginning and an end, so we must painfully accept that we cannot control part of our projected future: we are finite. The burden of an authentic existence is rooted in accepting what Heidegger considers our *finite freedom*—being aware of our thrownness into a situation with a past toward our own individual deaths, yet deliberately existing free of the impersonal illusions of inauthenticity. This finite freedom is not just human freedom limited by certain circumstances or experiences, but the finite character of our freedom from the very beginning of our existence. In "Tomorrow Never Knows," the Beatles tell us to "play the game 'Existence' to the end / of the beginning." For Heidegger, this is what makes our unique experience of the world possible. While we must exist alongside a shared world because of the conventions it provides to let us relate to each other, we do not have to lose our individual identities to it. We can choose to experience the world authentically.

Seeing the Love There that's Sleeping: The Admirable Compassion of the Beatles

The eruption of uncanniness brings us face to face with our participation in an empty world. Because inauthenticity can blind us to our own circumstances, "Blackbird" (*The Beatles [White Album]*, 1968) employs the image of sunken eyes learning to see, as a means of liberation. In his later writings, Heidegger elaborates on our capacity to illuminate authentic meaning through language. Just as the Blackbird sings "in the dead of night," we encounter objects and people in the context of a world with shared conventions. But if we really try to understand and illuminate the meaning of events as they unfold, then we can "fly / into the light of the dark black night." The most difficult encounter is finding ourselves in the darkness of inauthenticity, but the Beatles support our flight to a more meaningful existence: "Take these broken wings and learn to fly." The Beatles, so often in their songs, try to alert us of our potential to be free from absorption in an inauthentic existence.

In "While My Guitar Gently Weeps" (*The Beatles [White Album]*, 1968), the Beatles compassionately call us from our slumber. The Beatles "see the love there that's sleeping" and they wonder at the fact that "nobody told you how to unfold your love." They continue: "I don't know how someone controlled you. / They bought and sold you," like the people from "Within You Without You" who lost their souls to the ease of conventions. The Beatles not only struggle to live authentically, they also engage us in this endeavor. They try to alert us of the possibility of an authentic existence. The Beatles find us falling, but they keep singing with the hope of reaching us.

From the impersonal identity provided by an inauthentic existence in "I Me Mine," we hear: "No one's frightened of playing it. / Ev'ryone's saying it. / Flowing more freely than wine." The flow of participating in a shared world takes on a deceptive guise: If everyone else is playing this game of life, we should just let it take us away, too. "Across the Universe" (*Let It Be*, 1970) tells us about the enticing world of conventions and how we can lose ourselves to the flow of the three elements of fallenness we saw earlier: idle talk, ambiguity, and curiosity. The words of idle talk flow "like endless rain into a paper cup," but they slither away without creating meaningful discourse. Ambiguity is like the inauthentic moods and drifting emotions that take hold of us and control how we experience the world. Curiosity is like the blind tumbling of restless thoughts that never delivers authentic understanding.

Instead of reaching authentic discourse or understanding, we fall into the seemingly "limitless undying" world that "calls me on and on across the universe," away from recognizing our finite freedom. We tend to participate too much in the shared world of conventions because we are drawn into our everyday concerns. However, we've seen that we don't need to isolate ourselves from the lure of ordinary life in order to live authentically. In "While My Guitar Gently Weeps," the Beatles sing about an aware existence alongside the shared world. They observe mundane qualities and everyday events, like noticing the world turning around them as they continue to create and play their music: "I look at the floor and I see it needs sweeping." We can authentically interact with the tasks of everyday existence as long as we struggle to understand our motivations and maintain our own identities. "My Guitar" also tells us that "with every mistake we must be learning." We will make mistakes, and we continue to fall into the average and conventional standards of inauthenticity. However, whether or not we accept the burden, we are ultimately responsible for forging our own authentic existence.

The Beatles could see us as the "silly people" of "Fixing a Hole" who "run around" and never wonder "why they don't get past my door." These people are complacent and "disagree and never win." But, instead, the Beatles see our potential and compassionately call to us. Remember the hope they express in "Let It Be," that even though "the broken hearted people" (like the isolated and alienated characters we've come across who are trapped in self-deception) "may be parted there is / still a chance that they will see." But, like we saw in "I've Just Seen a Face" and "The Fool on the Hill," we must be ready to hear the lyrics while listening to the Beatles. We must be reticent in order for the message to break through our fallen and scattered existence, and that's the chance that we might see the answer in living authentically. Further, the significance the lyrics have for us can change depending on our individual perspectives, our evolving experiences, and our own continuing struggles against inauthenticity.

The shared conventions of an inauthentic existence may seem boundless and overpowering, like the "inciting and inviting" world in "Across the Universe." We should try to emulate the Beatles and be resilient in our struggle against getting lost in inauthenticity by striving to live our own lives in the face of easy answers and everyday routines. We cannot escape fallenness, but we can direct ourselves toward authenticity by making a home for ourselves alongside average everydayness. To do this, we must endeavor to hold onto our own identities while we come together in our shared Nowhere Land. Answering the call to authenticity can shake our foundations, but the Beatles encourage us to remember our individuality and take ownership of our lives by building a better understanding of the social world in which we must participate. If we approach our everyday lives with care and hold on to the truth we discover, we can resolutely sing along with the Beatles: "Nothing's gonna change my world."

10

George on Being and Somethingness

MICHAEL H. HOFFHEIMER and
JOSEPH A. HOFFHEIMER

George Harrison was too good a poet to have much use for Philosophy with a capital P. Yet he worked out a consistent view of the world that influenced significant life choices and inspired the lyrics to his songs.

This chapter explores George's ideas of life by comparing them to Existentialism, a system of philosophy popular in the 1950s and 1960s. Existentialism promoted values prevalent in youth culture, yet George's vision of life offered an alternative to the central tenets of Existentialism. But before we look at George's counterpoint to existentialism, we have to understand his childhood and his involvement in Indian religion.

The Harrison Family Curse

Freudian psychoanalysis traces adult problems back to early childhood experiences. For example, Freud would trace John's rebelliousness back to his mother leaving him in early childhood. Behind many great Beatle love songs lies a fear of being abandoned by girlfriends—"Run for Your Life" is a conspicuous example. As John laments in one of his post-Beatle songs, "Mother you had me but I never had you."

Unlike John and other geniuses who suffered as children, George inherited the curse of a happy childhood. His parents did not abandon him. His mother encouraged his early interest in music. His father booked the Quarry Men in 1959 and later accompanied his son on tour.

George's mother helped him get his first electric guitar. This, for Freud, would help explain why George never could smash guitars on stage like Pete Townsend and did not found Punk. It also explains how George avoided the occupational disease of lead guitarists, egomania. George had a modest opinion of his own technical skills. His licks are short and reserved, his style a perfect match for the other Beatles.

Early fanzines, with a core of truth, labeled Beatle George the Quiet Beatle. Beatle biographer Hunter Davies wrote that "George is the one who has an absolute mania about any publicity of any sort."[1] George later described Beatlemania: "it's like 'Cuckoo's Nest,' you know, where you are sane in the middle of something and they're all crackers."[2] At the height of the feuding that would lead to the demise of the group, John and Paul were fantasizing about renewing live tours. The horror of new tours helped reconcile George to the band's dissolution.

The curse of a happy childhood explains several of George's outstanding failures. A quick surf of the Web proves that many fans revere *Sgt. Pepper* as Beatle achievement supreme. The Lennon-McCartney songs on that concept album and those that followed are driven not so much by Monty Pythonesque absurdity as by nostalgia. Lyrics over anachronistic musical styles and studio-added cellos, trumpets, and sound effects evoke communal memories of some lost past. Paul mined this genre for years, peopling his songs with family characters like "Uncle Albert."

But the Harrison family curse kept George from joining John and Paul in spinning out false-memory hits like "Strawberry Fields" and "Penny Lane." His spare contributions provided important balance to the late Beatles compilations. Think of *Abbey Road* without "Something" and "Here Comes the Sun." George's single effort at Mean-Mister-Mustard-moonshine was "Savoy Truffle" (1968), a eulogy to a dessert inspired by Eric Clapton's dental-destructive dependence on chocolate bon-bons.

After many years of deep analysis (not covered by your health plan), Freud would have concluded that George was incapable of fantasizing about his absent mother for the simple reason that she was still alive and kicking. Indeed she (literally)

---

[1] *The Beatles*, revised edition (New York: McGraw Hill, 1978), p. 315.
[2] *I, Me, Mine*, second edition (San Francisco: Chronicle Books, 2002), p. 43.

contributed the "damn good wacking" line to "Piggies" (1968) when George was stuck for a rhyme. George's even-tempered disposition explains other abnormal psychological traits, notably his sordid interest in the ukulele, the instrumental emblem of the Anticool which he collected and played privately.

"For You Blue" (1970) shows the family curse at work. The song's original title ("blues") and George's reference to Elmore James indicate that he intended the song as homage to the bluesman. Yet despite its twelve-bar structure and slide guitar, the mood remains irrepressibly upbeat.

Early childhood memories likewise explain George's positive attitude towards religion. John gave voice to the rage of his generation at the unfairness of reality and the absence of God in the world. George, in contrast, kept a soft spot for religion and devoted much of his life to a religious quest. Roots of his attitude lie in his childhood experiences with Roman Catholicism, encouraged by his mother and tolerated by his agnostic father. To be sure, hypocrisy rankled and doctrine failed to satisfy. But in his memory, "I liked . . . the smell of the incense and the candles. I just didn't like the bullshit."[3]

India

At the end of his life George remarked that everything could wait but the search for God. George's personal search altered the course of Western culture and changed the direction of the Beatles. At the height of worldwide youth rebellion in 1967–1968, George devoted himself to Indian religion. He persuaded the Beatles to travel to India to study with the Maharishi. Their visit was cut short by scandal, memorialized in John's ode to Sexy Sadie making "a fool of everyone."

George played a historic role in bringing Indian culture to the West. By the early 1960s sitar master Ravi Shankar was touring and recording in the West and Alan Watts was publishing popular accounts of Buddhist and Hindu thought. But South Asian culture was not widely understood or respected. Consider the fact that George first saw a sitar on the set of "Help!" (1965) where the instrument was being deployed for comic effect. In the 1960s

---

[3] The Beatles, *The Beatles Anthology* (San Francisco: Chronicle Books, 2000), p. 26.

Indians were still serving as butts of humor in British media. Indian stereotypes are both exploited and exploded in Peter Sellers's over-the-top characterization in "The Party" (1968).

George was drawn to the sitar precisely because it was exotic. In 1966 he began study of the instrument under Ravi Shankar, and his Beatle songs soon reflected his growing knowledge of North Indian raga patterns, modalities, and instrumentation.

His lyrics likewise began to incorporate themes and ideas from South and East Asian philosophy and religion. "Love You To" (1966) announced the theme of the transitory character of life with its opening line, "Each day just goes so fast, I turn around, it's past." His *anti-Pepper* "Within You Without You" (1967) explored the idea of *maya*, the 'wall of illusion' that causes suffering according to Hindu and Buddhist teachings. "The Inner Light" (1968) set lines from Taoist scripture to music accompanied by Indian classical instrumentalists recorded in Mumbai. Even "Long, Long, Long" (1968), a love song laden with multiple meanings, reflected his religious interests: he later revealed that the "you" addressed in the song is the Lord. His solo *Wonderwall* album (1968), mixed traditional Indian instrumentation recorded in Mumbai with popular Western sounds recorded at Abbey Road.

George's interest in South Asian sounds and ideas began to infect other members of the band, and John recorded George on sitar for the first time on "Norwegian Wood" (1965). John introduced "Across the Universe" (1970) with the memorable image: "Words are flowing out like endless rain into a paper cup." The verse ends with the Hindi refrain *Jai Guru Deva, Om*, a chant in praise of guru Dev. John exposed his conflicted feelings about the lure of the Hindu in the first ex-Beatle million seller "Instant Karma" (1970).

George resumed serious guitar work on the final Beatle albums, but his borrowings from Asia changed forever the imagery, modalities and instrumentation of rock. He celebrated the Hindu-inspired search for God in "My Sweet Lord" (1970). And *The New York Times* coverage of George's death singled out his popularization of South Asian culture as his greatest legacy.

Dr. Freud would diagnose even George's openness to foreign musical sounds as symptom of the family curse of a happy childhood. George remembered how his mother tuned the family radio to foreign broadcasts, "Arabic or something." This taught him to delight in things that sounded different. He carried around the childhood memory of a record with an off-center hole that "sounded weird. Brilliant."[4]

Existentialism

In the years the Beatles rocketed to fame, Existentialism was the hot fashion in Philosophy. Unlike most academic trends, Existentialism also attracted wide interest among people who were not required to read it for credit.

Part of Existentialism's appeal, like that of the Beatles, lay in its bold defiance of authority. Existentialism's forefathers included the devout Danish thinker Søren Kierkegaard (1813–55) and the German philosopher Martin Heidegger (1889–1976). But in the 1950s, "the English army had just won the war," and Existentialism became most closely identified with left-leaning French intellectuals who had opposed the Nazis.

The way-coolest Existentialist was French philosopher Jean-Paul Sartre (1905–1980). Sartre was no songwriter, but he was a paperback writer who published readable novels and plays. He popularized the term "Existentialism," related his ideas to real-life ethical problems, and made his points by discussing moods familiar to his readers. It didn't hurt that he wrote a lot about sex.

Sartre's magnum opus *Being and Nothingness* appeared in 1943, the year George was born. The book provides a systematic explanation of the world of experience. One of Sartre's main points is that existence precedes essence. By this he means to reject the idea that people have some fixed "human nature" that is revealed in their acts. George similarly ridicules a reductive essentialism in the words of "Savoy Truffle" (1968), where he comically applies the adage "You are what you eat."

Sartre believes people confront an unavoidable freedom in acting. Moreover, he believes people experience anxiety—the famous "Existential *Angst*"—when they face the need to act in the world. Woody Allen made a career parodying Existential *Angst* in films about obsessively reflective people paralyzed by indecision. Sartre's point was not that indecisiveness causes

---

[4] *Beatles Anthology,* p. 26.

anxiety but that people cannot help relating to the world in a way that requires decisions. George neatly expressed this Existentialist insight in a line in "While My Guitar Gently Weeps" (1968). When he looks at a dirty floor, the singer does not see a surface with dirt on it but rather "a floor that needs sweeping." What he sees in other words is a floor, perhaps standing more generally for the world, which requires action.[5]

Sartre supports his rejection of human essence by long discussions of being and nothingness. Writing in a tradition of German philosophers, Sartre believes existence is a sort of mental projection because its features like stability, continuity and endurance can never be deduced from a person's experience of an ever-changing world.

George would agree in part. In "Within You Without You," he emphasizes how the self helps define reality: "Try to realise it's all within yourself." The song warns against the danger of thinking perceptions of the world are real.

Sartre goes far towards rejecting all supernatural explanations. He imagines with John "no hell below us, above us only sky." But where John challenges heaven on the moral ground that it keeps people from living for today, Sartre rejects supernatural forces for theoretical reasons. First, God has no place in Sartre's catalog of being. Second, God undermines Sartre's premise that people experience unconditioned freedom in acting.

Nothingness

Like John, Sartre views imagination as a basic requirement for human freedom. Sartre even sees it as an irreducible feature of human thought, "an essential and transcendental condition of consciousness."[6]

Sartre delights in exposing the paradox that for something to be imaginary it is necessary that it not exist. Since something that is imagined stands in a negative relation to the existing

---

[5] George discovered the image of "weeping" in the *I Ching*. He retained the image of the unswept floor through extensive revisions to the lyrics (*I, Me, Mine*, pp. 120–24); Walter Everett, *The Beatles as Musicians* (New York: Oxford University Press, 1999), Volume 2, pp. 200–01.

[6] Jean-Paul Sartre, *The Psychology of the Imagination* (New York: Philosophical Library, 1948; originally 1940), p. 273.

world, he concludes that the existing world is negative from the standpoint of imagination.

> The gliding of the world into the bosom of nothingness and the emergence of human reality in this very nothingness can happen only through the position of *something* which is nothingness in relation to the world and in relation to which the world is nothing. By this we evidently define the structure of the imagination.[7]

Sartre defines freedom as the ability of people to exist in negative relation to the existing world.[8] Imagination forces them to think of a different world and forces them to act, to change the existing world. This thought is echoed in "Revolution" (1968), where by revolution or evolution "we all wanna change the world."

Sartre explains how freedom causes unhappiness. "I am condemned to exist forever beyond my essence, beyond the causes and motives of my act. I am condemned to be free . . . we are not free to cease being free."[9] Beatle songs repeatedly capture the fate of people trapped in a world without essential meanings. "Nowhere Man" (1965), penned while John was idle and bored, describes a person lacking purpose and direction who "doesn't have a point of view, knows not where he's going to." "Two of Us" (1969) recounts the aimlessness of two lovers riding aimlessly, thoughtlessly, and pointlessly.

Sartre insists that freedom does not consist in achieving one's goals. On the contrary, he sees all people's lives as failures when measured by their goals, because such goals are routinely frustrated.[10] Paul layered this sense of frustration along with other meanings in "Blackbird" where the wingless bird, identified with the singer, is given broken wings and asked to learn to fly. "Eleanor Rigby" related the bitter fate of an aging woman whose life's dreams remain unfulfilled.

---

[7] *Psychology of the Imagination*, p. 271.

[8] The human being "must be a being who can realize annihilating rupture with the world and with himself" and "the permanent possibility of this rupture is the same as freedom." *Being and Nothingness* (New York: Philosophical Library, 1956), p. 439. "This constantly renewed act is not distinct from my being . . ." (p. 461).

[9] *Being and Nothingness*, p. 439.

[10] He observes that a personal life "whatever it may be, is the history of a failure." *Being and Nothingness*, p. 481.

Sartre argues that people must also choose how to imagine themselves in relation to past events. Just as in "Two of Us" the lovers posses memories longer than their future. Sartre proposes that all history is a projection of an individual's self-identity (p. 502). While history is in one sense a projection of free choice, the conditions of choice are themselves affected by the chosen past. The past "imposes itself upon us and devours us" (p. 503).

Bad Faith

Sartre claims people turn their capacity to negate existence inwardly as a way of escaping from reality. He calls such self-denial "bad faith" and explores how people lie to themselves, know they are lying, and then engage in further self-deception to avoid knowing they are lying.

The classic example Sartre gives is of a woman who allows herself to be seduced while pretending not to notice that her companion is trying to seduce her while really wanting him to do so. John refuses to participate in a similar seduction in "Norwegian Wood" (1965). Sartre does not restrict bad faith to prudish hypocrisy. He sees it in other common postures, including sincerity and role playing.

Sartre's theory commits him to a sort of courageous atheism that replaces God with people who are solely responsible for their conduct. His critique of bad faith commits him to championing lives of authenticity. Perhaps nowhere is it more clear how Sartre embraces both the Modernist optimism in the possibility of all-comprehensive theory and the Modernist faith in the transformative power of theory. As John and Paul put it in "The Word" (1965), "Say the word and you'll be free!"

Existentialism's principles were custom-made for the ethos of youth culture in the 1960s. Its theory of "Existential *Angst*" described young people's feelings of isolation, misunderstanding, and sexual frustration. Its theory of "bad faith" fit stereotypes of hypocrisy and conformity attributed to the older generation. Its bold rejection of essentialist explanations seemingly endorsed the repudiation of traditional authority of all sorts. Its idea of authenticity was philosophical rock'n'roll, a long-winded version of Sixties slogans like "Be real!" or "If it feels good, do it!"

The Big I

George repeatedly responded to the central concerns of Existentialism, not because he ever read Sartre but because Existentialism privileged experiences of anxiety and isolation that were major cultural concerns. Themes of Existentialist philosophy were addressed by James Dean's character in *Rebel without a Cause* (1955), by Allen Ginsberg's beat poem "Howl" (1956), and by Jagger and Richards in "Paint it Black" (1966).

In hindsight, George was always the most ambivalent about such cultural trends. His early songs embody a guarded narcissism that contrasts with the expressions of rage and lust in other Beatle songs. His first song, "Don't Bother Me" (1963), steers so clear of despair it is not even very sad. His second, "You Like Me Too Much" (1965) avoids hot words like "love," "girl," and "baby," and employs the understated, laconic line "you like me too much and I like you." According to several accounts, including George's, this song was not romantic in origin. His more melancholy "If I Needed Someone" (1965) communicates similar emotional restraint, detachment, and resilience.

George's self-restraint informed fateful biographical choices from his sober response to the dissolution of his first marriage to his invitation to Eric Clapton to play lead guitar on "While My Guitar Gently Weeps" (1968).

Like Sartre, George recognized both the illusory character of the outer world and the power of the ego to deceive itself. In 1967 he penned the lines, later set to music, "It's easier to tell a lie than it is to tell the truth . . . It's easier to criticize somebody else than to see yourself."[11]

George acknowledged the power of the ego's demand for supremacy, but he also recognized that this demand was wrongheaded and could even lead to insanity. "I looked around and everything I could see was relative to my ego—you know, like 'that's *my* piece of paper' and 'that' *my* flannel,' or 'give it to *me*,' or '*I* am.' It drove me crackers; I hated everything about my ego" (p. 158).[12]

---

[11] *I, Me, Mine*, p. 110. George completed the song and recorded it in 1976.

[12] The importance of this experience for George is suggested by the fact that he selected the song it inspired for the title of his autobiography.

George responded by affirming the primacy of the non-self. Just as in "Love You To," he suggested that an individual's self lacks stability and can not be named—"you don't get time to hang a sign on me"—so in "I, Me, Mine" (1970), he expressed the idea that the self is itself an illusion. But rather than denying all reality to selfhood, George sought its truth in a really existing self-hood that was greater than the perceptions of self that proved so illusory and false. He realized, "there *is* somebody else in here apart from old blabbermouth."

Identifiying underlying truth of the self with a supernatural reality or "big 'I,'" George gave poetic form to his mixed feelings about the big and little, false and true, ego: "All through the day / I, Me, Mine, I, Me, Mine, I, Me, Mine / All through the night / I, Me, Mine, I, Me, Mine, I, Me, Mine / Now they're frightened of leaving it / Everyone's weaving it / Coming on strong all the time."

The lyrics of this song counter the self-centered materialism celebrated by contemporary pop groups like the Beach Boys.

Inner Light and Outer Sun

George's idea of the "Big 'I'" embraced a variety of super-individual realism that is alien to most modern philosophy but which the German poet Wolfgang Goethe expressed in observing that the eye must be something like the sun to be able perceive the sun. Like Goethe, George also saw light as a force of nature that symbolized the reality linking the individual self with the "Big 'I'." For him inner light was a spark of the divine in the individual.

George employed light imagery in many of his best songs. Already "Think for Yourself" (1965) associates closed eyes with ignorance and misery. The "fog upon L.A." in "Blue Jay Way" (1967) obscures vision, causing friends to lose their way. "Inner Light" (1968) advises turning one's vision within and claims, "Without looking out of my window, I can know the ways of heaven."

The most brilliant example of light imagery is "Here Comes the Sun" (1969). Lyrics hint at the illusory character of perception with the words, it "seems like years" since the periodic reappearance of the sun. The title announces the song's optimistic theme, reinforced by images of "ice slowly melting," the passing of the "long winter," and the return of the sun after a "long time." Its light imagery invites interpretation at the level of symbols. Light from the sun provides happiness, love, peace. It dispels the cold, lonely winter of oppression and evil. With its lilting melody, one of the most memorable of any Beatle song, "Here Comes the Sun" evokes freedom and serves as the perfect anthem for the end of school or the fall of a tyrannical regime.

George's most grandiose vision of uniting inner and outer light occurs at the end of "Within You Without You" (1967): "When you've seen beyond yourself / then you may find, peace of mind, is waiting there— / And the time will come when you see / we're all one, and life flows on within / you and without you."

Vision imagery also appears in "While My Guitar Gently Weeps" (1968), George's ode to the perennial suffering caused by human delusions. The song repeats the words "I look" four times. It depicts unrealized love as "sleeping," suggesting closed eyes, and personifies the guitar weeping, suggesting eyes filled with tears. In George's greatest songs like "Here Comes the Sun" and "While My Guitar Gently Weeps," images of light and vision help keep the meanings suggestive and evocative. These songs avoid the concrete representations and narrative yet manage to convey a seriousness of purpose and depth of meaning that reward close, repeated listening.

Ineffable Somethingness

In the end, it may not be George's convictions that distinguish him from Existentialism so much as his lack of faith in the power of language to capture the experience of even the small portion of reality allotted to a single person. George shares with Sartre the belief that the truth of reality differs radically from its appearance. He parts company from Sartre in believing there is truth beyond appearance and in accepting that such important truth cannot be expressed adequately in words. In a word, truth is ineffable. He put this idea bluntly in "What Is Life?" (written as a Beatle but recorded later): "What I feel, I can't say" (p. 162).[13]

---

[13] George wrote the song "What Is Life?" for Billy Preston in 1969 and recorded it himself on his first solo album.

George's most moving tribute to ineffability is his one super-hit single "Something" (1969). In it *something* attracts the singer, but the singer neither specifies what the something is nor identifies the "she" who inspires. He refers only to his lover's acts of moving, wooing, and smiling. The song beautifully pairs lyrical uncertainty with a melody that descends over accompanying chords that become increasingly dissonant. Despite its elusive quality, the song stands as a supreme, affirmation of love, the attraction of the Other, and the reality of that something that connects one with another in the universe.

VI

They All Want to Change Your Head

The Beatles and
Consciousness-Raising

11

Realizing It's All Within Yourself: The Beatles as Surrogate Gurus of Eastern Philosophy

RONALD LEE ZIGLER

Since the 1960s many Beatles fans have suspected that the title of John Lennon's song "Lucy in the Sky with Diamonds" was really a clandestine reference to the psychedelic drug LSD. Lennon himself tried to put such speculation to rest through his own personal disclaimer.[1] However, in June of 2004 Paul McCartney resurrected this issue asserting that "Lucy in the Sky With Diamonds" really was a reference to LSD.[2]

Whether or not we choose to believe Lennon's or McCartney's take on this particular song's inspiration, it is clear that the Beatles did encounter LSD and were transformed by its influence—and transformed in ways that were clearly reflected in their music. This transformation of the Beatles followed a pattern that was repeated among many members of the youth culture of the 1960s: intense hallucinatory experiences inspired by LSD, and exposure to the ideas expressed in the texts of Eastern Philosophy. The consummation of this combination of experiences for the Beatles was a trip to India and a course of study under the guidance of the Maharishi Mahesh Yogi.

Yet, even before the Beatles encountered LSD or Maharishi, they had already begun to develop an interest in Eastern culture. This interest, John Lennon tells us, was inspired by the Indian musicians who were employed during the making of the movie

---

[1] *The Beatles Anthology* (San Francisco: Chronicle Books, 2000), p. 242.
[2] *Los Angeles Times* (3rd June, 2004), Home Edition, Calendar Weekend; Calendar Desk, p. E5.

Help! (*Beatles Anthology*, p. 171). The contributions of these Indian musicians can be seen in a restaurant scene in the movie, and can be heard on the film's musical soundtrack as well. Their resulting influence was apparent on the Beatles next album *Rubber Soul* which featured George playing a sitar on "Norwegian Wood." With their next album *Revolver* the Beatles had clearly gone beyond the adoption of a sitar and had begun to take a deeper interest in Indian Philosophy.

Two books, with which the Beatles became familiar, may explain why their experiences with LSD prompted an interest in Eastern Philosophy. The first book is Aldous Huxley's *The Doors of Perception*, perhaps the first instance of a major author examining his own experiences with psychotropic substances from within the context of the tenets of Eastern Philosophy.[3] Not surprisingly Huxley appears in the crowd on the *Sgt. Pepper* album cover and *The Doors of Perception* became quite popular in the 1960s. Perhaps even more important was *The Psychedelic Experience: A Manual Based on the Tibetan Book of the Dead,* a book published by Timothy Leary, his Harvard colleague Richard Alpert (later "Baba Ram Dass"), and Richard Metzner. This book, offered a very explicit interpretation of the relationship between Eastern thought and the hallucinatory experiences produced by LSD.[4] John Lennon refers to *The Psychedelic Experience* in explaining the inspiration for his song "Tomorrow Never Knows" from *Revolver* (*Beatles Anthology*, p. 209). A consideration of this book, as well as Huxley's book, is indispensible to any effort at deciphering principles of Eastern philosophy in the music of the Beatles.

Surrendering to the Void

What makes *The Psychedelic Experience* so important in its influence on the Beatles (outside of the credit John Lennon gives to it), is that it was based on a text which emerged from Tibetan Buddhism—*The Tibetan Book of the Dead*.[5] In this text we find

---

[3] Aldous Huxley *The Doors of Perception* was first published in Great Britain by Chatto and Windus in 1954.

[4] Timothy Leary, Ralph Metzner, Richard Alpert, *The Psychedelic Experience: A Manual Based on the Tibetan Book of the Dead* (New York: Citadel Press, 1964).

[5] *The Tibetan Book of the Dead: Or, the After-Death Experiences on the Bardo Plane,*

the expression of a host of ideas and concepts which are common to several Eastern traditions: especially the Buddhist and Hindu traditions. First and foremost is the idea that the human soul is engaged on a journey of increasing self-realization which spans many lifetimes.[6] *The Tibetan Book of the Dead* is a guide for those souls who, while approaching death, may have either failed in the task of self-realization during their present lifetime, or may yet have the potential to "see the truth" at their moment of death and, through such self-realization, escape the never ending cycle of death and re-birth—the meaning of *nirvana* (or freedom from re-birth) and the ultimate goal of human life. Individuals approaching death are in need of guidance for negotiating the transition into the very different reality we encounter after death, and before our subsequent re-birth.

According to Timothy Leary and his colleagues who wrote *The Psychedelic Experience* this "different reality"—described in this ancient text—resembled the reality *experienced* following the ingestion of LSD and other psychotropic substances. In other words, these substances have the potential to induce an experience which simulates all of the *psychological* significance of death—"ego death" and *transcendence* of our ordinary worldly experience. The "manual" Leary and his colleagues created was specifically aimed at guiding and directing an individual who was engaged in such a "trip" and thus approaching transcendence or "ego death." As John Lennon recalled "we followed his instructions in his 'how to take a trip' book" (*Beatles Anthology*, p. 209). This kind of guidance was deemed necessary to help direct the individual through the awe—and sometimes panic—which was often induced during the most intense stages of the psychedelic experience.

According to Lama Kazi Dawa-Samdup's English Rendering; compiled and edited by W.Y. Evans-Wentz (Oxford: Oxford University Press, 1960). Also see *The Tibetan Book of the Great Liberation: Or, the Method of Realizing Nirvana through Knowing the Mind,* edited by W.Y. Evans-Wentz (Oxford: Oxford University Press, 1968).

[6] As director and screenwriter Harold Ramis once explained, Bill Murray's movie *Groundhog Day,* was an attempt to capture the meaning of this idea in a novel way. The difference is that rather than reincarnating into different lives, Murray's character "Phil Conners" is trapped in one day—Groundhog Day. The effect is to portray the same situation assumed by *The Tibetan Book of the Dead*—we are condemned to life in this world (albeit in different bodies) until we, so to speak, "get it right"; which means we realize our true inner self.

It was at these stages of the LSD trip that death, from a psychological—or what philosopher's term *phenomenological* perspective—appeared most imminent. Phenomenology is a form of philosophical inquiry concerned with descriptions of any phenomena by means of direct awareness and our subjective experience. An appreciation of the phenomenology of the psychedelic experience goes a long way toward explaining the meaning of a bad trip—where the individual will alternately experience a range of frightening thoughts and hallucinations which can inspire intense panic, depression, and paranoia, and which led more than one seeker to conclude his or her trip in a hospital.

The message and guidance offered by John Lennon in "Tomorrow Never Knows" is the same provided by *The Tibetan Book of the Dead* and *The Psychedelic Experience.* When the Beatles sing "Turn off your mind, relax and float down stream, it is not dying," they are repeating the advice of those books. In spite of the onset of the subjective experience of death—and accompanying panic—the seeker is encouraged to close the eyes, and "relax." Likewise, the lyric "lay down all thoughts surrender to the void" echoes the advice of these texts. Yet, one may still ask, what value lies in "surrendering to the void"— other than overcoming the panic and paranoia of a bad trip? The answer is a fundamental theme of Eastern thought which emerges in more than one Beatles song: by surrendering to the void, we encounter a spiritual revelation of life's fundamental reality through an experience of transcendence—also known as the "Clear Light" which is, as the Beatles sing, "shining." The elucidation of this fundamental reality characterizes the metaphysics, theory of reality, of the *Vedanta* branch of Indian Philosophy.

Even from a purely musical perspective, it must be added, John Lennon was quite clear about the purpose of the unusual sound of "Tomorrow Never Knows." He was trying to recreate the sound of "thousands of monks chanting."[7] While John felt unsuccessful in his attempt to recreate that sound, the fundamental inspiration for the song's lyrics remains. "Tomorrow Never Knows" marks the beginning of the Beatles' numerous

---

[7] Hunter Davies, *The Beatles*, second revised edition (New York: Norton, 1996), pp. 277–78.

expressions of ideas that characterize *Vedanta*. For this reason, before we discuss the Eastern philosophical concepts embedded in this and other Beatles songs, let's consider some of the major ideas emerging from Vedanta.

Vedanta and the Beatles

Vedanta is concerned with metaphysics, life's ultimate reality: the underlying unity of all of creation, and the role of *maya*—illusion—in undermining our comprehension of this fundamental reality. The relationship between *maya* and *Brahman* (*the ultimate reality*) is traditionally depicted as analogous to the relation between the ocean (*Brahman*) and its transitory waves (*maya*). Yet, this is *only* an analogy. This ultimate reality must be *experienced* to be understood.

As we are taught in "Tomorrow Never Knows," by surrendering to the void, we "see the meaning of within" which is the nature of existence itself: shining, universal being, the fundamental unity from which all life emerges. The unity or totality of all creation is what Vedanta Philosophy refers to as *Brahman*. The Beatles may have become enamored with Vedanta because of a passage in Huxley's *The Doors of Perception*.[8] Huxley explains a theory originally advanced by the French philosopher Henri Bergson, subsequently treated sympathetically by the British philosopher C.D. Broad.[9] According to this theory, the main function of the brain and nervous system is *eliminative* and not productive—functioning like blinders on a horse. Thus, each person is at each moment *potentially* capable of remembering all that has ever happened to him and of perceiving everything that is happening everywhere in the universe (*Brahman*, the ocean of life).

The function of the brain and nervous system, then, is to protect us from being overwhelmed and potentially confused by this flood of knowledge, which would be irrelevant to the day-to-day tasks of ordinary living in our everyday world. To make biological survival possible in the mundane world, Mind at

---

[8] George's comments indicate that he and the other Beatles had in fact read *The Doors of Perception* (*Beatles Anthology*, p. 267). And as already mentioned, Aldous Huxley appears among the crowd on the *Sgt. Pepper* cover.

[9] C.D. Broad, "The Relevance of Psychical Research to Philosophy," in Broad, *Religion, Philosophy, and Psychical Research* (London: Routledge, 1953).

Large (*Brahman*) has to be "funneled" through the reducing valve of the brain and nervous system (our *de facto* blinders). For this reason, our everyday ordinary awareness is *reduced* awareness and a measly trickle of consciousness—only that which will help us to stay alive in our everyday world. Huxley concludes by speculating that the function of "spiritual exercises" and certain psychotropic substances may be to create a "by-pass" that circumvents this reducing valve—thereby exposing the individual mind to a greater awareness, Mind at Large, or what Vedanta terms *Brahman*, life's ultimate reality. Following Huxley's explanation of Bergson's theory, we see that the notion of "surrendering to the void" is an invitation to encounter this larger reality.

"Tomorrow Never Knows" affirms the never-ending cyclical nature of life in which birth follows death just as certainly as death follows birth. The song reminds us that it is only through "ignorance" and "hate" that we "mourn the dead" and that the cycle of birth and death commit us to "play the game existence to the end, of the beginning"—whereupon a new cycle emerges. This never ending cycle is the reason why, according to Eastern texts like *The Bhagavad-Gita*, one is not to "mourn the dead"—as the ignorant and "unenlightened" do.[10] Rather, life or "existence" is a never ending series of "games" in which *Brahman* alternately becomes manifest and un-manifest, forming a perpetual cycle of beginnings and endings. Indeed, also on *Revolver* the song "She Said, She Said" shares the belief that death is not a singular event ending one life, but a cyclical event that few can recall. "She said, I know what it's like to be dead." John tells us that this line was inspired by the actor Peter Fonda whose obsession with his own LSD experience led him to repeat this phrase ("I know what it's like to be dead") repeatedly to the Beatles during one of their own LSD encounters while visiting California (*Beatles Anthology*, p. 190).

George Harrison has offered a contrasting interpretation of the meaning of "Tomorrow Never Knows." In *The Beatles Anthology* he suggests that what Lennon was really getting at, is what meditation is basically all about (p. 210). George's analogy to meditation has merit since the goal of meditation is also an

---

[10] Maharishi Mahesh Yogi, *On the Bhagavad-Gita: New Translation and Commentary* (Baltimore: Penguin, 1989), p. 90.

experience of transcendence—the shining "void" of Being (albeit without the intensity and hallucinations of a drug-induced experience). Nonetheless, given John Lennon's confession about the inspiration for this song, George's comments reveal his attempt to separate this song from its drug-induced context and origin. This perhaps reflects George's own well-founded disillusionment with psychedelics which was, in part, brought on by his visit to San Francisco's Haight-Ashbury district in the 1960s. Rather than finding "hippie" spiritual seekers, he found a lot of kids virtually homeless and strung-out on drugs. What George had discovered is a point underscored more recently by religious scholar Huston Smith: while there is little doubt that certain kinds of psychotropic substances may induce religious or spiritual experiences, nonetheless, it is equally clear that these experiences alone do not necessarily lead to a more religious or spiritual life.[11]

Realizing It's All Within Yourself

In George Harrison's song "Within You, Without You" we find the consummate expression of Vedanta and Indian Philosophy in the Beatles' songbook. Indeed, by employing Indian musicians to accompany this song, George left little doubt about the underlying message.

In keeping with Vedanta, this song addresses the "wall of illusion," otherwise known as *maya*, that undermines our capacity to "glimpse the truth"—*Brahman*, the universal, absolute unity of all things. When the Beatles sing of the "space between us all," they are cleverly identifying the reality of "reduced" awareness. From the perspective of the expanded awareness of Brahman, "we are all one" and there is no "space between us all"—that perspective is part of maya, illusion. In the song, George also offers a somber reminder: most people do not encounter life's deepest truth until it's "far too late, when they pass away." Yet, the hope offered by this song is the same message that emerges repeatedly in *The Bhagavad-Gita,* a principal text of Indian Philosophy. While the individual, alone, is responsible for his or her own predicament in life on account of past

---

[11] Huston Smith, *Cleansing the Doors of Perception: The Religious Significance of Entheogenic Plants and Chemicals* (New York, Penguin Putman, 2000).

actions or *karma*, the individual is also empowered with great potential and, consequently, responsible for his or her own salvation as well (*Bhagavad Gita*, p. 395). It's entirely up to the individual, as George's song instructs "to realize that it's all within yourself" since "no one else can make you change."

For many, the somber mood of "Within You, Without You" interferes with the otherwise positive message: "peace of mind" is waiting there for those who embark on the necessary spiritual journey. In marked contrast to the mood of "Within You, Without You" is another George song which appears in the *Yellow Submarine* movie and sound track: "It's All Too Much." While "Within, You Without You" appears as a warning to our failure to "see the truth," "It's All Too Much" is a celebration of the joy and bliss which accompanies the illumination provided by a vision of life's ultimate reality.

Though the song appears to begin as a personal love song (and in many ways may still be seen as such) it quickly becomes obvious that this song is about much more. One line in particular may have two meanings, confirming the idea that the song is about both personal and cosmic love. "And the more I go inside, the more there is to see." This line can be interpreted as a reference to both what is seen in the eyes of a loved one, as well as the inner vision fostered by the inner directedness of meditation. It's in meditation, after all, as taught by Yoga Philosophy, that we nurture a vision of *Brahman*, the absolute, ultimate reality. Another lyric, significantly, repeated twice, "Everywhere, it's what you make," underscores the relation between the karma of our past lives and the circumstances under which we currently live. Perhaps the most relevant lyric to our current inquiry "Show me that I'm everywhere and get me home for tea," refers to the reality of *Brahman*: a reality which, while accessed by going within during meditation, is omnipresent. When we realize the truth of *Brahman*, we realize that we *are* in fact, simultaneously everywhere and everything *as well as* an individual personality engaged in mundane existence—even one having tea. The central purpose of *Yoga* Philosophy is to bring about the full *integration* or *union* of these two seemingly contradictory realities: awareness of the ultimate truth, or Brahman, and awareness of the reality of our mundane existence (the term "yoke" has the same root meaning as the term yoga—to bring together, to integrate).

In other songs by John and Paul, some of these same themes emerge. "The Fool on the Hill" and "Across the Universe," complete our look at the most important lyrical preoccupations of the Beatles with Eastern Philosophy.

The Fool on the Hill Glides Across the Universe

The fool on the hill, while exhibiting his "foolish grin" is "keeping perfectly still"—as one does in meditation. In later years, Paul McCartney acknowledged that the inspiration for the song was in fact the Maharishi Mahesh Yogi—or, at least, someone "like" him: an individual whose perception of reality is at once, more complete and more accurate than the average person (being a knower, as it were of *Brahman*).[12] To "see the world spinning round" captures the idea that the "fool's" grasp of reality is larger and more inclusive than the ordinary individual's perception. Yet, by virtue of such a perspective, this individual places him or herself at odds with the rest of humanity whose vision of the "truth" is limited to the "reduced" awareness described by Huxley. Here's an individual who sees the world as it *really* is.[13]

With "The Fool on the Hill" we also find a clearer expression of the goal of a life of self-discovery and self-realization. Experiencing *Brahman* is to experience the deepest reality within one*self*, distinguishing it as a state of *Self*-consciousness. This ultimate experience of Self-consciousness is said to bring with it the characteristics and qualities of *Sat-Chit-Ananda*: the pure absolute state of bliss-consciousness, and hence accounts for what may appear as a "foolish grin" to the unenlightened (*Bhagavad Gita*, pp. 440–41). In "Across the Universe," these sentiments find their most mature expression.

"Across the Universe" was written by John Lennon in India while the Beatles were staying at Maharishi's ashram. The song thus marks a period of time in which the Beatles were, at once, most immersed in Indian Philosophy, and also most free of

---

[12] See Paul McCartney's 1990 press conference in Chapter 8 of the DVD *The Beatles: A Celebration*, written, by Geoffrey Giuliano (Delta Entertainment, 1999).

[13] This idea that a wise individual may nonetheless be perceived as an old fool is not uncommon. It emerged in Herman Hesse's story *Siddhartha*. By the end of this story Siddhartha, the narrative's principal character has come to full self-realization—awareness of Brahman. Nonetheless his mentor and he are a mystery to most people who alternately describe them as either wise men or fools.

drugs. "Across the Universe" represents the clearest expression of John Lennon's take on Maharishi's many discourses on *The Bhagavad-Gita.*

Among the principal features of *The Bhagavad-Gita*, is a delineation of the meaning of an integrated, enlightened life of full Self-realization. While the philosophy of Vedanta occupies portions of *The Bhagavad-Gita*, it is equally concerned with the basic tenets of *Yoga* Philosophy. As mentioned, the Sanskrit term *yoga* has the same root meaning as our term "yoke": a word for uniting or bringing together. Yoga Philosophy is concerned with the techniques that foster the integration or union of the individual with cosmic life—Brahman.[14] In the yoga of meditation, a *mantra* is used as a technique for fostering an experience of transcendence (*Om* or *aum*, being the most widely known mantra). The various disciplines and techniques of Yoga Philosophy comprise a body of knowledge which is, traditionally, passed on from master to disciple for the purpose of experiencing the truth embodied in Vedanta. After all, this is a truth that goes beyond words and must be experienced to be understood.

In "Across the Universe," John Lennon pays tribute to these ideas. Most noticeable are the words which introduce his chorus: "Jai Guru Dev." The literal meaning is "praise" or "all glory" to Guru Dev. "Guru Dev," literally, "divine teacher" or spiritual guide, is a term which expresses both respect and devotion to the memory of a departed master. Unlike the parting of ordinary individuals—requiring the form of guidance offered by *The Tibetan Book of the Dead*—the departure of an enlightened master is deemed an occasion in which the manifest individual merges most fully with the unmanifest, divine world: *Brahman.* There are no more rebirths. The master's devotees subsequently, are said to experience the master as waves of bliss from the unmanifest—otherwise known as *Brahmanandam.* The expression "Jai Guru Dev" was—and still is—invoked regularly by Maharishi in memory of his own master as a greeting or salutation to all visitors.

---

[14] What most westerners think of when they hear the term "yoga" is that which comprises *hatha yoga*: according to classical Indian Philosophy, this is the practice and study of yogic postures and positions which are aimed at "purifying" the body and preparing the mind for Self-realization. Equally important, however, is what is termed *dhyana* yoga, the yoga meditation.

The refrain that occupies the most significant part of the chorus also captures a central message from *The Bhagavad-Gita*. When the Beatles sing "nothing's gonna change my world," they're expressing an important theme of this text which defines a central characteristic of Self-realization: a profound state of equanimity. According to *The Bhagavad-Gita*, such equanimity is equally "unshaken" in "the midst of sorrow" and "pleasures." Such an individual neither "greatly rejoices on obtaining what his dear to him" or her, "nor grieves much on obtaining that which is unpleasant" (*Bhagavad-Gita*, pp. 154–58, 360–63). Consequently, even while (as the Beatles sing) "pools of sorrow and waves of joy are drifting through" your mind, "possessing and caressing" you, nonetheless, in the enlightened state of consciousness, "nothing's gonna change" your world. One's awareness is, so to speak, stabilized on Brahman, and integrates the experience of our mundane world along with reality at its deepest, most profound state, where "limitless undying love . . . shines . . . like a million suns." From a purely musical perspective, John Lennon's score for this song reinforces this sense of equanimity. Unlike most Beatle songs "Across the Universe" features no contrasting bridge (or middle eight). There is just the constant alternation of verse and chorus.

And in the End

There are other Beatles songs in which we can trace the influence of Eastern Philosophy. Often this influence was more brief or more subtle. A good example is the opening line of "I Am the Walrus." This is the Beatles' most succinct affirmation of the metaphysics of Vedanta which underscores our basic spiritual unity: "I am he as you are he as you are me and we are all together." Vedanta makes this point more concisely in the Sanskrit expression *Tat tvam asi* which is translated "Thou art that" (*Bhagavad-Gita*, p. 357). The origin of this aphorism is the *Chandogya Upanishad*—among the most ancient sources of Indian Philosophy.[15] A good summary of the entire *Chandogya Upanishad* might well read: "I am that, thou art that, all of this,

[15] Juan Mascaro, *The Upanishads: Translations from the Sanskrit with an Introduction* (New York: Penguin, 1965), pp. 117–19.

is nothing but that." Lennon's rendering is, perhaps, easier to sing.

Another noteworthy song is George's "The Inner Light." Here, however, George borrowed the entire text for the song's lyrics directly from the *Tao Te Ching*—an ancient text of Chinese philosophy. And in the later solo music of George Harrison we find a lifelong preoccupation with the type of spiritual quest that defines these Eastern traditions.

In some of their other songs, we can discern yet another more subtle legacy of Eastern Philosophy's influence on the Beatles: the alternating expression of two values which may appear paradoxical on the surface. On the one hand, many songs project a positive, optimistic view of the human potential and especially of individual self-efficacy—*it all lies within yourself no one else can make you change.* Yet there is a current of Eastern fatalism, which periodically emerges in Beatles songs. This fatalistic dimension is linked to the laws of *karma* which dictate much of our fate. Our inevitable karmic fate is being underscored in "All You Need Is Love," when the Beatles intimate that there is nothing one can do that can't be done nor is there anyone one can save that can't be saved, and most importantly, there is nowhere one can be that isn't where one is meant to be. And in "Revolution", we not only hear that our principal concern should be to "free our minds" but that when all is said and done, everything is "going to be alright."

In the final analysis, whether it's mantras or meditation, the Beatles' embrace of Eastern Philosophical ideas—however briefly they may have appeared in the group's music—went a long way toward establishing these interests in popular culture today, making the Beatles surrogate gurus in their own right for a tradition of ancient teachings that has been going in and out of style, and will continue to do so, for many years to come.

12

I'd Love to Turn You On: The Beatles and the Ethics of Altered States

JERE O'NEILL SURBER

During the 1960s and into the 1970s, the Beatles, as a major icon of the era, served as a flashpoint for a number of moral, political, and cultural issues. None was as passionately contested, from both sides, as that of their experimentation with altered states of consciousness, first through drugs and later through meditative practices.

While the Establishment vilified them as pied pipers of psychedelia and godless gurus and the Counterculture celebrated them as holy prophets of a New Age, the Beatles themselves seemed always to defy the images promoted by either side, often by the recognizably philosophical maneuver of posing new questions rather than advocating entrenched views and values.

The decade of the Sixties was itself a time of intense questioning about some of the most fundamental assumptions that had dominated philosophical thought, social practice, and political policy since the beginning of the Enlightenment in the seventeenth century. One of the most well entrenched and rarely questioned assumptions, which can be found already fully developed in the philosophy of René Descartes (1596–1650), was that there is a single, clearly evident, and "normal" state of consciousness that we all share as thinking, rational human beings.

Descartes himself recognized at least one other state of consciousness—that of dreaming—in the famous "dream argument" in his first *Meditation*. But he invoked the dream state ultimately to reinforce his conviction of the normality and rationality of waking consciousness against the abnormal and irrational qualities of dream experiences. It was not until late in the nineteenth century that thinkers such as Freud and Nietzsche first appeared as lonely and often derided challengers of this long-unquestioned philosophical assumption. However, by the 1960s, this small stream of doubt, fed by a growing number of other currents—Husserl's and Heidegger's phenomenology, Lacan's revisions of Freudian psychoanalysis, Mircea Eliade's studies of non-Western religions, and Foucault's radical historical studies, to name but a few—converged to produce a widespread questioning about whether any one state of consciousness could be singled out as somehow normal or foundational for all other alternatives.

Since Descartes had linked the privileged "normal state of consciousness" with rationality, then skepticism about the former immediately called into question the possibility of drawing any clear line between rational and irrational states of consciousness. If this were merely a theoretical matter, it might have provided just another topic for philosophers and intellectuals to debate. But it had vitally important ethical and political implications as well, because both ethical and political thought since the Enlightenment had, for the most part, been based upon the very assumption of a normal, rational state of consciousness underlying the judgments, decisions, and actions of human beings. Put simply, the most fundamental ethical assumption, clearly evident in such an important moral philosopher as Immanuel Kant (1724–1804), was that acting morally meant acting rationally, and that acting rationally presupposed the lucid, self-aware "normal" state of consciousness.

Though there had certainly been significant ethical and political disagreements among philosophers operating out of these shared assumptions before the decade of the 1960s, during this period philosophers and policy makers came to face a host of new, largely unsuspected challenges that went to the heart of their enterprises. Many, both intellectuals such as Professor Timothy Leary and Norman O. Brown as well as representatives of the Counterculture such as Ken Kesey, the Grateful Dead, and Jefferson Airplane, viewed experimentation with "alternative states of consciousness" as ushering in a new era of human liberation and self-realization, an "Age of Aquarius" as it was sometimes called. Others, usually representing "the Establishment," responded by sustained attempts to discredit these "New Age" experiments and movements devoted to "consciousness alter-ation" and began a cycle of legislative repression that assumed that any other than the normal, rational state of consciousness was ethically wrong and politically subversive.

To their credit, the Beatles rather consistently refused to align themselves with either group. Although there are clear refer-ences to altered states of consciousness in their lyrics, inter-views, and films from about 1965 onward, and they made little attempt to conceal their own experimentation with drugs and, later on, various forms of meditation, they communicated in their works a sort of critical reserve that is mostly absent in so much of the Counterculture and its representatives. What, then, were some of the ethical questions posed by the Beatles?

How 'Normal' Is 'the Normal State of Consciousness'?

The 1967 album *Sgt. Pepper's Lonely Hearts Club Band*, with its experimental recording techniques, psychedelic art and word imagery, and famous last line ("I'd love to turn you on . . ."), was the Beatles' first large-scale, fully explicit, and perhaps still most spectacular invocation of drug-induced altered states of consciousness. Whatever might have been the actual story behind the song, the initials of its second cut, "Lucy in the Sky with Diamonds" (LSD), were clearly understood as such a refer-ence by almost everyone who listened to the album upon its release. What is less apparent is that, even prior to this landmark album, especially in *Rubber Soul* (1965) and *Revolver* (1966), the band had begun to explore states of consciousness other than the rational, normative one of lucid awareness that had domi-nated so much of the philosophical tradition stemming from Descartes.

Two such states, those defined by emotional memory and intense love, dominated the first of these albums and would remain recurrent themes throughout their active period as a band (and even beyond in their solo careers). The very title of this album, *Rubber Soul*, with its deliberately distorted photo-graph of the band, suggests the sort of warped extension of con-sciousness involved in attempting to recall long past events or viewing another person "through the eyes of love." In fact, such existentialist philosophers as Martin Heidegger (1889–1976) and

Jean-Paul Sartre (1905–1980) had, several decades before, already proposed that consciousness, in its very structure, "stands out from" (a literal translation of "exists") or "transcends itself" toward something other than itself, rather literally abandoning the "normal" self-contained and present-oriented state privileged by Descartes. Both themes intertwine in what is probably the most popular song of this album, "In My Life," where memories of past times and places are constantly compared to a present love the two themes woven together to form a tapestry of naturally occurring and entirely familiar "altered states of consciousness" reflecting the visual distortion of the album cover.

The Beatles' next album, *Revolver*, goes much further in the same direction. To the states of memory and love are added sleep ("I'm Only Sleeping") and a sort of basic cosmic vision ("Here, There, and Everywhere"). But its most remarkable cut, the final one on the album, "Tomorrow Never Knows," anticipates what will appear overtly in their next album (*Sgt. Pepper*). Though mostly unnoticed at the time, it is, in fact, based upon a text from *The Psychedelic Experience* by Dr. Timothy Leary, and invites the listener to "turn off your mind, relax and float downstream." As if to summarize this period of their work and anticipate the next, the song ends, "So play the game 'Existence' to the end, Of the beginning, of the beginning."

If we accept the idea presented in these works that there is a broad and rich variety of "states of consciousness" (whether naturally occurring or drug-induced), this immediately suggests that the sort of lucid, rational consciousness assumed by Descartes and the tradition following him is, at most, one among many such states. Now we might be tempted to claim that, in such a situation, it simply wouldn't be possible to regard one such state as somehow privileged over the others. But there is a dilemma lurking here. If we want to claim that there is a single "normal" state of consciousness among the various possibilities, then don't we somehow have to make such a claim from *outside* the state that we are judging as "normal"? Otherwise, if we remain entirely within it, how would we ever be able to prove that it, among all others, is the single privileged state of consciousness? In other words, in order to assert that a particular state of consciousness is "normal," it seems that we could only do so from "outside" the "normal" state of consciousness itself, which would undercut our claim that the state in question is actually "normal." On the other hand, if we want to claim that "consciousness" is more a tapestry or kaleidoscope of various states of consciousness, then don't we have to argue this point from a particular position, which would presumably be some "baseline" state that would make such a rational argument possible? But wouldn't this be exactly the "normal," rational state of consciousness that we are trying to dispute? Maybe John Lennon best expressed our bewilderment in the face of such a dilemma in a song recorded just after *Revolver*, "Strawberry Fields": "I think I know I mean a 'Yes' but it's all wrong—that is I think I disagree."

How 'Ethical' Is the 'Normal State of Consciousness'?

The underlying logic of the first dilemma, that we may not be able to certify some particular state as "normal," mainly revolves around ambiguities in the terms "normal" and "abnormal." The logical problem involves attempting to distinguish the two by applying the term "normal" to some particular state of consciousness and then regarding all others as somehow "abnormal." But, since "normality" had, since Descartes, been equated with "rationality," another, more distinctively ethical set of issues immediately arises. We might, that is, further challenge the dominant assumption about some "normal state of consciousness" by asking, "Even if some particular state of consciousness could be established as 'normal,' why should we assume that it is also 'rational'?"

Several decades before the 1960s, the question of whether a "normal" state of consciousness (supposing that it makes sense to speak of one) must necessarily also be "rational" had been explored in considerable detail within two bodies of philosophical thought, existentialism and the Frankfurt School of Critical Theory. Already in the 1920s, in his seminal work *Being and Time*, Martin Heidegger had suggested that our natural, "everyday" state of consciousness, that state of mind in which we go through our daily activities and routines with little reflection or self-awareness and mostly "follow the crowd" when ethical or political issues arise, is (to use his term) "inauthentic." By this, he meant to suggest, among other things, that our ordinary daily lives are lived in a sort of "neutral state" where, for the most part, we "go about our business" avoiding assuming any responsibility either for our own lives or for those of others. Though such a state may give us a bit of moment-to-moment comfort in familiarity and shield us from having to think too much or confront any upsetting moral issues or commitments, it also renders life passive, empty, and meaningless. If this is a fair description of our "everyday state of consciousness," the "normal" state in which we live, then it represents anything but the sort of aware, self-conscious, active, rational state that the tradition assumed to underlie any genuinely moral or political activity. In fact, one might well be tempted to regard this version of a "normal" state as itself irrational and potentially immoral.

Clearly registering this more "existentialist" line of thought, the Beatles created a fairly extensive cast of characters whose lives lack self-responsibility, commitment to others, and ultimately any meaning at all. Just to name a few, on *Rubber Soul* we meet the "Nowhere Man, living in his nowhere land, thinking all his nowhere thoughts for nobody." A bit later, on *Revolver*, there are perhaps the most pathetic of the Beatles characters, Eleanor Rigby and Father MacKenzie. As *The Beatles: The Rough Guide* summarizes the song, "A lonely spinster, a lonely priest; she dies, he buries her." Then, at the end of the drug-driven mayhem of *Sgt. Pepper*, the Beatles confront us with one of their most memorable dress-downs of everyday life, its intrinsic meaninglessness now complicated by a sort of neurotic mania fueled by the constant bombardment of depressing media stories. It is hard to hear "A Day in The Life," with its concluding crashing and sustained chords, as anything but a massive "downer" induced by the return to empty "normalcy" from the fantastic psychedelic carnival that had gone before. Finally, while the Beatles' attitude had, up until then, gone from a sort of pity to sad resignation ("I read the news today, oh-boy . . ."), the *White Album* finds them blatantly contemptuous of the "little piggies" who lead self-satisfied "piggy lives" while the world around them is collapsing. Clearly, for the Beatles, these "normal lives" would not be something that anyone would "rationally" choose if they could discover other alternatives.

The second strand of philosophical thought questioning the assumption that our "normal" state of consciousness must be "rational" is that of the so-called Frankfurt School, a group of social theorists and critics active in Germany during the 1920s and 1930s who escaped Nazism to live in the U.S. On their view, there is, in fact, a certain "rationality" characteristic of normal, everyday consciousness but it is a one-sided, myopic, and ultimately self-defeating one. They called this "instrumental reason" and linked it with the rise of science and its technological applications. On their analysis, instrumental reason reduced any ethical or political thought about genuine human values and aims, considered in the broadest sense, to decisions about the technical means of achieving immediate personal or social goals usually already dictated by existing economic or political structures.

Perhaps the Beatles, too, had something like this in mind in contrasting their own harmonious communal life in the Yellow Submarine with their mechanistic, Nazi-like antagonists, the "Blue Meanies." The members of the Frankfurt School also held that, in the time since the Enlightenment, instrumental reason had come to install itself even within the psyches and lives of individuals, so that anyone who rejected such a way of thinking would be regarded by society at large as "abnormal" and "irrational." You might think here of the way "Hippies" seeking communal ways of life, rejecting potentially successful careers, and protesting the war were regarded by "the Establishment."

Put simply, instrumental reason was concerned with achieving dominance and power over nature and other human beings and, if this was not your goal, then "you must be crazy (irrational)." Against this, the Frankfurt School asserted that there is another kind of rationality that they called "critical," whose aim was to reveal the very irrationality of instrumental reason both at the individual and political level. (To see the contrast between the two types of rationality, think, for instance, of the difference between asking what the relative costs and benefits are of building a new retail development on open land, versus asking whether doing so, whatever its relative economic advantages, actually improves the environment and lives of the people living in the area.)

During the Sixties, there was a direct connection between the earlier thought of the Frankfurt School and the development of the Counterculture. One member of the Frankfurt School, Herbert Marcuse (1898–1979), accepted a permanent position in the U.S. as a professor of philosophy and provided theoretical justification and practical encouragement of the Counterculture's experimental lifestyles, musical and artistic innovations, and political activities. In his at the time very popular work, *An Essay on Liberation*, Marcuse asserts that "critical rationality" includes precisely the sort of imaginative experimentation practiced by the Counterculture in the realm of popular culture. Through such cultural activities and productions, the Counterculture was able to break loose of the dominant instrumental-rational mindset of the dominant culture by exploring new ways of life, forms of expression, and modes of consciousness which served as positions from which the actual irrationality of the dominant culture could be exposed and undermined.

The Beatles, with their immense popularity and prodigious creative output, played a significant role in this formation of a "critical consciousness" which came to regard the "normal" state of instrumental-rational consciousness as itself irrational and, ultimately, immoral. (The perverse and wildly exaggerated "body count" of the "enemy" on the daily news during the Vietnam era was a case in point.) In one sense, simply as highly creative and innovative artists, the Beatles succeeded in opening a critical distance between the dominant form of rationality and new worlds of imagination (like "The Yellow Submarine") from which the limitations and irrationality of the former could be revealed. More specifically, the two major avenues of drug use and, slightly later, Eastern meditation and mysticism also came to play such a role for them.

What then was the dilemma that the Beatles highlighted for the popular culture of their day? If, on the one hand, we think that the normal or dominant mode of consciousness is irrational or immoral, producing such clearly immoral practices as racial bigotry, unjustified warfare, and the destruction of the environment, then it seems to follow that we are, in a broader sense, *morally obligated* to produce and occupy alternative states of consciousness that can counteract the "normal" one while not producing such results themselves. Put in this way, one might well, along with such figures as Timothy Leary, Aldous Huxley, and William Burroughs, come to regard even drug use, exotic religious rituals, and sexual experimentation as themselves a sort of "moral action." On the other hand, it is by no means clear that such alterations of consciousness are without their own immoral consequences, as the "Helter Skelter" scenario of the

Manson family or later the Jim Jones or Branch Davidian cults made very clear. But more, if both the "normal" state of consciousness and other "non-normal" states are equally capable of producing results that most of us would regard as immoral, where are we standing when we make such moral judgments about these consequences?

In the face of such a dilemma, the Beatles once again maintained (or perhaps evolved toward) a sort of critical balance. If they first appeared, within limits, to endorse drugs and, later, meditation as providing potential platforms for the critique of "normal" consciousness, and disavowed political revolution in favor of "changing your minds instead" on the "White Album," their last word seems to come on their final testament, *Abbey Road*, with the chorus of its first track, "Come together over me." Despite their personal problems with each other, the entire *Abbey Road* album seems a new departure that has left behind the dilemmas based upon subjective states of consciousness in favor of interpersonal communication ("Come Together"), joyous affirmation ("Here comes the sun"), humor ("An Octopusses' Garden" and "She came in through the bathroom window"), and even a concluding wink at the Queen herself.

Can I Treat Myself Immorally?

Considered from the viewpoint of philosophy as well as popular culture, Descartes's assumption about a privileged "normal" state of consciousness did not fare well over the course of the 1960s. Especially for the Counterculture and its apologists, the earlier lines between "normal" and "abnormal" states of consciousness and "rational" and "irrational" actions and policies seemed increasingly questionable. This in turn provoked a predictable counter-movement as established political authorities stiffened anti-drug laws, increased penalties for their violation, and ramped up enforcement efforts, eventually issuing in the "War on Drugs" that remains the basis of federal policy even today. (Though no laws seem to have been enacted against the practice of various other forms of consciousness alteration such as meditation, evidence later emerged that some groups involved with them did come under surveillance by government agents.)

The Beatles were not exempt from such measures, and John Lennon's dubious arrest for possession of a small amount of marijuana, followed by problems with travel and immigration, made headlines around the world. John registered his bitter response to such treatment in his song of 1969, "The Ballad of John and Yoko, wryly anticipating his own crucifixion. It was a refrain with which legions of fellow members of the Counter-culture could readily identify.

Judging by the direction taken by public policy then and later, the counter-response appeared to be that, even if we grant that it is difficult to distinguish between "normal" and "abnor-mal" states of consciousness, and that it's questionable whether some forms can be shown to be more "rational" than others, we can at least draw a distinction between "naturally occurring" and hence morally permissible states of consciousness and others that are deliberately induced by the ingestion of psychoactive substances and hence are morally blameworthy. Considerable evidence can be offered attempting to link chemically altered states of consciousness with socially harmful consequences (for example, automobile fatalities, a rise in the crime rate, failure in school, or generally anti-social behavior). But such arguments are rather easily answered by pointing out that there are many things that produce the same results (corresponding to each of the examples cited above, cell phones, unemployment, poor parenting, and the mass media might be mentioned), most of which no lawmaker would ever attempt to outlaw or ban.

This suggests that the fundamental *ethical* argument (as opposed to questions of practical social policy) against the prac-tice of "artificially induced" consciousness alteration must take the form of showing that such a practice is somehow intrinsi-cally wrong apart from its consequences. But, shorn of all con-sequences, this amounts to demonstrating that there are certain things that are intrinsically wrong to do to our own selves. Once again, when viewed from a critical philosophical perspective, a perplexing dilemma arises, one that goes to the heart of what we mean by ethical or moral agency and actions.

On one approach, most famously represented by the philosopher Kant, among our moral duties are certain duties that a person owes to him- or herself. One such duty is to refrain from deliberately physically harming ourselves, which would render such things as suicide and self-mutilation intrinsically immoral (as Kant himself concluded). But this presupposes a distinction between myself as a material, physical being and myself as a conscious rational agent, a distinction by no means as straightforward as it seems. And, of course, it once more invokes Descartes's now questionable assumption of the latter as itself "normal" and "rational." But, even more, on this argument it would still remain to prove that the alteration of one's own consciousness is in any way harmful in the way that mutilation or suicide is to the body.

An alternative approach, represented earlier by David Hume (1711–1776) and today by most libertarians, is to claim that moral or ethical action exclusively concerns our relationships with other persons. (The underlying protest against violations of privacy expressed in "The Ballad of John and Yoko" clearly falls under this heading.) To speak of any distinctive moral duty to myself is simply nonsensical, this view would insist. Certainly we sometimes speak of someone "lying to himself" or "breaking a promise to himself" or even "harming herself," but such claims tend to fall under the heading of psychopathology rather than immorality.

The implicit argument, then, is that if an action is "victimless" (that is, doesn't involve harmful consequences to other persons) then it can't possibly be a "crime" and shouldn't be treated as such. But if the former approach turned on an assumed divisibility of the self into a rational agent and a body acted upon, the latter seems unjustifiably to ignore such a difference in the face of the impact of physiological changes, caused by conscious decisions, upon consciousness itself. Addictive dependency is perhaps the clearest example, but nervous exhaustion, disorientation, and various temporary (or in extreme cases permanent) neuroses or even psychoses would be others.

The Beatles were not philosophers, so we should not expect to find any clear answers to these questions in their work. Rather, they were gifted artists, part of whose genius was to have, with subtlety and intelligence, expressed some of the major dilemmas of our time and opened a creative space wherein we can confront them on our own. The Beatles are no more but the songs—and the questions—still remain.

VII

We Can Think It Out

The Beatles on the
Practice of Philosophy

13

But I Can Show You a Better Time: The Beatles and the Practice of Philosophy

JAMES B. SOUTH

> The results of all the schools and of all their experiments
> belong legitimately to us.
> —Friedrich Nietzsche

Two Beatles songs: "You Won't See Me" and "I Want to Tell You." On the surface, both are fairly straightforward songs about love affairs gone awry. While both point to frustration on the part of the spurned or disappointed lover, the songs have different points of view. The first is an anguished love song from the point of view of a discarded lover, while the second is a song of consolation to the one spurned.

In the first song, the singer, frustrated that his lover won't respond to his calls, finally, and with some desperation, pleads that he will lose his mind if she doesn't relent. In the second, the singer knows the problem is his—he's sending mixed signals—and makes that clear. He comforts the one who seems distressed over the failure of the relationship: "But if I seem to act unkind, / it's only me, it's not my mind / that is confusing things." There is, in short, an air of resignation, but not desperation, in the latter song.

One way of thinking about the difference between these two songs is to fall back on the recognition that a standard convention of love songs is the love affair that is unequal, one in which one person loves the other in a qualitatively different way ("let's be friends") or a quantitatively different way ("I love her more than she loves me"). We might look at these two songs as merely what Paul McCartney, later in his life, referred to as "silly love songs." But what if we look at these two songs, and many other Beatles songs, in a way that renders them rather less silly?

You May Be Awoken

Writing in the eighteenth century, Immanuel Kant expressed a certain exasperation with the way philosophy was being done: "One must not just speculate for ever; one must one day also think about actual practice."[1]

"The Fool on the Hill" gives a description that initially seems relevant to the person who wants to speculate for ever: "Well on the way, head in a cloud / The man of a thousand voices talking perfectly loud / But nobody ever hears him, / Or the sound he appears to make, / And he never seems to notice. . . ." I suspect many people view the practice of philosophy in exactly this way: it's endless speculation that makes no real difference in our lives.

In response to such concerns, professional philosophers today draw a distinction between "Philosophy" and "Applied Philosophy." So, for example, there's a difference between ethics as a theoretical discipline, a branch of philosophy, and ethics as it can be applied to decisions in business (Business Ethics) and medicine (Medical Ethics). The former might typically be concerned with issues such as the justification of moral principles, the formal nature of moral judgment, and the like, while the latter might be more concerned about the relation between the interests of particular corporation and the interests of its shareholders.

Such a distinction between types of philosophical problems is important and explains why hospitals have philosophers on their Ethics Committees. It's a help to patients and their families to have people trained to provide clarification about the very practical issues of patient consent, confidentiality, and various end-of-life issues. But Kant was not suggesting that we should give up theoretical ethics and do applied ethics in its place. Anyone who has read very much Kant would know that he never abandoned his commitment to discussing, and criticizing,

[1] Immanuel Kant, *Lectures on the* Philosophical Encyclopedia, quoted in Pierre Hadot, *What Is Ancient Philosophy?* (Cambridge, Massachusetts: Harvard University Press, 2002), p. 267.

the traditional theoretical problems of philosophy. But if Kant wasn't advocating that we all become applied philosophers, what was his point about "actual practice?"

The Beatles' description of the Fool on the Hill can give us a pointer. What if the Fool on the Hill isn't really a fool? One way to see why the Fool isn't really foolish is to note how Kant continues his discussion of the actual practice of philosophy: "Nowadays, however, he who lives in a way which conforms with what he teaches is taken to be a dreamer" (*What Is Ancient Philosophy?*, p. 267). Kant's "practical" philosopher, then, refers not to the type of philosophical issue one considers (applied versus theoretical), but to the relation between what the philosopher teaches and how the philosopher lives. In the same way, the Fool on the Hill's blindness to the practical affairs of the world around him is not the reason he's called a fool, but rather the Fool is considered by most of us to be foolish because he lives according to what he thinks.

Confirmation for this reading of the Fool (and Kant's practical philosopher) can be seen in the contrasting descriptions given of the Fool with the person described in "Nowhere Man." The Nowhere Man is "as blind as he can be" and "just sees what he wants to see." The Fool on the Hill, though, is not blind: he "sees the sun going down / and the eyes in his head / see the world spinning round." The starkness of these two descriptions is striking. The Fool on the Hill may be considered a dreamer by the rest of us, but his feet are firmly planted and he sees, even if his seeing is described by others as dreaming.

Just as Kant does, the Beatles try to call us to a recognition that true wisdom may look like foolishness or idle dreaming to most of us, but that's not because of the content of what's being thought or seen; rather, it's because it's so rare to see someone whose beliefs and actions are in harmony. The obvious next question to ask is why Kant and the Beatles think such harmony is so rare.

Now That You Know Who You Are, Who Do You Want to Be?

In another of his works, *The Metaphysics of Morals*, Immanuel Kant provides a useful distinction that can aid us in understanding why conformity between beliefs and actions is rare. He does so within the context of an interesting discussion of the way that we judge ourselves as moral agents. He compares our conscience to an inner judge and argues that this inner judge must be considered as *another person*. In explicating the notion of another person within us, he goes on to say, "A human being who accuses and judges himself in conscience must think of a dual personality in himself, a doubled self which, on the one hand, has to stand trembling at the bar of a court that is yet entrusted to him, but which, on the other hand, itself administers the office of judge that it holds by innate authority." He concludes by naming the self as judged a "sensible being" and the self that judges an "intelligible being."[2]

Returning to our two songs, Kant's distinction between intelligible self and sensible self, between judge of actions and the one whose actions are judged, is structurally analogous to the distinction the singer makes in "I Want to Tell You" between "my mind" (the intelligible self) and "me" (the sensible self). The singer is judging himself, and the nexus of the judgment is the distinction between belief and practice. It's the singer's 'me' that is confusing things. But in judging himself, the singer also offers this distinction to his dissatisfied lover.

In this way, the singer is trying to lead his lover, and by extension, the listener, to a deeper awareness of the relation between the self and its desires. By contrast, the singer in "You Won't See Me" has no such distinction available for his self-understanding, and it is this lack of distance between his desires for his lover and his self that accounts in great part for the sense of desperation present in his song. His sensible self, as it were, is in danger and the unavailability to him of his intelligible self means he risks destruction of his mind.

Thus, one lesson we can learn from "I Want to Tell You" is a method for becoming philosophers. In this connection, it's significant that "I Want to Tell You" provides us no substantive description of the "mind" or "me," instead relying on the intuitive plausibility of the distinction. The song asks us to recognize the distinction as one we can use in our everyday practice. That is, before we can provide some positive conception of these two

---

[2] Immanuel Kant, *The Metaphysics of Morals*, Part II, Section 1 (ß13) (Cambridge: Cambridge University Press, 1996), p. 189. This passage is discussed by Hadot, *What Is Ancient Philosophy?*, p. 201.

selves, we have to see that there are such selves. And even once we see there are such selves, it's an easy matter to forget the distinction. If we're going to become people whose beliefs and practices cohere in the way Kant suggests and that the Fool on the Hill exemplifies, we need ways to be reminded of our tendency to separate these two areas of our lives.

The Ancient writer Plutarch strikingly describes the practice of philosophy that I see present in many Beatles songs. He writes: "Most people imagine that philosophy consists in delivering discourses from the heights of a chair, and in giving classes based on texts. But what the people utterly miss is the uninterrupted philosophy which we see being practiced every day in a way which is perfectly equal to itself" (*What Is Ancient Philosophy?*, p. 25).

The core distinction we drew from "I Want to Tell You" between "me" and "my mind" helps us understand Plutarch's point. The lyrics of the song don't seem to be philosophical in the usual sense of the term, since there is no argument presented and no explanation provided for the distinction. If we distinguish, though, between two types of philosophical style, we'll have a better grasp of what's at stake in the quotation from Plutarch. In addition to a standard philosophical style of presenting rigorous arguments for positions, there's another style present in philosophy throughout its history. It's this daily practiced philosophy, perfectly equal to itself, that some Beatles songs perfectly capture.

Nothing to Get Hung About

The Stoic philosopher Epictetus writes: "Wherever 'I' and 'mine' are placed, to there the creature inevitably inclines: if they are in the flesh, the authority must be there, if in one's volition, there, if in external things, there."[3]

In "Rain," the Beatles make a similar point: "Rain I don't mind / Shine I feel fine." There are multiple ways we can position ourselves to rain and sunshine. We can think about rain and sunshine as they affect our flesh, by making us cold or warm.

---

[3] All my quotations from Epictetus are from A.A. Long, *Epictetus: A Stoic and Socratic Guide to Life* (Oxford: Oxford University Press, 2002). This one is on page 222.

We can think about rain and sunshine as "external things" that help or hinder our getting along in the world. But the song makes it clear that the 'I' need not be located in the flesh or in external things. Instead, it can be located in what Epictetus calls "volition," but which the Beatles colloquially render in such a way as to make clear that it's simply a matter of the perspective the 'I' takes on either the flesh or external things. Talking about the weather may seem too trivial to be of philosophical significance. In fact, how we react to the weather shows a great deal about how the way we live coheres with our speculation and in its everydayness it fits with the practice of philosophy Plutarch recommends.

Thus, while we might want to object to "Rain" as working at a too elementary level to be philosophically significant, the Beatles won't let us, nor should they. Consider the opening lines of the song: "If the rain comes, they run and hide their heads / they might as well be dead." In linking together such a "natural" reaction to the rain as running and hiding one's head with *death*, the Beatles are forestalling the objection about banality. But do they run now the opposite risk? Are they engaging in exaggeration? I don't think so, and the passage from Epictetus helps us to see why. After all, what's under discussion is the 'I' that doesn't mind the rain or shine. It's that 'I' that is not present to those who let the weather determine their actions, or, in other words, it's the singer in "You Won't See Me" whose 'I' is wrapped up in external things outside of his control. The 'I' that is not attached to the flesh or external things is the 'I' of volition. It's where human freedom resides. So too, although "Rain" continues—"Can you hear me / That when it rains or shines, / It's just a state of mind"—this shouldn't be read in the sense that our mind determines whether it's raining or not, but rather in the sense that how we let the rain effect us is a state of mind over which we have control. So, in a very strict sense, the 'I' of volition does die when it's controlled by the flesh or by external things, just as the singer in "You Won't See Me" is right to see the possibility of his mind's collapse given his attachment to an external thing outside his control. There are, it seems, multiple ways we can die. The 'I' without volition, the 'I' that can't control how it reacts to the rain, is not really alive.

All this talk of the 'I' and its relation to flesh is not meant to present a metaphysical position that the 'I' is somehow separate from the body any more than the assertion that rain is a state of mind is meant to propose an epistemological position concerning the mind and its objects. The purpose of the song and its example is better read as an expression of practical philosophy in the Kantian sense. The Beatles are trying to get us to close the gap between speculation and practice. And the notion of "volition" helps us see that what the Beatles are teaching us in the songs I've discussed is an approach to thinking about freedom and self-control.

Nothing to Do

So far, then, the Beatles are doing what Kant and various Stoic philosophers have encouraged us to do: close the gap between speculation and everyday life. We now need to be a bit more specific about the state of mind that the Beatles point to in "Rain" and that the Stoics have called "volition." The everyday term for it is "freedom." Epicetus explains:

> The unconstrained person, who has access to the things he wants, is free. Whereas he who can be impeded or thrown into anything against his will is a slave.
>
> *Who is unconstrained?*
>
> The person who seeks after nothing that is not his own.
>
> *What are the things not one's own?*
>
> Everything that is not up to us to have or not to have, or to have thus and so qualified, or thus and so disposed. Therefore the body is not one's own, nor its members, nor property. If, then, you attach yourself to any of these things as if it were your own, you will pay the appropriate penalty of one who seeks after things that are not one's own. (Long, p. 202)

The lesson here is that freedom is a matter of being unconstrained. This is a straightforward claim and it coheres nicely with an everyday notion of freedom. It's a notion of freedom that's available for everyone.

It's all very well to provide these concepts and show that they're readily available to anyone who wants to be a practical philosopher. But one problem remains, namely, how we come to recognize these concepts. After all, as John Lennon sings in

"Strawberry Fields Forever:" "Living is easy with eyes closed / misunderstanding all you see." What can convince us to open our eyes? Lennon is well aware that opening our eyes to the world around us can be difficult. And in "And Your Bird Can Sing" he makes this point explicitly. So, we clearly need to do more than provide arguments; we need to do more than tell ourselves, as it were, that events are insignificant. We need to realize that all of this is, in the end, within our power. Only then can we recognize that how we view events matters more than the events that occur.

Songs like "I Want to Tell You" give us three-minute philosophical exercises that help us to recognize what is and what is not within our control. "I Want to Tell You" doesn't just tell a story; it's also talking to us. Two features of the song lend support to this reading of it.

First, it's notable that the singer never actually explains the difference between "me" and "my mind." We don't have in this song a worked out philosophical theory about the two kinds of selves. What this fact points to is the almost pre-philosophical disposition needed to get any philosophy started at all. However one may end up defining these two selves, the distinction must come first. In drawing our attention to the problem, then, the song performs a philosophical function.

Second, we respond to this song on more than one level. On one level, it's merely a song about some relationship George Harrison had that didn't work out well. On another level, however, the song works because we can recognize a universal element to the story told in the song. There's a symbolic value to the "I" and "my mind" in this song and other songs like it that, again, seem doctrinally neutral but point to a universal condition of human nature. By furnishing us a quick philosophical lesson in a three minute pop song, the Beatles are doing just what Epictetus suggests philosophers should do: "We should not conduct our training through unnatural or out of the ordinary means; otherwise, we who claim to practise philosophy will be no different from circus performers" (Epictetus, p. 111).

I've Found a Driver and That's a Start

"Drive My Car" shows that the Beatles know perfectly well that the starting point is crucial whatever the end or goal we might have. It also shows that the practical philosophical lessons about the self and freedom they provide are philosophically substantive in that they show us how to be autonomous and happy agents. After all, the end or goal we have may very well be one of those "external things" that remains forever outside our power: "I've got no car and it's breaking my heart." But if we arrange our desires in such a way as to be satisfied with what is in our power, then the starting point may just be all we need: "But I've found a driver and that's a start." And how do the Beatles end this song? They do so with one of the most joyous affirmations one could hope for: Beep Beep m'Beep Beep Yeah!

14

Take a Sad Song and Make It Better: The Beatles and Postmodern Thought

JAMES CROOKS

I discovered the Beatles at the age of four. My neighbor, a year older and far more sophisticated, told me, through the backyard fence, that although they were mostly famous in England, she already knew all their songs. When I ventured the opinion that the name seemed kind of stupid, she blasted me with a spirited chorus of "She Loves You," turned on her heel, and marched back into her house. To the best of my recollection, this was my first discussion of culture.

The night John Lennon died, about seventeen years later, I talked for hours on the phone with my old college roommate. By that time, the music of the Beatles had sewn itself so deeply into the fabric of our lives that the sudden tragic certainty there would be no more of it felt like an end *for us* the meaning of which we struggled to fathom. Hung up between sadness and gratitude I thought of my sophisticated neighbor. And it occurred to me that in my life a circle was closing, that a frame of reference for making sense of the wider world I lived in, sketched in outline behind my old house, was now complete.

The technical name for such frames of reference—for the broad tapestry of reflective experience we use to make global sense of particular things or events—is "meta-narrative." The wider world I lived in, the one you and I still share—as frighteningly serious as Islamic fundamentalism, as numbingly frivolous as *Entertainment Tonight*, and so, not surprisingly, always on the verge of falling to pieces—philosophers and culture critics now characterize habitually as "postmodern." What I was groping toward in conversation with my friend the night John Lennon died was the thought that the Beatles had managed, in a lightning flash of about seven years, to produce a meta-narrative of postmodernism; to gather up in popular songs the strange logic of the reality academics, poets, activists, and others had struggled to express in less accessible media. I certainly think now, in any case, that we have something to learn from the Beatles about *philosophical* postmodernism. As I'll try to show in a moment, their lyrics display its basic features.

But something else, ultimately, is just as important. Postmodern philosophers tend to read the catastrophes of the twentieth century—at Auschwitz and Hiroshima, more recently in Africa and the Middle East—as the inexorable conclusion of modern science, bourgeois politics and global capitalism. As a result, they're deeply pessimistic—offering us either last rites for a disappearing tradition (the title of Martin Heidegger's famous *Spiegel*-interview was "Only a God Can Save Us Now"[1]) or the assisted suicide of an all-out war on rationality and its attendant values (Jacques Derrida's friendly summation of Michel Foucault's *Madness and Civilization* is that "reason is madder than madness"[2]).

The Beatles, on the other hand, always represent culture's failures as a passing moment. We may well begin with a "sad song." But the point of intellectual, artistic and political activity—the point of life itself—is to "make it better." In retrospect, I think my neighbour's pedagogy could have been a little more patient and expansive. But even her testy "She Loves You" pretty much cuts to the chase. Beatle-postmodernism retains the possibility of being healed by love. They are, in this respect, physicians of the culture their philosophical counterparts regard for the most part as terminal. And a little reflection on the opti-

---

[1] *Der Spiegel* is the German equivalent of *Time*. Heidegger granted the magazine an interview in 1966. In it, he addresses, among other things, lingering questions about his association with National Socialism in the 1930s. The piece was published shortly after his death ten years later.

[2] See Derrida's "Cogito and the History of Madness," in *Writing and Difference* (Chicago: University of Chicago Press, 1978), p. 62.

mism of their meta-narrative can help us understand the limits of postmodern thought. I'll save that for the very end. First, like the singer in a tribute band, I'd like to warble in Beatle-speak the song of philosophical postmodernism. It involves some cutting and pasting of ideas. But then the Beatles themselves did that regularly.

Verse One: Postmodernism and the Revolution Effect

In the slow version of "Revolution" on the "White Album" John wavers between a political activism that sanctions violence and one that forbids it: "when you talk about destruction, don't you know that you can count me out / in." He took a lot of flack for this from the organized left. And indeed, in the wider context of 1968—that year of unparalleled protest in the bourgeois West, of the marches on the American Embassy in London, the riots at the Democratic convention in Chicago, and the student uprisings in Paris—the song is surprisingly ambivalent. In fact, though, four decades on, John's indecision—count me out of / in on the "revolution"—is a perfect epitome of philosophical postmodernism.

Like the student radicals of the Sixties, postmodern thinkers want to break from the past. They protest the nineteenth- or twentieth-century faith in technology, social progress, and free markets, rejecting the values and methods of the modern philosophical tradition that developed in tandem with it as inadequate for understanding and criticizing its monumental failures. But on closer inspection those values and methods—already in the seventeenth century and even more explicitly later—are themselves revolutionary.

Descartes makes a point of breaking from the devotion to religious and philosophical authorities characteristic of Medieval thought, of rejecting the entire store of past opinion and resolving to build a new science from the ground up on the foundation of indubitable truths. Kant makes a point of breaking from the consensus, well established since Aristotle, that the rationality of the mind mirrors that of the cosmos, of swearing off all knowledge of things apart from human consciousness and resolving to limit understanding to the world of appearances. With the specialization of scientific disciplines and the corresponding transformation of the university, the expansion of markets, and the accelerating secularization of the state in the second half of the nineteenth century, we see more radical breaks with traditional intellectual, social, political and religious ideals. By the time Nietzsche dies in 1900, no office of the tradition that had run from Plato to the Renaissance retains its powers. Modern philosophy has become the unapologetic revaluation of all values.

Here, then, is the central quandary. The gesture of criticism—of breaking from tradition—is what needs to be criticized. The revolt against modern culture and its philosophy is a revolt against revolution. That means: philosophical postmodernism *must* be, like John's lyric, fundamentally ambivalent. Rejecting what it takes to be the substantive *content* of revolutionary thinking—its premises, arguments and conclusions—its message is clearly: "count me out." But—recognizing in rejection itself the enduring *form* of revolutionary thinking—and so the inescapability of modernism for all would-be critics—its message can only be some version of: "count me in." What sense can we make of this ambivalence? And what are its consequences? Let's look a little more closely at the moments ("count me out" / "count me in") of the "Revolution-effect" taking guidance as we go from elsewhere in the Beatles' songbook.

Verse Two: "Count Me Out!" or the Nowhere Man Effect

The words "count me out!" express alienation—a central theme for the Beatles from beginning to end. The narrative voices of "Misery," "I Call Your Name," "You Can't Do That," "I'm a Loser," "I'm Down," "Run for Your Life," and "I'm Looking Through You" belong to alienated lovers. The women portrayed in "Eleanor Rigby," "Lady Madonna," and "She's Leaving Home" are alienated friends and relations. The folks in "Paperback Writer," "A Day in the Life," "Taxman" and "Piggies," are either alienated workers or alienated consumers. Harping on this theme isn't itself particularly remarkable. The rhythm 'n' blues groups that spawned rock and its offshoots were already, collectively, a culture of complaint nourished and sustained by a cast of characters who had been counted or counted themselves out of relationships, families, and mainstream society. What's impressive is the range of variations. The Beatles "count me out" anthology seems to include every mode of alienation—including the one clearly audible in the works of Heidegger (1889–1976), Foucault (1926–1984), and several generations of followers dedicated to thoroughgoing criticism of modern thought and its institutions. It's reproduced elegantly and simply in the lyric of "Nowhere Man."

On John's account, this song was prompted by frustration with his own writer's block ("Nothing would come. I was cheesed off and went for a lie-down, having given up. Then I thought of myself as Nowhere Man—sitting in his nowhere land"[3]). A little reflection on the quandary I sketched a moment ago, however, shows us a wider reference. If modern thought and its institutions are already essentially revolutionary, if the modern world is defined by a series of crises and reforms, then a thoroughgoing critic—one who is absolutely serious about dissent—has no place to stand. For Heidegger, Foucault, and kindred spirits, the problem with modernity is that, like *Star Trek*'s Borg, it assimilates all opposition—or more technically—that it "totalizes" its own values and methods. Serious postmodern thinkers, precisely in order to *be* serious, must report on the state of the world as if they had refugee status elsewhere; asylum in a kind of philosophical "nowhere-land."

Practitioners of the "Nowhere-Man-effect" face two problems. The first is concrete: Having counted themselves out of the modern world completely, they have no rationale for intervening in it. Among other things, this makes politics difficult. Reviewing the history of philosophical postmodernism in France, Vincent Descombes says: "almost no important political thinking as such can be seen to thrive within it."[4] A colleague of mine once asked far more bluntly: "What are they going to do when the tanks roll in?" The second is abstract but for our purposes more compelling: Opposing modernism in all seriousness amounts to perfecting it. That's because the desire for thoroughgoing criticism drives modern thought from the beginning. In relation to the Medieval consensus that reason must be subordinate to revelation, Descartes is a "Nowhere Man." In relation

---

[3] See Steve Turner, *A Hard Day's Write* (Carlton: Harper Collins, 1994), p. 91. I'm grateful to Dave Millard for the "long-term loan" of this book.

[4] Vincent Descombes, *Modern French Philosophy* (Cambridge:Cambridge University Press, 1980) p. 7.

to the Aristotelian consensus that the rationality of the human mind must reflect the rationality of the cosmos, Kant is a "Nowhere Man." It's not so much particular configurations of modern thought that threaten. It's the story of the philosophical refugee that looms up behind all of them. The serious postmodern thinker, "making all his nowhere plans for nobody," is a modern intellectual, a modern self, *par excellence.* In the matter of genuinely opposing modern culture and its Borg-like assimilation of criticism, it seems—to paraphrase John McEnroe—"you cannot be serious!"

Verse Three: "Count Me In" *or* the Glass Onion Effect

But must postmodernism be serious? Part of the magic of the Beatles' meta-narrative is the seamless accommodation of what I just dubbed the "count me out" anthology by a wider "count me in" delight in the world that welcomes foolishness like a joke between friends. This attitude is evident in virtually any Beatlemania-era exchange with the breathlessly earnest entertainment press (Reporter: "What do you think of Beethoven?" Ringo: "I love him—especially his poems"[5]), in the childlike whimsy of songs such as "Yellow Submarine," "Octopus's Garden," and "Bungalow Bill," and the gentle parody of other genres in "When I'm 64," "You're Mother Should Know," "Honey Pie" and "Back in the U.S.S.R.." The Beatles' voice the modes of playfulness, of irony in a broad sense, as deftly and comprehensively as those of alienation—including the one clearly audible in the works of Jacques Derrida (1930–2004) and others for whom the alternative to the "Nowhere-Man-effect" dogging the hyper-serious criticism of modern thought is "deconstruction."

The exemplar here is "Glass Onion." By the late 1960s the band wanted to discourage the legion of fans who were scouring their lyrics for some kind of cosmic code. John does it in this song by re-reading some of his own earlier lyrics explicitly as flights of imagination. That, in turn, produces an ingenious form of artistic self-consciousness. The words themselves renounce the powers attributed to them. The creative process becomes

---

[5] Hunter Davies, *The Beatles* (London: Arrow, 1992), p. 273.

completely transparent—like so many layers of glass. Derrida and his followers want to skirt the dangers of modern philosophy by stirring up a similar awareness. For them as for John, language is playful. What it gives us, at bottom, is not a representation of stable identities (objects, selves, institutions, and states) but the primordial flux of *non*-identity—the *no*-thing or abyss—from which identities emerge.

The work of postmodern thinking, on this view, consists in undermining and taking apart the entire range discursive forms in which cosmic codes or determinate meanings of any kind—masks of language's original *in*determinacy—find accommodation. Among these, certainly, are the values and methods of traditional revolutionary thinking; but also a series of more comprehensive oppositional relations virtually all previous thinkers would have regarded as axiomatic: argument versus free association, author versus reader, text versus world. Deconstruction peels away these oppositions. Under its regime, postmodern philosophical writing becomes a patchwork of puns and etymologies, jokes, extended quotations and commentaries—cajoled out of the modern tradition or imposed on it—the consistent aim of which is to dissolve all determinate significance into wordplay, to reproduce in the medium of thought a "Glass Onion effect."

As a point of intellectual history, this approach develops in response to the perceived failures of the philosophical "Nowhere Man effect." And it certainly sidesteps the unintended irony of doling out hyper-serious criticism of a tradition of hyper-serious criticism. Still, deconstructionists face a set of problems not unlike those confronting Heideggerians or followers of Foucault. Concretely: if thinking boils down to play the world and everything in it becomes frivolous. Nothing has weight. Here not only politics but reflective engagements of any kind are endangered. The Hegelian dialectic has no more right to our attention than the dismally repetitious formulas of reality T.V. More theoretically: the one thing a committed ironist is *serious* about is the moral necessity of his renunciation of authority.

Practitioners of the "Glass Onion effect," in spite of their playfulness, persist in thinking prescriptively. They *recommend* deconstruction of the world as a model for living ("Well here's another place you can be—listen to me"). But that means the postmodern ironist's renunciation of authority amounts to a kind of self-promotion. Ironically, nothing could be more modern. Since Descartes made the "I that thinks" philosophy's point of departure, it has been self-centered, bent on understanding the world as a byproduct of human subjectivity. The revolutions of modern thought are anchored in the conviction that the self is unsurpassably real. Its Borg-like assimilation of criticism turns on our refusal to question this reality.

Verse Four: "Count Me In" or the I Am the Walrus Effect

But must postmodernism be either alienated or ironic? Must it, in other words, remain self-centered? One of the most remarkable things about the revolution framed in the Beatles' songbook is the variety of its forms. Their "count me in" playfulness is certainly not exhausted in irony and its latent self-promotion. On the contrary, they often take aim at egoism explicitly. Think of George's self-criticism in "I Me Mine," for example, or his plea for a kind of Eastern self-transcendence in "Within You Without You."

Casting a wider net, think of the range of songs on later albums—including "Lucy in the Sky with Diamonds," "Hello Goodbye," "Wild Honey Pie," "Revolution #9," "I Dig a Pony" and "Come Together"—that, one way or another, shatter the unity of narrative consciousness suggesting very strongly that our discrete sense of self and world is illusory, that what's real is an arbitrary conjunction of fragments. The Beatles are masters of what we might call, from the standpoint of the "I that thinks," non-sense, including the modes of nonsense developed by Gilles Deleuze (1925–95), Felix Guattari (1930–92), and others, in reaction to the perceived failures of both thoroughgoing criticism and deconstruction, under the heading of "post-structuralism."

The paradigm lyric in this case comes from "I am the Walrus." Its body consists of "ludicrous images ('semolina pilchards, elementary penguins') and nonsense words ('texpert, crabalocker')"[6] the order and connection of which is absolutely random (Looking back on the filming of "Magical Mystery Tour," which contains the only performance of the song, Paul himself says: "we just put all these ideas in and it was very haphazard").[7]

---

[6] *A Hard Day's Write*, p. 146.

The representation of anything like traditional meaning is accordingly scuttled. And the veil of the self—which had managed to retain its philosophical status as an unsurpassable reality even through the revolution of deconstruction—is lifted in the song's first line: "I am he as you are he as you are me and we are all together."

Post-structuralism packs exactly the same one-two punch. Books such as *Anti-Oedipus* (Deleuze and Guattari) or *Dialogues* (Deleuze and Parnet) are studied assemblages of thought-fragments—some taken up and developed, others simply registered—with no traditional argumentative structure. They spread out in front of us like a philosophical yard sale—a collection of thought-items in the very basic sense that one stands beside another. This "effect," in turn, follows from the breakdown of the discrete author—the "I that thinks"—as a principle of organization. In fact, we might read the beginning of *A Thousand Plateaus*—Deleuze and Guattari's last and most ambitious work—as a prosaic repetition of the beginning of "I am the Walrus": "The two of us wrote *Anti-Oedipus* together. Since each of us was several, there was already quite a crowd."[8]

The breakdown of the discrete author by practitioners of the "I am the Walrus effect" sidesteps both the obvious self-centeredness of modern philosophy and its subtler persistence in the figures of the intellectual "Nowhere Man" and the "Glass Onion" deconstructionist. At the same time, it creates for philosophical postmodernism a kind of political mandate. For Deleuze, Gauttari, and other poststructuralists, the point of social action is to disrupt the outdated and morbid global culture of self-promotion that drives everything from shopping at Walmart to "carrying pictures of Chairman Mao," to kick over all institutions and customs, all *structures*, in which the "I that thinks" might find refuge. But if, in the strange logic of postmodernism, this is how philosophy truly counts itself in on revolution, it does so at considerable risk. Deleuze in particular saw the danger. "How," he asks, "can one avoid [self-transcendence's] becoming identical with a pure and simple movement

---

[7] *The Beatles Anthology* (San Francisco: Chronicle Books, 2000), p. 274.
[8] Gilles Deleuze and Felix Guattari, *A Thousand Plateaus* (Minneapolis: University of Minnesota Press, 1987), p. 3.

of self-destruction: Fitzgerald's alcoholism, Lawrence's disillusion, Virginia Woolf's suicide, Kerouac's sad end?"[9] As if to frame this question for us, elevating it above all others, he finally took his own life.

Coda: The Hey Jude Effect

I suggested earlier that philosophical postmodernism is a "sad song." Warbling its verses in Beatle-speak helps bring out the source of the pessimism: In the long shadows of the bloody twentieth century, thinkers seem typecast in one of three ultimately unsatisfying roles: the intellectual "Nowhere Man," the "Glass Onion" deconstructionist, or the "Walrus" post-structuralist. The first, for reasons we gave above, is too frighteningly serious, the second too numbingly frivolous. The third too easily conflates thinking and suicide. Sad, indeed! But the saddest thing of all is that, for the last twenty years or so, philosophy has been unable to conceive of other, more fulfilling roles—like that friend most of us have had at some point in our lives who's become so adept at describing the illusions of human intimacy that he's incapable of having a decent relationship. Unbridled intellectual sophistication sometimes condemns us to misery.

On just this point, though, the Beatles' meta-narrative achieves its greatest insight. Their critique of culture is grounded and framed on all sides by an enduringly *naive* celebration of love. Beneath the cagey ambivalence of "Revolution," the thoroughgoing alienation of "Nowhere Man," the clever irony of "Glass Onion," the studied nonsense of "I Am the Walrus," and the critical surface of dozens of other songs that offer playful social comment or issue serious calls to action, a kind of bedrock hopefulness, a marvelous spirit of optimism, permeates the entire songbook offering immunity from despair.

You might think of it as the "Hey Jude effect." As far as I'm concerned, Paul's advice in the opening verse of that brilliantly simple track—". . . take a sad song and make it better. Remember to let her into your heart . . ."—is an epigram for everything the Beatles accomplished in the end. Their bottom

---

[9] Gilles Deleuze and Claire Parnet, *Dialogues* (New York: Columbia University Press, 1987), pp. 38–39.

line, surely, is that our pessimism, no matter how sophisticated, our sadness, no matter how deep, is soothed and sheltered by the simple opening of the heart. Is such naivety doomed to fail? Possibly. But more than three decades after the Beatles stopped recording, their brand of it still captures our imagination. Perhaps that's because we've yet to give it a try. At this point in my life, I'm prepared to side with my childhood neighbor. Love seems as promising a cure for modernity's self-centeredness as despair.

VIII

Zarathustra's Silver Hammer

The Beatles
and Nietzsche

15

Fixing Metaphysical Holes: The Beatles, Nietzsche, and the Problem of Incompleteness

RICK MAYOCK

Nothing gets us thinking like a riddle. A good riddle grabs us, hooks us in, and forces us to think about familiar things in an unfamiliar way. Consider this riddle: How do you fix a hole where the rain gets in and stops the mind from wandering?

The Beatles' "Fixing a Hole" seems to imply that holes can derail our thinking and need to be fixed. Similarly, the philosopher Friedrich Nietzsche (1844–1900) suggests that an examination of our thoughts will reveal that they are full of holes, and lead us into vacuous "abysses" of intellectual paralysis. According to Nietzsche, what stops the mind from wandering is philosophy itself, at least in the traditional way it has been done, by forcing us to see the world through rigid concepts that distort our picture of reality. Consequently, we need to construct a world view that enables us to live with the troublesome holes, emptiness, and incompleteness of our experience and our conceptual framework. We can call this the problem of incompleteness.

Many of the Beatles' songs and album covers contain riddles and clues that seduce us to listen carefully and look beneath the surface for hidden meanings. When we start interpreting and piecing together clues, looking for the subtext beneath the text, we become experts and "texperts." But what if there are no hidden meanings intended—don't we know the joker laughs at us?

Yet we cannot help but interpret—we dig for clues. We have, as Nietzsche suggests in *Beyond Good and Evil*, a "will to truth."[1]

---

[1] Friedrich Nietzsche, *Beyond Good and Evil* (New York: Random House, 1966), p. 9.

Understanding Nietzsche is a bit like solving riddles. He writes in a style that induces us to think in new and different ways in order to free us from using concepts that stop the mind from wandering. With Nietzsche as our guide, let's look for clues along the way in Beatles' songs, which, like many of Nietzsche's teachings, compel us to interpret familiar things in an unfamiliar way.

And When My Mind Is Wandering

"I'm fixing a hole where the rain gets in, and stops my mind from wandering . . ." Every time I hear this puzzling lyric I wonder what the riddle could possibly mean. What kind of hole needs fixing, what is the "rain" that gets in, and how does it prevent the mind from wandering where it will go? Why do the cracks that ran through the door need to be sealed and what is it that needs to be kept out? The lyric seems to suggest that the wandering mind (thinking or consciousness) is possible because we set up the conditions for thinking. We fix the holes, fill the cracks, and paint the rooms of our consciousness. This allows the mind to wander, to be free.

Nietzsche suggests that one of the goals of philosophy is to free the mind, to allow it to wander without conceptual restrictions that inhibit thought. He urges us to become a different kind of philosopher, a "free spirit," who does not fall victim to the seductions of dogmatic philosophy and fundamentalist thinking. The "free spirit" is the free mind that is allowed to wander where it will go. Nietzsche thinks the trick is to free our minds from the seductions of a philosophical tradition that promises impossible ideals.

The Beatles knew something about being seduced by an impossible ideal. John Lennon sings about a girl he knows he will never win, and marvels at his own naive persistence in "Girl!" According to Nietzsche, we are always in danger of being seduced by the comforting thought of "truths" that are "fixed" and stable, but we don't know why. Philosophical ideas can be seductresses that lure us to a state of blissful ignorance. "She's the kind of girl you want so much it makes you sorry, still you don't regret a single day."

"Metaphysics," according to Nietzsche, is the pursuit of this false sense of a "fixed," privileged account of the universe, which assumes that facts exist independently of our knowing them, and that reality is independent of our interpretations. Plato's idea of a fixed set of truths, and Christianity, which Nietzsche calls "Platonism for the people" (*Beyond Good and Evil*, p. 3), are examples of the worst kind of seduction. According to Nietzsche these are forms of dogmatism: erroneous inventions that present otherwise arbitrary interpretations of the world as "fixed." Dogmatic philosophers try to stabilize and concretize a shifting, porous, and incomplete picture of reality. They "fix" the truth in such a way that gives it the illusion of permanence and universality.

As is often the case with riddles, there is something backwards suggested by these lyrics. I usually think of the mind as wandering away in flights of fantasy, which requires opening a hole in our consciousness, not fixing it. But if we think of ourselves as Nietzsche's "free spirits," the riddle makes more sense. As free spirits we know that notions of "truth" and "reality" are our constructions, the result of fixing holes and plastering cracks. We are aware that we set up the conditions for thinking, and that we're only fooling ourselves if we believe that truth is something "out there," beyond the cracks and holes of our mental sanctuaries. The rain that gets in and stops the mind from wandering numbs our thinking with its false assumptions of a fixed reality. Fixed ideas are like the "fixed stars" of the ancient astronomers, which only appear fixed from our limited perspectives. The free mind realizes that all truths are dependent on perspectives, and that there is no "reality" independent of our perspectives.

It Really Doesn't Matter if I'm Wrong I'm Right

The bridge or "B" section of "Fixing a Hole" gives us some musical relief from the minor chordal constructions of the verses. It lifts us up to a sense of reassurance and optimism with its exchange of major chords: "It really doesn't matter if I'm wrong I'm right." But this looks like another riddle that needs to be solved. One interpretation is that truth is completely arbitrary. Whatever I think is true, is true. This position was held by the ancient Greek philosopher Protagoras (490–420 B.C.E.), who maintained that truth is relative to the understanding—whatever I believe is true, is, in fact, true. Nietzsche says something like this, raising the question of the "value of truth," and implying that there is something suspicious about our "will to truth." "Suppose we want truth," he writes, "*why not rather* untruth? and uncertainty? even ignorance?" (*Beyond Good and Evil*, p. 9). The riddle for Nietzsche is this: what causes our drive for truth? He asks us to question our motives for seeking the truth and warns us that solving riddles is not always in our best interest.

According to Nietzsche, the will to truth is a characteristic of dogmatic philosophers who are both perplexed and seduced by the enigmatic character of truth. He writes: "Suppose truth is a woman—what then?" (p. 2). It seems that philosophers have been "inexpert" and clumsy in winning her heart. "Sexy Sadie . . . what have you done? You've made a fool of everyone." We try to display her (truth, that is) in a public way, to expose her and strip her naked. But in doing so, we fail to respect her mysteries and secrets. We experts or "texperts" fail to see that the truth is not a "naughty girl" who "lets her knickers down." We have been seduced by the prospect of an objective glimpse of the truth, free of our perspectives and interpretations. But such a prospect may result more from our desires than from any truth that is revealed.

The Beatles' lyric could be suggesting the extreme relativism of Protagoras, or, perhaps something more profound: Nietzsche's idea that we need to examine our motives in seeking the truth. Do we want her to look a certain way before we even encounter her? "One sunny day, the world was waiting for a lover . . . she came along to turn on everyone."

There's a Place Where You Can Go When You Feel Low, and It's Your Mind

"We created *Sgt. Pepper* to alter our egos, to free ourselves and have a lot of fun," Paul McCartney said, "we were fed up with being Beatles."[2] The Beatles had become too big, too vulnerable, too porous and full of holes that needed to be "fixed." It's understandable that they would want to retreat from a chaotic world and conceal themselves from the people who

---

[2] Paul McCartney, "Fifty Moments that Changed the History of Rock and Roll," *Rolling Stone* 951 (24th June, 2004), p. 119.

"disagree and never win, and wonder why they don't get in my door."

But it looks as if our song presents us with another riddle. Who are these people, what are they arguing about and why don't they get in my door? The lyric seems to suggest that if we control the atmosphere we can create the intellectual space that keeps out indeterminacy and disagreement. But does this mean that we retreat into our own private thoughts, and, if so, what's the point of that? "If the rain comes, they run and hide their heads, they might as well be dead."

The Beatles' idea of keeping out the rain by creating a sanctuary has a biblical motif found in the book of *Genesis*. Fixing holes and cracks is a way of preserving an ordered and safe cosmos, free from chaos. Painting a room in a colorful way represents the rainbow, the sign of God's covenant and promise of protection. Just as Noah builds the ark to protect the sacred space, which must be sealed against cracks and holes, our mental sanctuaries offer protection against chaos, an ark against a sea of holes. Chaos could be disagreement, arguing and never winning, the impossibility of finding the truth. Nietzsche writes: "Every choice human being strives instinctively for a citadel and a secrecy where he is saved from the crowd, the many, the great majority—where he may forget 'men who are the rule'" (p. 37). But if we create a mental sanctuary to escape a world of harsh realities, are we not simply creating our own personal prisons, and, if so, is the mind really free?

I'm Painting a Room in a Colorful Way

The Beatles gave us not only their music, but an artistic vision and a different way of perceiving the world. Album covers, posters and other art forms used colors in new and exciting ways (except, of course, the "White Album"), enticing us to see things from new and different perspectives. A psychedelic experience may envision holes and cracks as windows or doors to a separate reality or set of perceptions into which the mind wanders. In this light, the experience need not be distorted or negative, but may expand the possibilities of perception and shake us out of our commonplace presuppositions.

Painting a room in a colorful way can be thought of as a challenge to overcome our static precepts. To some extent we create our own world. We choose the colors to paint the rooms through which our minds can wander. The Beatles call upon us to recognize that we are artists and that we have creative control of the world that we perceive.

Nietzsche also suggests that we arrange the world selectively for our purposes. All human practices involve artistic selection and simplification. Just as a painter can never paint "everything" and attain representational completeness, we too, in our understanding of the world, select, simplify and arrange our knowledge of the world. There's no "real" world behind appearances ("nothing is real . . ."); rather, reality is simply the totality of our arrangements and selections. Certain "truths" are pulled into the foreground while others are pushed back. Since we cannot grasp all things at once we must assume an illusion for the sake of a common perspective. In this way we "falsify," we plaster the cracks and fill in the holes, thereby creating the illusion of artistic completeness in our cognitive vision of the world. This arranging and selecting induces us to forget that truth is created, not discovered. But we free spirits are aware that we designate "truth": "you can indicate anything you see . . ."

Nietzsche says that we remain ignorant of the exact ways in which our views are simplifications. But we shouldn't fool ourselves by thinking that our concepts are *the* truth in any permanent sense. A certain amount of *untruth* is necessarily part of our perspective.

There is no truth independent of our perspective, no possibility of a perspective-free view of the world. The person who has no perspective is the "Nowhere Man," who "doesn't have a point of view." Nietzsche's position is that all we have is a point of view, or points of view. There is no view from Nowhere; no unbiased, pure, objective point of view. The "Nowhere Man" is as "blind as he can be," and he "just sees what he wants to see." But, according to Nietzsche, this is what we all do. ". . . isn't he a bit like you and me?" We decide what to focus on. By filling cracks and holes in our metaphysical world view, we attempt to complete that which is incomplete, to make coherent that which is fragmentary and to keep at bay the horror of an otherwise formless and chaotic world. The orderly and purposeful world in which we live is our creation, our sanctuary. We shelter ourselves from a formless world that pursues its course without any regard for our views, our values and our desires. Fixing a hole is, in this sense, recognizing the untruth and created nature of our mental sanctuaries.

I'm Taking the Time for a Number of Things

In the second bridge of "Fixing a Hole" there are some interesting changes in the lyrics. The people are no longer "standing" and disagreeing. Now they "run around" and "worry me." Is this another riddle to add to our confusion? Let's see if we can interpret this puzzling lyric and make some sense of it.

The first part of "Fixing a Hole" is illustrated with static imagery: *fixing* a hole, the rain *stops* the mind from wandering, I'm right *where I belong,* people are *standing there, disagreeing* and never winning. In the second part of the song, the language is active. Now the singer is *painting* a room and when the mind is *wandering,* there he will *go.* Now people *run around,* and now we can take the *time* for important things. The song's lyrics have shifted to include a temporal dimension, indicating a process unfolding. We have moved from static notions of "being" ("standing" in bridge 1) to active notions of "becoming" ("running" in bridge 2).

One of the most damaging errors of dogmatic philosophers, according to Nietzsche, is the attempt to impose "being" on "becoming." Rigid, static concepts arrest and distort the dynamic and fluid aspects of reality. The ancient Greek philosopher Heraclitus (around 500 B.C.E.) maintained that the only real thing is change, or "becoming," and that permanence, or "being" is an illusion. Nietzsche aligns himself closely with Heraclitus and criticizes philosophers who try to characterize the change and flux of reality (what he calls the "will to power") as static notions of "being." In other words, they try to coerce "becoming" into "being." In doing so, they create metaphysical monsters, like Plato's eternal and unchanging notion of "the Good," and Christianity, with its fixed dogmas and beliefs. According to Nietzsche, there is no "being" behind "doing" or "becoming;" no lightening behind the flash. Dogmatic philosophers fail to see this because they do not look with suspicious eyes at the origins of their concepts to see that they are sailing on a "sea of holes."

The first part of "Fixing a Hole" is about creating a mental space that allows the mind to wander. Once space is created, time follows—the time for a number of things that weren't important yesterday. Space and time, according to the philosopher Immanuel Kant (1724–1804), are conditions for the understanding, conditions required for all rational thought. If we did not have the space, the sanctuary, the conditions, we could not take the time to think. Nietzsche's spiritual hero, Zarathustra, retreats to his cave to be restored and renewed. So too, we need to create our own caves, our own sanctuaries, our own time, so that we can have rational concepts. But this is not the end of the story. Every set of concepts, every metaphysical construction must be eyed with suspicion and tested for cracks and holes.

Four Thousand Holes in Blackburn, Lancashire

As the closing bars of "Fixing a Hole" fade in a repeating minor chordal interplay, we're left wondering if we have fixed anything at all. The melody becomes less assured, drawing out tension and anticipation and leaves us questioning the optimism of the bridge. Paul's voice sounds less confident, perhaps an omen of things to come. As the mind wanders "where it will go," so does the melody. There is no neat, optimistic ending to the song, no satisfied reassurance that any holes have been fixed. We are led uneasily into the next song: "Wednesday morning at five o'clock as the day begins . . ." After the ebullient triumph of "Getting Better," "Fixing a Hole" has taken a dark and worrisome turn that disturbs our confidence in the "Sgt. Pepper" masquerade, which, like all masquerades, must come to an end.

In the "Reprise," we leave the "Sgt. Pepper" fantasy and its fictitious audience, and are immediately ushered into the harsh realities and dark dealings of "A Day in the Life." The stark landscape of the daily news, car crashes, and wars stands in sharp contrast to the illusory world of "Sgt. Pepper." The ominous wavering of Paul's voice at the end of "Fixing a Hole" may have been a clue to the riddle and a foreshadowing of this turn of events. We may have fixed a hole but now we are in the world of four thousand holes in Blackburn, Lancashire.

When we abandon our masquerades and fantasies, we leave our caves and sanctuaries, and try to disrobe the seductress "truth" in the light of the Platonic sun. But in so doing we enter into the world of "being," the world of static and "fixed" concepts. Once a riddle is solved, the mind ceases to wander and becomes stagnant, satisfied with stale, uninteresting, hallow "truths." These "truths" are what Nietzsche calls "idols" that need to be "touched with a hammer as with a tuning fork," since they are full of holes and dissonance and do not resonate.[3]

John Lennon's statement that the Beatles are more popular than Jesus responds to Nietzsche's understanding of "idols" that reach their "twilight" and are always on the brink of being replaced with new, more popular idols. For Nietzsche, Christianity has become a dogmatic tyranny, but is an idol in its twilight. We may take our interpretations for granted, but they are in danger of becoming idols, and we must be prepared to abandon them when the need arises. The masquerade must come to an end when we realize that our ideals are thinly veiled and full of holes.

Come Together . . . Right Now

John's voice comes to us as if in a dream: "I read the news today, oh boy . . ." The opening verses are followed by orchestral swirls, lifting us into the void of chaos and dissonance. The ascending maelstrom gains momentum as the song's familiar structures deteriorate. The orchestra climbs, building to the point of madness—we have left our fantasy of disguises, fixed holes and fixed truths.

The orchestral buildup occurs over twenty-four bars. Classically trained musicians were instructed by George Martin to begin on the lowest note on their instrument and to slowly ascend to an E-major chord. They were also told to not listen to the other instruments, creating the effect of musical dissonance.[4] The middle section brings some uneasy relief and assurance amidst the discord. An alarm clock, and confident, repeating piano chords introduce a new voice: ("woke up, got out of bed . . .").

Paul's voice inserts a song within a song, a play within a play. Hamlet remarks: "the play's the thing, wherein I'll catch the conscience of the king." Does the interlude catch our conscience,

---

[3] Friedrich Nietzsche, *Twilight of the Idols*, in Walter Kaufmann, ed., *The Portable Nietzsche* (New York: Viking, 1954), p. 466.

[4] Mark Lewisohn, *The Beatles' Recording Sessions* (New York: Harmony, 1988), p. 96.

and, if so, how? The "Paul" section of the song introduces a more optimistic melody, as we accompany a new narrator preparing for his daily commute. Perhaps the optimism is false, though, predicated on a lack of awareness of the times and the tragedies around us. Paul's brisk and melodic narration of rushing to catch the bus arises from the orchestral dissonance but remains unaffected by John's haunting account of the horrors of the daily news. Which is a dream and which is reality? The alarm clock takes us out of a dream, or a nightmare, but isn't the reality of the day to day routine a dream of sorts or a waking slumber? Isn't the daily commuter a "Day Tripper," except that for her there's no good reason and no easy way out? When somebody speaks and we go into a dream are not the distinctions between reality and illusion blurred?

According to Nietzsche, each phase of our lives is an illusion, a construction, a new form of life, an interpretation or perspective. As artists we have an awareness of what features we are including and leaving out. We recognize that we need illusions and that we depend on simplifications. Living a day in the life requires our artistic intervention. When we find ourselves "in the thick of it," we help ourselves to a bit of what is all around us. The problem of incompleteness induces us to pull together our perspectives in the illusion of completeness. It is not solved by fixing holes that never stay fixed. Our attempts to fix them underscore the difficulties of solving the problem. Nietzsche's position is that any attempt to complete that which is incomplete requires us to become artists. Of free spirits, he writes: "Their 'knowing' is *creating*, their creating is a legislation, their will to truth is—*will to power*," (*Beyond Good and Evil*, p. 136).

In the early days of the Beatles' fame, people often could not tell them apart, as if their haircuts synthesized them into clones of each other. But later in their career they have to force themselves to work together. The "Beatles" become more fragmented and less of an entity as the fiction of unity and completeness is undermined by four individuals seeking their own unique creative voices. "I'm looking through you, you're not the same . . ." During the recording sessions for the "White Album" Ringo Starr temporarily quit the band.[5] In his solo

---

[5] Philip Norman, *Shout: The Beatles in Their Generation* (New York: Simon and Schuster, 1981), p. 342

album, John sings: "I don't believe in Beatles." Yet, amidst the dissolution they "come together" to make records. Side Two of *Abbey Road* is a medley of incomplete songs, seamlessly woven together to produce a "complete" whole. The artistry of the Beatles produces an aesthetic totality out of an otherwise fragmentary patchwork of pieces. When the cracks are filled, we maintain the illusion of completeness.

Tell Me the Answer

An orchestral crescendo wakes us out of the dream and we are deposited back into the world of the daily news, the bedrock of reality. Reading the news may be an attempt to bring us back to reality, but the story is full of holes. John's final "I'd love to turn you on . . ." is a gentle invitation, perhaps not to a drug experience, but an invitation to become conscious of our potential for enlightenment, to ground us in a world that is ungrounded, to anchor us in a sea that is full of holes, and to see the blandness and incompleteness of a life of waking to alarm clocks and catching buses. The orchestral swirl ascends again and we are caught in another chaotic crescendo, intimating the angst of the void, the anxiety of a day in the life of limited assurances and fragmented structures.

The solution to the riddle of "Fixing a Hole" may be more promising. The way the song ends provides us with musical and lyrical clues. First, let's consider the musical clue. Each verse begins on a major chord and progresses through an interesting chordal structure (major–augmented–minor seventh–dominant seventh). This musical phrasing suggests a plaintive and wistful tone, needing resolution. Only the first words of each verse are hopeful and land on major chords: "fixing," "filling," "painting," "taking (the time)." But each verse diminishes into a minor chordal "wandering," the same chords on which the song fades. There is no optimistic musical resolution, no ending to affirm or confirm the theme of fixing holes—an odd construction for a song, but perhaps intentionally odd.

The second clue lies in the repeated lyrics that the mind will wander "where it will go . . ." Where it *will* go. Will it wander away, and if so, where? The suggestion is that the mind will not remain content in any artificial construction or mental sanctuary that we have erected and patched. If we stay in the sanctuary we run the risk of again building metaphysical edifices based on flimsy foundations. Nietzsche calls such a construction a "columbarium," a dome of concepts on an unstable foundation, a grave, full of recesses and holes.[6] If we remain in a sanctuary of spider webs and porous constructions we create a graveyard of concepts, a dead philosophy. The lyrical and musical clues allow the song to move us out of "fixed" structures to "wandering" processes—from "being" to "becoming." Without such a move, we run the risk of writing the sermons that no one will hear, and wiping the dirt from our hands as we walk from the grave—but no one was saved!

Nietzsche's philosophical autobiography, *Ecce Homo* is subtitled: "How One Becomes What One Is." To become what one is, according to Nietzsche, requires constant reinterpretation and reinvention, a continual fixing and painting and rising above ourselves. To do so, we need to build new sanctuaries and fix new holes. If we leave our sanctuary, we cannot check back in. If we do check back in only to find a copy of Gideon's bible, we discover that the room has changed: Gideon has checked out, perhaps pursuing Rocky's spiritual well-being. We, like Rocky Raccoon, need to *revive* and reinvent ourselves. As the world changes with our changing perspectives, we too change. Building a sanctuary allows us to take the time for the things that weren't important yesterday, but they will not be important tomorrow, either. The Beatles revive and reinvent themselves as their masquerade becomes too burdensome. John assimilates himself into the dual entity of "John and Yoko," Paul creates the "Wings" project, George and Ringo begin solo careers.

Nietzsche affirms the theme that our mental constructions are temporary forgings. Behind every cave there is another, deeper cave, a more comprehensive, stranger and richer world beyond the surface. Every philosopher makes arbitrary judgments: "There is something arbitrary in his stopping *here* to look back and look around, in his not digging deeper *here* but laying his spade aside; there is also something suspicious about it" (*Beyond Good and Evil*, p. 229). Man is evolving, Zarathustra teaches, and is on a tightrope, on his way to becoming the next

---

[6] Friedrich Nietzsche, "On Truth and Lies in a Nonmoral Sense," in Daniel Breazeale, ed., *Philosophy and Truth: Selections from Nietzsche's Notebooks of the Early 1870s* (Atlantic Highlands: Humanities Press, 1979), p. 85.

step, beyond man—the *ubermensch*. To stop here is arbitrary, "a dangerous shuddering and stopping."[7]

Help Me Get My Feet Back on the Ground

Another approach to the riddle of "Fixing a Hole" is to leave it unsolved, to let it remain a puzzle, so that the mind can wander and not stagnate. Solving riddles can be a dangerous business, as history and literature have shown. The Manson "family" fell under a dogmatic and "fixed" interpretation of "Helter Skelter." Oedipus solves the riddle of the sphinx, but when he solves the riddle of his life the result is devastating. He learns of his hidden tragedy and is ultimately blinded. Nietzsche proposes that we too become blinded when we settle for "truth" or worse, when we believe we have conquered the seductress "truth." We should leave the veil before the goddess, and not peek beneath, for we may not like what we find. Maybe the riddle is best left unsolved because it is more fun to constantly reinterpret it from our ever changing, ever evolving perspectives, better to leave the story incomplete than to "solve" it. If there are enough "holes" in the lyrics, we can supply endless meanings—who is the walrus, anyway?

---

[7] Friedrich Nietzsche, *Thus Spoke Zarathustra*, in Walter Kaufmann, ed., *The Portable Nietzsche* (New York: Viking, 1954), p. 126.

16

The Beatles as Nietzsche's Music-Playing Socrates

PAUL SWIFT

The Beatles may be considered as philosophers—according to Friedrich Nietzsche's view of philosophers as earth-shaking events. Nietzsche's idea that the genuine philosophers of the future will be rare visionaries who tune us into important things about life is not universally accepted, but is useful for identifying a type of greatness that the Beatles embodied.

Nietzsche's emphasis on the importance of music, dancing, and laughter for philosophy offers an expectation for philosophers to be rare models of greatness, in contrast to the standard academic view in which philosophers are basically scholars, argument technicians, or bookworms. Nietzsche challenges philosophers to develop themselves intellectually, but also stresses a need for human beings to affirm life through music and laughter.

In the *Birth of Tragedy out of the Spirit of Music*, Nietzsche reflects on the significance of Socrates's attempt to compose music after Socrates had been sentenced to death. Socrates was charged for corruption of the youth and not believing in the correct gods in ancient Greece, a conflict which invites comparison to the attacks of the Beatles that occurred in the southern United States in 1966. While Socrates was incarcerated and waiting for his execution he attempted to compose music, an "irrational" activity that he had derided while he was still a free person. The Beatles and Socrates both opened new possibilities for thinking about the future, and both were attacked for corrupting the youth. However, Socrates never wrote great music, and Nietzsche reflects on this aspect of Socrates character: how important is it for a wise man to write music? Nietzsche suggests that the relationship of philosophy to music is very important and calls for a new legion of future philosophers, a type of "music-playing Socrates" for the future. Music and laughter are important for Nietzsche's view of the philosophers of the future, and the Beatles, especially John Lennon, seem to answer this call.

Philosophic Training Outside Academia: Will the Real Philosophers Please Stand Up?

As free-spirited intellectual pioneers, the Beatles were collectors of a special type. Some people collect sports cards, Beatles memorabilia, figurines, or coins, but the Beatles collected diverse experiences, a key for expanding one's horizons and training oneself as a philosopher in Nietzsche's non-standard view of the philosopher.

The Beatles journeyed the world to seek out alternative perspectives on what is real. Their well documented experimentation with LSD and other drugs, as well as their training with the Maharishi show how they sought out new experiences to challenge their worldviews. Even if such mind-bending trips ultimately achieved little or nothing to unveil any type of truth or reality (the discipline of philosophy still seeks truth), such episodes were nonetheless important for challenging the limits of the Beatles' ordinary experiences, a key expectation for Nietzsche's philosophers of the future.

Such a path is not advisable for everyone, since seeking out such experiences may serve to make one less aware rather than more aware, not to mention the fact that many persons mess up their lives badly with drugs.[1] However, intoxication is not always contrary to the goal of philosophy according to Nietzsche, since he suggests that some insights can be triggered through *Rausch*, or *the rush* of intoxication. Nietzsche proposes that this type of experience allows one to understand his concept of the Dionysian.

---

[1] Ringo Starr was attuned to this danger when he said "I hope the fans will take up meditation instead of drugs." Later the Beatles (especially John Lennon) became painfully aware that both intoxicants and meditation gurus can be life-negating crutches and sources of self-deception.

Although "life" is sometimes viewed as a hopelessly vague philosophic concept, it is not empty. Nietzsche connects his idea of life-affirmation to his concept of the Dionysian. Dionysus is the wine god of ancient Greece, and Nietzsche uses Dionysus to refer to a dimension that academic philosophers traditionally say little about: intoxication, frenzy, creativity, passion, and sex. At one point he declares: "I would only believe in a God who could dance."

At times the Beatles embody a sense of Nietzsche's Dionysian philosopher and also seem to fit into Nietzsche's larger view that philosophy should be in the service of life. Saying "yes" to life means that one should avoid life-negating practices such as harboring resentment, pettiness, vindictiveness, and greed.

The Beatles, along with other musicians such as Jimi Hendrix, the Grateful Dead, and the Doors, offer examples of the timeless pulse of the Dionysian. Nietzsche thought a musical remedy is needed for academic philosophy, since philosophy within academia has frequently become stuffy, sterile, overly abstract, and disconnected from life: the philosopher's quest for truth needs to include and recognize the value of music, dance, and laughter.

For those who aspire to become professors in the field that purports to love wisdom—philosophy comes from the Greek words *philo* (love) and *sophia* (wisdom)—in the twenty-first century, there is no mandate to trip on acid or experiment with meditation techniques. Yet such activities need not be viewed as antithetical to philosophy at all, and Nietzsche suggests at times that there is an important distinction between the academic philosophy professor and the genuine philosopher. Consider Nietzsche's view of the genuine philosopher as an extraordinary dreamer, a condition that is not necessary as a qualification to be a professional philosophy scholar:

A philosopher—is a human being who constantly experiences, sees, hears, suspects, hopes and dreams extraordinary things; who is struck by his own thoughts as from outside, as from above and below, as by his type of experiences and lightning bolts; who is perhaps himself a storm pregnant with new lightning; a fatal human being around whom there are constant rumblings and growlings, crevices, and uncanny doings. A philosopher—alas, a being that often runs away from itself, often is afraid of itself—but too inquisitive not to "come to" again—always back to himself. (*Beyond Good and Evil,* p. 292)

As creative visionaries the Beatles embody the dangerous earth-shaking philosophic ideal for which Nietzsche hopes. John Lennon specifically identifies himself as a dreamer in his later years in the "good" sense of dreaming—not as a form of escapism, but a type of artistic viewing of the world to consider new possibilities for the future. During the 1960s the Beatles were often a radical force that undermined the authority of the traditional establishment. It's precisely this radical questioning of prior authorities which is important for addressing the connection of the Beatles to philosophy, since some of the early Beatles' encounters with religious fanaticism reveal a kinship to some of Nietzsche's deepest philosophic concerns, a somewhat neglected yet important part of the Beatles' story.

As a free thinker outside of the establishment John Lennon especially seemed to embody Nietzsche's sense of the philosopher. John worked hard at trying to get people to think and act to change the world, even if his hopes for peace and feminist empowerment diverged from Nietzsche's philosophic aspirations.

Forbidden Knowledge: Dionysian Frenzy

Nietzsche devoted much of his life to music by continuously composing and reflecting on the significance of music. While barely fourteen years old, in 1862, he began writing about "the Demonic in Music" to try to explicate the uncanny power that music seems to have over human beings. Nietzsche's desire to become a professional musician never materialized, but he was still struck with the same impulse as a teen that vented itself through John, Paul, George, and Ringo as well, the dream of transforming the world by bringing new music to life.

By the late 1860s Nietzsche's encounter with Schopenhauer's theory of music and his personal acquaintance with Richard Wagner helped provide impetus for his first book (*The Birth of Tragedy out of the Spirit of Music*), in which Nietzsche presents his own concept of the Dionysian. As an aesthetic and psychological category to describe frenzy, excess, passion, intoxication, and wild sex, Nietzsche ventures into a forbidden area of discourse. Nietzsche contrasts the dangerous Dionysian dimension with the Apollonian (named after the Greek God Apollo) which represents balance, order, reason, beauty, civilization. Western philosophy has told us much about the Apollonian, but there is a provocative sense of the Dionysian which philosophers have ignored, one that suggests an affinity to the Beatles.

The *mania* of Beatlemania is an important psychological and philosophic phenomenon that intersects with Nietzsche's concept of the Dionysian. There is much historical precedent connecting dithyrambs (wild dances) to the Dionysian origins of ancient Greek tragedy, but Nietzsche intimately connects the Dionysian to music in a sense that may not be present in the historical tradition. How is it that some music is able to trigger such a mania, a frenzied feeling that seems to border on the demonic? The other arts, such as sculpture, poetry, painting, architecture, and literature (arts which Nietzsche identifies as primarily Apollonian) do not unleash the frenzy of the Dionysian. How does music offer this strange power, one that is different from other arts, one that seems to bare a similar relationship to the sex drive's relationship to abstract thought?

Has the philosophic significance of sex, music, and intoxication been repressed by a tradition which invariably has viewed frenzied mania as contrary to reason and therefore irrelevant to philosophy? Nietzsche uses the analogy of the feeling of intoxication as a physiological experience that is the key to understanding the Dionysian, an invitation to break free from repressing the wild inner nature that is buried in all of us. Nietzsche and the Beatles both recognized that intoxication can indicate an unhealthy escapism at times, but does this mean that all types of intoxication are unhealthy? Is Mardi Gras or Carnival always unhealthy?

The Beatles' odyssey explored the possibility of a healthy frenzied mania, a feeling of freedom that allows one to feel herself as part of a larger work of art, unlocking an original feeling of life. In diverse times and places each young generation rocks out to the Dionysian party impulse of the springtime drive. Sex, drugs, and rock'n'roll have been blind spots in the history of academic philosophy. Dionysus is bigger than the individual. Nietzsche views Dionysian celebration as an expression of life-affirmation. He stammers to convey the sense that there is a wild wisdom in such freakouts, even though such revelry would be viewed as a sign of decadent deviance by later religious traditions. The oldest Greek tragedies were both more satyric (satyrs are half-human, half-goat mythological beings infamous for mischief and sex) and more musical according to Aristotle (*Poetics*, line 1449), a repressed explosive force with which both Nietzsche and the Beatles experiment. In spite of the peculiar differences we have as individuals, there is a primitive communal feeling that is shared in music and the Dionysian experience, a feeling of an underlying oneness. The frenzy of Beatlemania is very close to Nietzsche's Dionysian.

Nietzsche is controversial for his suggestion that all religions are deceptive about their historical origins. If Nietzsche is correct, virtually all religious perspectives are also deceptive about organic life and sex. Nietzsche believes that human beings frequently seize upon religion as a way to repress their bodily desires and console themselves by inventing purposes and directions for life. According to this view, most authorities from academic philosophy and theology are untrustworthy sources to provide any meaningful insights into the best types of music, sex, or intoxication. Moreover, such institutional authorities are forbidden from speaking truthfully about the nature of the Dionysian.

Like Dostoievski and Marx, Nietzsche at times conceives of religion as a type of escapism, an unnatural coping mechanism to deal with the pain of life. John Lennon and Nietzsche both described god as a concept by which we measure our pain. God can be thought of as a projection capacity to calculate punishment and guilt or God can be thought of as an ethical symbol to allow one to cope with suffering. How are suffering and pain connected to the meaning of life? Nietzsche and John Lennon both pose this as the first philosophic question.

Do all priests deceive themselves and others about sex and nature in their zeal to subvert nature's deepest impulses? Is the vow of chastity a virtue or a vice? The Dionysian view of sex as natural, healthy, and life-affirming rather than filthy and forbidden is often in direct conflict with theological accounts of sexuality. Dionysian philosophy attempts to reclaim natural desires without the anxiety of imaginary sin or eternal guilt-trips. The Beatles also discard the conventions of the theological view in their musical question: why don't we do it in the road?

Nietzsche writes that he would only believe in a god who could dance, proclaiming laughter as the most holy in his later work *Thus Spake Zarathustra*. The frenzy created by "Twist and Shout" and other Beatles rockers reveal an animating force that encourages life-affirmation in Nietzsche's sense. Moreover, the Beatles' clever use of humor also speaks to Nietzsche's desire to affirm life through laughter. In spite of being megastars, the Beatles were able to laugh at themselves and often connect with ordinary people, whether joking over their dandruff or poking fun at the "Paul is dead" hoax. Humor has a way of bringing one back down to earth, a strategic means to communicate and enliven others that requires a special type of intelligence.

Nietzsche and the early Beatles offered a new order of values by laughing off a type of sterile seriousness present in many dominant religious and philosophical views of the world. Even if the Beatles do not go as far as Nietzsche to suggest that all religion is deceptive superstition, there was a legitimate threat which the Beatles posed at times for religious leaders who demand unconditional obedience from their followers. Nietzsche and John both ask us: from where would values come—if we imagine there is no heaven?

Darwin's theory of natural selection appeared in 1859 and shortly thereafter Nietzsche also found himself writing about *how* the origin of life emerged, a portrait that clashes with theological accounts of creation during this time. Schopenhauer pointed out that almost no universities permitted openly atheistic philosophers to hold jobs during this time. This is a primary reason why Nietzsche suggests that there is an important distinction between philosophy scholars and philosophers.[2] In 1867, a hundred years before the summer of love, Nietzsche writes about academic philosophers:

> The ruling establishment appoints no one who contradicts religion. Consequently the philosophy of the universities conforms to the religion of the land. An example of this is the Hegelians and their failure. Another one of the ruling establishment's purposes is to appoint philosophy professors who promote the interest of the state. Consequently genuine philosophy goes unrecognized and is silenced to die.[3]

---

[2] See *Thus Spake Zarathustra*, "On Scholars," Part 2: "When they pose as wise, their little epigrams chill me: their wisdom often has an odor as if it came from the swamps" (*The Portable Nietzsche*, p. 237).

[3] Friedrich Nietzsche, *Frühe Schriften* (Stuttgart: Beck), Volume 3, p. 395 (my translation).

Nietzsche's suspicion that only "yes men" are dealt philosophy professorships suggests that there is only an illusion of academic freedom. Philosophers who refuse to pretend that it is reasonable to believe in religious dogma had been weeded out of the mix of philosophy professors. If this view is correct, philosophy within the universities is inherently political and certainly not done in a value-free context.[4] Power structures influence the space in which philosophy is done.

If we were to understand "philosophy" in the very broad sense of considering and evaluating conflicting and controversial ideas, Nietzsche and the Beatles both became sensitive to the idea that the medium or public space in which philosophy takes place directly permits or bars certain issues from consideration. Such an issue is important for contemporary media studies, since it raises the larger related question of whether there can be value-free media (both within the sense of news media, as well as any other region of discourse). Many forums that claim to be nonbiased actually promote or repress certain questions or issues based on value judgments and specific agendas lurking in the background—such forces still mold the type of ideas that are presented and discussed publicly.

Southern Cooking: Eliminating the Corruptors of Our Youth

In an interview with Maureen Cleave in March 1966, John Lennon remarked offhandedly that the Beatles were "bigger than Jesus."

> Christianity will go. It will vanish and shrink. I needn't argue with that; I'm right and I will be proved right. We're more popular than Jesus now. I don't know which one will go first, rock'n'roll or Christianity. Jesus was all right, but his disciples were thick and ordinary. It's them twisting it that ruins it for me.[5]

---

[4] Like Nietzsche and Schopenhauer, Spinoza was also a great philosopher who got into much trouble for controversial views about God, so much so that he declared himself unfit to be an academic philosophy professor, evidenced by his comment: "I do not know how to teach philosophy without becoming a disturber of the peace."

[5] *Evening Standard* (London: 4th March, 1966).

Cleave's article appeared in London's *Evening Standard*, without any incident in England. However, when the article appeared in the United States several months later, in *Datebook*, a furor resonated in the Bible Belt. In the southern United States, Beatles' records and memorabilia were smashed and thrown into public fires. John Lennon's candid remarks were the impetus behind the Beatle Burnings, and numerous death threats were directed at John as well as the other Beatles in the deep South, shortly before and during their 1966 American tour. Oddly enough, this southern cooking was triggered by comments that may have been taken out of context, and if we are to believe the later explanation in Lennon's apology, such comments had neither the tone nor intention that were attributed to them. Nonetheless, such a reaction shows how the environment directly conditions which types of ideas, music, and art are permitted to flourish in the public space. There's a power structure that conditions the "free" exchange of ideas.

The Beatles offered apologies in an attempt to calm the fanaticism that had targeted them in the name of religious virtue. The fallout created anxiety for John, Paul, George, and Ringo during their U.S. tour, as Ku Klux Klan members publicly expressed the intention of whacking (putting a hit on) the Beatles. The hostility toward the Beatles during this phase was not confined to radical terrorist groups like the Ku Klux Klan, but also found broader support from more mainstream communities in parts of the United States. After they had been accused of being Communists who planned to brainwash the youth, as well as Satanists, John Lennon mustered up an apology:

> I'm not anti-God, anti-Christ, or anti-religion. I was not saying that we were greater or better. I believe in God, but not as one thing, not as an old man in the sky. I believe what people call God is something in all of us. I believe that what Jesus, Mohammed, Buddha, and all the rest said was right. It's just the translations have gone wrong. . . . I wasn't saying whatever they're saying I was saying. I'm sorry I said it, really. I never meant it to be a lousy antireligious thing. From what I've read, or observed, Christianity just seems to me to be shrinking, to be losing contact.

This part of his apology was able to smooth things over enough to defuse most of the organized political movements against the Fab Four, but can we take this apology at face value? Could "I'm sorry" mean "I'm sorry you are so fanatical that you threaten my life and burn my music?" John also claimed that *Lucy in the Sky with Diamonds* was simply about Sean Lennon's drawing, but there seems to be good reason to infer that there is more going on in both cases—there is a hidden meaning or subtext. Was John's apology coerced, like the Dixie Chicks' apology for their criticism of George W. Bush in comments made at a London concert in March 2003? After publicly claiming they were ashamed that George W. Bush was from their home state of Texas, the Dixie Chicks (like the Beatles) were met with death threats, boycotts, and orchestrated public burnings of their work. Beatle burnings and the more recent Dixie Chicks episode indicate how political conditions directly influence the transmission of art and ideas. Although it's not overt censorship, such conditions show how the "free" domains of art and philosophy really may not be free.

Through his apology John conveyed that his comments were a criticism of Christianity rather than Christ, and his negative comments were actually aimed at a type of inauthentic institutionalized religion. If this is really what he meant in his original comments, such a view is considerably less offensive. In this sense, he could be viewed as a religious reformer who sought to dispense with institutionalized rules that divide rather than unite people. By claiming that God is "something in all of us," Lennon offers a way out by offering a *way in*, a vision of religious life that cuts out the middle man of organized religion to seek a direct spiritual relationship with the ultimate. By eliminating the mediator between God and humanity, the Beatles were able to shake the collective conscience of an entire generation by demanding a type of ethical responsibility that points directly back to the individual.

Lennon's comments were sufficiently well received to squelch the Beatle-burnings and death threats toward the Beatles. The Fab Four are neither the first nor the last to have their artwork torched in the name of a calling toward a "higher" moral purpose. Unlike most pop-icons, the Beatles were actually able to challenge an entire generation to question and think, activities which are almost always met with public hostility. Like Socrates, the Beatles' vision of the world was at one time in conflict with popular religion and was met with hostility and death threats.

Dangerous John

Unlike the widely prevalent view that considers anyone who has a philosophy Ph.D. to be a philosopher, Nietzsche thought there was a dignity in philosophy to which thinkers needed to measure up. His view distinguishes philosophy scholars from genuine philosophers, as the latter frequently are not sanctioned by the ruling establishment (dominant state or religious powers). This type of genuine philosopher is often perceived as dangerous, since this type of thinker frequently undermines accepted authorities in the quest for truth. John Lennon is a philosopher in this Socratic-Nietzschean sense. By undermining the idea that institutionalized religions have a privileged access to divinity (above and beyond the individual), John Lennon suggested a new path in the quest for knowledge of God and self.

As someone who embodied courage, strength, reflection, and personal freedom, John Lennon was a dangerous philosophic force in the Nietzschean sense, more so than the other Beatles. Insofar as political and religious leaders are accepted authorities who want to rule over others and make them obey, this special type of philosophic individual poses a legitimate danger. In his work *Schopenhauer as Educator*, Nietzsche raises the question of what the optimum number of philosophers for a state should be: if the only thing a leader wants is obedience, then the correct number of philosophers is zero, since genuine philosophers expose weak arguments and undermine traditional authorities that demand unconditional obedience. In this sense, the genuine philosopher must have a special type of courage to attack weak but popular arguments that promote illusions, whether they are partisan, nationalistic, religious, or historical. Nixon's attempt to deport John Lennon due to his later mobilization of the anti-Vietnam war vote is but one aspect of this dimension; freethinkers pose a danger to rulers who desire blind obedience.

Nietzsche suggests that the philosopher can be an agent of change, rather than simply be a writer of scholarly books that less than one percent of the population can understand. John and the other Beatles were not just dreamers, but philosophic types in Nietzsche's "good" sense, agents who made a difference by changing the world and offering a hope for the future. However, there are also some general differences with the Beatles' aspirations for peace and Nietzsche's view that there will always be wars among human societies. Even if both Nietzsche and the Beatles tried to construct philosophies in the service of life (toward empowerment, encouragement of music, dancing, and laughter), there are real differences between them as well.

The divergent tendencies in the Beatles' philosophy of peace and Nietzsche's philosophy of war admittedly put the Beatles in a different camp than Nietzsche in terms of envisioning what is best for this world. Nonetheless, both offer radical new musical visions of the world. Although this was the case with the Beatles, I have tried to show that this is true of John Lennon especially. Both Nietzsche and John asked us to imagine there's no heaven, but Lennon had a universal brotherhood and sisterhood of humanity in mind. Yet John's question (and Nietzsche's question) still remains: From where would human values come if heaven were only a psychological projection? Human beings would need to look within themselves for meaning, rather than to seek it in some supernatural destination. "You say you want a revolution?" "Around the creators of new values the world revolves."[6]

Later Lennon seemed to suggest a need to look for an ethics which does not originate in other-worldly metaphysics or from appeals to nationalism, an Apollonian dream of a world living together as one. Yet the world still is a violent place. In a world where religious practices and groups sanction violence against others, pacifists often put themselves in greater danger. Lennon, Gandhi, and King are among the most famous proponents of peace, and all were murdered. Lennon's mandate to imagine a world with no afterworld recognizes a need to bring metaphysics back to earth. Yet is there a necessary connection between terrorism and religion? Religion can be blamed for murders, but there's no shortage of murder in decidedly atheistic environments either, as the Cambodian killing fields so gruesomely remind us.

---

[6] *Thus Spoke Zarathustra* ("On the Flies of the Market Place").

On a personal level, music was important for both Nietzsche and the Beatles as a means to dialogue with the world. Both the Beatles and Nietzsche used music and humor as a means to convey their messages. As free spirits, the Beatles were able to break free from a life-negating seriousness in order to affirm life with music and laughter.

The Beatles as Philosophical Visionaries

Although there are similarities between Nietzsche's view of the genuine philosopher and the Beatles, the radical nature of Nietzsche's thinking strives for conflict rather than harmony. Many contemporary scholars have suggested that Nietzsche, like Lennon, had no beefs with Christ, but only meant to criticize Christianity—institutionalized religion. This may make Nietzsche more amenable to the politics of academic philosophy, but I'm guessing that Nietzsche himself would probably not accept such an interpretation. After all, Lennon's comments that "I am not anti-God, anti-Christ, or anti-religion" are a far cry from Nietzsche's declaration, "I am in Greek, and not only in Greek, the Antichrist."[7] Nonetheless, the Beatles and Nietzsche both furnish us with an important alternative view of the genuine philosopher: he or she frequently takes the form of a visionary who questions traditional authorities and struggles for forbidden knowledge.

---

[7] Nietzsche, *Ecce Homo* ("Why I Write Such Good Books," II).

IX

Number Nine, Number Nine, Number Nine

The Play of Language and the Play of Differences in the Beatles

17

And of Course Henry the Horse Dances the Waltz: Lennon's Lyrical Language Games

ALEXANDER R. EODICE

John Lennon frequently scoffed at intellectual attempts to analyze the lyrics of his Beatles songs, asserting that there was no hidden meaning or secret message contained in them. He was particularly amused by the dogged effort to find encoded symbolic meanings about life, the universe, dead Beatles, what-have-you in the obscure lyrics of songs like "I Am the Walrus," "Glass Onion," "Come Together," or "Revolution #9." While it might have been the obscurity of certain lyrics that led interpreters to suspect there was deep and hidden meaning contained in them, to Lennon, himself, such lyrics were always playful attempts at stringing sounds together in such ways so as to make them only seem deeply meaningful.

Lennon suggests that, in this regard, he "had tongue in cheek all along," and meant to give only the *impression* that there is something more to the lyrics than is actually in the lyrics themselves. In commenting further, he suggests that whatever meaning is there is just "not that serious." Discussing the presumed symbolism contained in the lyrics to "I am the Walrus," Lennon says:

> the words don't mean a lot. People draw so many conclusions and it's ridiculous. I've had tongue in cheek all along . . . Just because other people see depths of whatever in it . . . What does it really mean, 'I am the eggman'? It could have been the pudding basin for all I care. It's not that serious.[1]

---

[1] *The Beatles Anthology* (San Francisco: Chronicle Books, 2000), p. 273.

Isn't it oddly ironic, then, that there should be a chapter in this book proposing to find certain connections between Lennon's writing and philosophy? John Lennon would rightly scoff at any over-intellectualized attempt to uncover a systematic philosophy or metaphysical theory in his song lyrics, as the meaning of the lyrics themselves may not be that serious. Yet Lennon was extremely serious about language and writing, and it is this level of seriousness that provides an opportunity to explore some philosophical themes associated with the *kind* of writing in which Lennon was engaged.

There are two fundamental aspects to his writing that are relevant in this respect: the first-person perspective and, what might be considered, a purely linguistic approach. In the first-person perspective, Lennon uses his lyrics not to make assertions or report facts about the world, but to attempt to display features of his own consciousness and inner mental states; in adopting the second approach, he seemingly demonstrates that while certain uses of language may not literally say anything, they may, in fact, show the limits of sense and the value of non-sense from a purely linguistic perspective. Lennon has the sense that there is no view of the world independent of what we are subjectively and of the language we use generally.

Nowhere Man and the View from Nowhere

Seminal pieces that mark a distinctive turn in Lennon's song writing include "Nowhere Man," "I'm a Loser," "Help!" and "In My Life." While the first of these is technically written in the third person (*He's a real nowhere man . . .*), it's a song in which Lennon compares himself to one who has no point of view (*doesn't have a point of view . . .*). Is it possible to have no perspective in particular, to have no point of view, or, borrowing a phrase from Thomas Nagel, to adopt a "view from nowhere"?[2] Some might argue that this is the only perspective from which it is possible to attain objective knowledge about

---

[2] Thomas Nagel, *The View from Nowhere* (Oxford: Clarendon, 1986). Nagel writes about "how to combine the perspective of a particular person inside the world with an objective view of that same world, the person and his viewpoint included. It is a problem that faces every creature with the impulse and the capacity to transcend its particular point of view and to conceive of the world as a whole."

the world; that is, one must free oneself from subjectivity in order to view the world as it actually is. Knowledge of the external world, under this strong conception of realism, is possible only by achieving a perspective that belongs to no one in particular; the realist suggests that, in this way, objectivity is preserved.

It may in fact be the case that the realist establishes a condition that is impossible to meet. While the idea of objectivity involves an external perspective on the world that is presumably shared by any rational knower or had by no one in particular, can such an external perspective be got entirely free from any reference to subjectivity or the internal aspects of one's own consciousness? If this criterion of objectivity is impossible to meet, then it follows that any knowledge that were conceivably based on this condition would itself be impossible. This radical form of skepticism seems to follow from the fact that the strong version of realism is untenable.

The continuing lyric in *Nowhere Man* points in this very direction. The "nowhere man" who "doesn't have a point of view" is incapable of viewing the world objectively and correctly, and so really *knows not where he's going to*. Moreover, he is not alone in his ignorance. It's not simply as if the "nowhere man" adopts an odd perspective on the world that inhibits his own ability to view things objectively; it's rather the case that in an effort to position himself from nowhere in particular, he demonstrates that it is generally impossible for anyone to attain objectivity and knowledge with a "view from nowhere"; the "nowhere man", in his inability to know, is *a bit like you and me*.

One approach to this problem is to recognize that an objective view of the world must involve, to some degree or other, the inclusion of the subject in the world itself. This is to say that while objectivity is achievable, it is neither possible nor necessary to have a completely external view of the world; it is necessary to arrive at the external only by including a measure of reference to the internal perspective of the subject who is included as something within the world. This is the view taken by Nagel, when he suggests that "the distinction between more subjective and more objective views is really a matter of degree, and it covers a wide spectrum. A view or form of thought is more objective than another if it relies less on the specifics of the individual's makeup and position in the world, or on the character of the particular type of creature he is."[3]

The point is, however, that it is not possible to exclude the subject completely. Nagel goes on to propose that "objectivity is both underrated and overrated, sometimes by the same persons. It is underrated by those who don't regard it as a method of understanding the world as it is in itself. It is overrated by those who believe it can provide a complete view of the world on its own, replacing the subjective views from which it has developed."[4] Somehow a proper view of the world must include both the external and the internal perspectives. Such a view recognizes that the external (objectivity) and the internal (subjectivity) are not complete opposites. To rely on one at the expense of the other would be to invite a radical form of skepticism on either side; one that makes knowledge impossible because the criterion of objectivity is impossibly demanding and the other that says we can only know internal states and there is no bridge from them to the external world.

It is, of course, a bone of philosophical contention as to whether this is possible in any number of respects. Is it possible to balance the external and the internal in the sense Nagel suggests? Can one have an objective view of the world that nonetheless includes some perspectival sense of the subject? Isn't it the case that viewing the world from the perspective of one's own internality, however minimally this might be employed, defeats objectivity and constitutes precisely what is meant by a subjective viewpoint?

John Lennon himself clearly favors the subjective perspective and seems unaffected by the extreme form of skepticism this might engender. From his first-person perspective, he views himself as the point from which the world is viewed. He declares himself a loser who is self-consciously aware of the difference between how he feels and how he appears; he makes pleas for help; and he reflects upon his past from the perspective of his memory. Declaring, plea making, and reflecting are significant examples of Lennon's "lyrical language games" that distinguish his lyrics from those which sim-

---

[3] *The View from Nowhere*, p. 5.
[4] *The View from Nowhere*, p. 5.

ply make assertions or tell a story and are indicators of his strong subjective viewpoint.

Lennon's First-Person Perspective: I Am He . . .

Lennon suggests that he is compelled to write in the first person because he knows himself in some unique way. His lyrics thus do not have a clear assertoric character; that is, his first-person locutions are never mere assertions or reports of feelings, but are instead expressions of feelings or emotive ejaculations. Beyond this, Lennon sometimes takes a deeply introspective Cartesian stance which leads, for instance, to lyrics which constitute solipsistic fantasies about living in a dream world or knowing what it's like to be dead.

This stands in marked contrast to McCartney's third-person perspective in writing lyrics, which generally have a naturalistic and traditional narrative structure. Lennon comments that he has no interest in writing songs like a novelist; that is, he is "not interested in writing third-party songs," but would rather write about himself, as he seems to have a sense of privileged access to his own inner states and a level of certainty about them that he cannot have about events in the external world.[5]

Descartes codified the first-person perspective as one of the fundamental characteristics of the modern concept of mind. In the *Meditations,* he famously argued that while it was possible to doubt the veracity of sensation, the existence of physical objects and all that he was taught, and possible also to entertain the hypothesis that God might be an evil genius out to trick us constantly, it is not possible to doubt the thinking of such thoughts themselves and in so thinking, he concludes that he must exist (*Cogito ergo sum; I think, therefore, I am*). Descartes, of course, meant to establish the independent existence of two kinds of thing—mental and physical. He's sure not only that he exists, but sure also that he is a particular sort of thing, a thinking thing. While bodies, if they exist, exhibit the fundamental physical property of extension; the mind does not share this attribute—it does not take up space—and it

---

[5] *The Beatles Anthology,* p. 247.

exhibits the fundamental property of thought, or more pre-cisely, self-consciousness.[6]

Necessarily associated with this dualism of the mental and physical are such notions as "private thought" and "privileged access." From such a perspective, the mental has an epistemo-logical primacy in that it is known directly, immediately and with the greatest certainty. In this regard, one's awareness of self has more value, so to speak, than experiences of external phe-nomena and third-party states of affairs. It's in this sense that John Lennon attaches supreme significance to his own inner states and uses them as musical and lyrical inspirations.

With increasing reflexivity, Lennon becomes more self-con-scious and writes imaginatively about inner states. In "I'm Only Sleeping," he implores that he be left alone with his fantasies; in "Tomorrow Never Knows," he suggests that by allowing con-sciousness to take its own course, one might come to "see the meaning of within" or synesthetically learn to "listen to the color of your dreams," and in "She Said She Said," certain lingering attachments to the outside world make him feel like he's "never been born." With this solipsistic tendency, Lennon's lyrics demonstrate the apparent ease of viewing one's inner states, not as objects in the world but as self-defining episodes, and the apparent difficulty of mapping one's thoughts onto the external world. In "Strawberry Fields Forever," this viewpoint is summa-rized in the lyrics: "Living is easy with eyes closed; Misunderstanding all you see." Reflexive self-consciousness pro-vides a clear glimpse of one's inner states, while sensation may always yield misunderstanding of the external world. In these songs, Lennon's lyrics constitute variations on the Cartesian theme of the primacy of the mental.

Descartes wonders, for instance, whether from the perspec-tive of conscious experience alone one could clearly demarcate waking states from dreaming states. Dreams present themselves as vivid conscious experiences and in "I'm Only Sleeping," Lennon seems to prefer the dream experiences to waking con-scious states. While he remains watchful of the passing show, the value of this particular experience is that he's immersed in his dream and prefers to be left alone in his hypnagogic state.

---

[6] Descartes, *Meditations on First Philosophy,* especially Mediations I and II.

As conscious experiences go, it may indeed be preferable to hold to the vivid character of the dream experience, as the outside world may be fleeting and lacking the qualitative nature of a purely "inner" experience.

Descartes, always skeptical of the ability of sensation to accurately represent the non-mental external world, hypothesized that it may be possible that the senses always deceive us, in a way that we cannot be deceived regarding the quality and character of our own internal states. Lennon echoes this skepticism in *Strawberry Fields*. The sense of vision may literally be deceptive; when we attempt to see the world as it is, it's possible we arrive only at misunderstanding, but "living is easy with eyes closed". Lennon believes that self-consciousness is not a sensory function and that it is "easier" to gain access to his own internal states than it is to represent the world through the senses.

Such experiences only serve to strengthen the idea that the only thing one knows with any real certainty is the content of one's own mind. This is a form of epistemological solipsism and not metaphysical solipsism; it is about what one can and cannot know, where knowledge is fundamentally limited to one's own mind, but it does not mean that one's own mind is the only thing that exists. Lennon recognizes the external world, the world outside his window so to speak, but he is never actually sure how to get from inside his mind to that world; more important, the world inside is, for him, far more interesting.

As he penetrates further into the recesses of his own consciousness, Lennon attempts to use his lyrics to portray what might be called "solipsistic fantasies." In "Tomorrow Never Knows," he suggests we may come to "see the meaning of within" in virtue of having certain deeply private kinds of experience; for instance, it may be possible to "listen to the color of your dreams." This is a clear instance of synesthesia, the idea that a sensation usually associated with one sense is joined with a sensation ordinarily associated with another sense. In this lyric, Lennon joins sound (hearing) and color (seeing). In ordinary experience, of course, colors don't make sounds. In the synesthete's experience, it is not simply that the two different kinds of sensation are regularly ordered in experience and that verbal descriptions of the sound of color, say, are really just metaphors, rather it's that colors actually do have tonal quality. Those who have synesthetic experiences understand the experiences as real and certain; according to some descriptions, such experiences have an emotional and noetic quality and are likened to mystical experiences.[7]

Lennon pushes his solipsistic tendency even further in "She Said She Said." In this song, there are references to self-directed fantasies of experiencing what, in ordinary terms, is impossible to experience. Having reached the limits of sensible awareness, he "feels like he's never been born" and indicates that one could "know what it's like to be dead." Can one actually "feel" like he's never been born or "know" what is to be dead? Is there something, some subjective thing, that it is like to be not yet born or never to have been born? Is a thing that has never been born capable of sensation and how does one who has been born come to understand what such capacities might be? Isn't any feeling an indication that one is already born and so the "feeling that one has never been born" cannot really be a feeling of never having been born, since in order to have the feeling in the first place, it is necessary to have been born? With the claim to "know what it is like to be dead," this problem is even more acute. Is death an experience or is it the annihilation of all experiences? If the former, then it seems there is no way to communicate what it is like to be dead as only the dead can know; and if the latter, then there is in fact nothing to communicate in so far as there is nothing that it is like or "feels" like to be dead.[8]

In Cartesian fashion, he declares in the opening line of "I Am the Walrus" that "I am he . . ." This is the same "he", the same

---

[7] See Richard E. Cytowic, *The Man Who Tasted Shapes,* especially pp. 73–79. Cytowic demonstrates the reality of synesthetic experiences and proposes to show how such experiences, while deeply subjective, alter general conceptions of human mentality and brain function. With a strong emotional component, synesthetic experiences involve functions associated with the limbic region of the brain and as noetic, they are experienced immediately and leave one with a deep feeling of certitude. Cytowic likens this to William James's idea of the mystical experience as having a noetic quality in so far as it illuminates with authority some aspect of the transcendent in such a way as is impossible through ordinary discursive knowledge and experience.

[8] In his famous article, "What Is It Like to Be a Bat?" *Philosophical Review* LXXXIII: 4 (October 1974), Thomas Nagel suggests that there is an ineliminable element in any experience that can be said to be subjective; namely, that it is necessary for there to be something that it is like to be that thing, to "feel" like that thing, as it were, from that thing's point of view. Nagel does not mean this in the solipsistic sense I'm using here; he thinks what while this phenomenological feature of consciousness is required for subjectivity, it's objectively possible for conscious creatures to entertain points of view other than their own.

subjective thing, that has the experiences described above. Like the Cartesian *cogito,* Lennon's *he* endures through time and is defined by the broad range of conscious experiences that characterize who he is as understood in the language of his lyrical form of self-consciousness.

All You Need Is Language

Lennon loves language and adopts another sensibility—a purely linguistic approach—when writing lyrics, one that was initially apparent in his non-musical, humorous writings, most notably, *In His Own Write* and *A Spaniard in the Works,* nonsense prose and poetry fashioned in the manner of writers like Lewis Carroll, Edward Lear, and to some extent the Joyce of *Finnegans Wake.*[9] In his brief introduction to the book, Paul McCartney writes that "there are bound to be thickheads who wonder why some of it doesn't make sense, and others who will search for hidden meanings. . . . None of it has to make sense and if it seems funny, then that's enough."

Some of Lennon's song lyrics are quite simply and intentionally playful uses of language that, from a literal point of view, might be taken as patent nonsense or gibberish, but which, from another perspective, display the wide and varied uses to which language itself can be put. This is itself a kind of "language game," one that Wittgenstein might suggest holds a special grip on our imaginations, and we should take it not "as a matter of course, but as a remarkable fact, that pictures and fictitious narratives give us pleasure, occupy our minds."[10] There are myriad ways in which language is used and one important and general use is for the pleasure of the sense of nonsense that the language itself portrays. In understanding this, one may come to understand something that initially appears as "disguised nonsense" as "patent nonsense."[11] The writer who enables us to move from the apparent sense of his language to its patent nonsense must be particularly adept at this game itself. Lennon is indeed one such writer, whose unique ability stems from his acute sense of the sense of language. For only

---

[9] Published originally in 1964 and 1965.

[10] Ludwig Wittgenstein, *Philosophical Investigations,* Section 1, Paragraph 524.

[11] *Philosophical Investigations,* Section 1, Paragraph 464.

one who has such a sense could create such a grand illusion of sense.

"Across the Universe," in its opening lines, conveys the idea that Lennon views language as a kind of infinite commodity: "Words are flowing out like endless rain into a paper cup; they slither while they pass, they slip away across the universe." The image here is one of Lennon plucking words from their natural context and putting them together in ways that simply make interesting strings of sounds or paint strange or fantastic aural pictures. Moreover, anything could serve as a prompt for Lennon to put words together to frame his lyrics. Sounds, newspaper articles, everyday discourse, old English ditties and nursery rhymes all provided Lennon with the words he needed to make his lyrics sound right. Perhaps most famous in this respect is the poster announcing a special performance of Pablo Fanques' Circus Royal which inspired the lyrics to "Being for the Benefit of Mr. Kite." When in this song Lennon writes "and of course Henry the Horse dances the waltz," it's not as if he is describing or reporting an event, proposing a hypothesis, or even telling a story. In the context of the song, with its surreal tonal quality, Lennon's lyrics create a fantastic imaginary world of fiery hogsheads, silent performers, and dancing horses; but, more than this, the aural picture the song creates, like fictional narratives, gives us pleasure; and, as Wittgenstein suggests, this is a "remarkable fact" indeed. Lennon's own comments on "I Am the Walrus" are especially instructive when he suggests "the words don't mean a lot . . . you stick a few images together, thread them together . . . I was just using the mind that wrote *In His Own Write* to write that song."[12]

To put a finer philosophical cast on this: While certain of Lennon's lyrics may give the illusion of having sense (or hidden meaning), thus making questions about their meaning meaningless, questions about their meaninglessness are not meaningless. While the words may literally say nothing, they do, in fact, do something. At the very least, they sound right when put together, but more, they may show something about the workings of language itself.

---

[12] *The Beatles Anthology*, p. 273.

18

Four Play with a Difference

RICHARD FALKENSTEIN and JOHN ZEIS

"I'll teach you differences"—The philosopher Ludwig Wittgenstein (1889–1951) considered using this line from *King Lear* as an epigram for his *Philosophical Investigations*. He didn't use it, but it would have been appropriate. Wittgenstein's philosophy in the *Investigations* teaches us differences by challenging many of the presuppositions that philosophers have made in framing the context of philosophical discussion, and by doing so he created a new philosophical "grammar." In a similar fashion, the Beatles taught us differences by continually challenging many of the presuppositions about what popular music is and can be. As George Martin said, "Whenever I said, 'Give them their heads, let them do different things,' they came up with things that were as good as, if not better than, the material they had done before."[1] It's incredible that, given their enormous impact upon music and culture, it was only for about six years that the Beatles enjoyed career success together.

Just what *is* it about the Beatles that makes them unique in the history of popular music? Although the tentacles of the Beatles' influence extended into many more venues of popular culture than just music, it's purely and simply their music and its mercurial evolution that grounds their pre-eminent status in popular music. The music of the Beatles, like all great art, is significant because it discloses certain basic truths about who and

---

[1] George Martin with William Preston, *With a Little Help from My Friends: The Making of Sgt. Pepper* (Boston: Little, Brown, 1994), p. 68.

what we are as human beings and what we take to be of absolute value. And if this is right, a discussion of the Beatles' music and the philosophy embodied in it is not a mere exercise in theoretical analysis, but a useful practical tool for enhancing our appreciation of the music itself. This is not to say that the philosophical aesthetic this essay will attribute to the music of the Beatles is something they were consciously aware of or even would assent to in retrospect. But just as the scores of their recordings produced by Hal Leonard (which they themselves could not read) enhance the understanding and appreciation of their music for those who can read it, so can its philosophical ground at another level of abstraction.

Act Naturally

Allan Bloom has argued that the revolution in popular music in the era of the Beatles has been a principal cause of "the closing of the American mind."[2] Bloom connects rock music with the rejection of the values of truth, beauty, and goodness. But Bloom's position is a failure of both perception and under-standing. Critics like Bloom do not or cannot *hear* what needs to be heard in the music of the Beatles because they have no adequate *conception* of what it is all about and what kinds of differences in musical expression they are supposed to be hear-ing. What's so important about the music of the Beatles is that it breaks down the rigid barrier between popular music and music as art, as well as the boundaries between different genres in pop music. The failure to recognize this in the music of the Beatles is caused and rationalized by a faulty philosophical view concerning what is distinctive of and of preeminent value in human nature and activity. Condescending critics like Bloom are misled because of an aesthetic that erects rigid barriers between pop music and music as art based on an exaggerated meta-physical dualist conception of human nature and a misapplied essentialism concerning the nature of art. Such critics are like the Greeks, who called all non-Greeks "barbarians" because, as the Greeks "clearly" perceived it, the others could not speak any articulate language at all: it was just "bar, bar, bar."

---

[2] Allan Bloom, *The Closing of the American Mind* (New York: Simon and Schuster, 1987).

Metaphysical dualism more often than not leads to a misperception of what is most distinctively human and what types of activities best exemplify our humanity. Metaphysical dualism is the thesis that the human person is composed of two radically different substances: mind and body. The mind is wholly immaterial and is of a noble, rational nature. The body, on the other hand, is material and is of a base and irrational nature. Given its deep roots and weighty authorities in western philosophy (Plato, Descartes, and Kant among others), the view has apparent justification, but as Wittgenstein and others have shown, its justification is illusory. It is a view in which the intellect and reason are opposed to appetite and the passions, and as such it entails a separation of what is best in human nature from what is the natural purpose of the human person.

You Can't Do That

Plato (around 429–347 B.C.) sees a division between our appetites, passions, and emotions on one side and our intellect and reason on the other. In Plato's view, the side of our nature that includes our passions and appetites is chained to the material world and governed by the laws of pleasure and pain rather than reason and truth. According to Plato, we ought to throw off our attachment to the material world and its pleasures and instead focus our commitment upon the world of Ideas, which includes the good, the true, and the beautiful. Our material or lower nature is blinded to what is really good, true, and beautiful and wallows in ignorance, illusion, and base appetites. And until we break the chains that bind us to the world, until we turn away from the pleasures of this world, we have no chance of attaining real value.

In such a dualism, there is a battle for control in the human person between the mind or soul, which is noble and supernatural, and the body, which is base and physical. When dualism is presumed as a basis of evaluative aesthetic judgment, it can lead to an exaggeration of the value of the formal elements embodied in the written score of music over the expressive, passionate, and emotional elements. Such an exaggeration often results in a devaluing of what is naturally human. Within such a scheme, it's predictable just how popular music and especially rock'n'roll—the lowest of "lowbrow" music—would be assessed. After all, the term "rock'n'roll," like "jazz," is just slang for sex—and there is nothing like sex for reminding us of our attachment to the world of matter and flesh! Hence, within a culture whose philosophical presuppositions are steeped in dualism, it's no wonder that when the Beatles captivated our lives, the result was a generation gap the likes of which has rarely been seen before or since. It is of course true that the Beatles were not alone in this revolution, and John Lennon expressed it best when he said:

> Whatever wind was blowing at the time moved the Beatles too. I'm not saying we weren't flags on the top of the ship. But the whole boat was moving. Maybe the Beatles were in the crow's nest shouting "Land Ho!". . . but we were all in the same damn boat.[3]

One of the principal features of the music of the Beatles and of white rock'n'roll in general is its roots in the music of Black America: its roots in blues and R&B. But what is so distinctive about the Beatles' transfusion of Black America's music is that their inspiration from this music did not result in mere derivation, "Blues Lite," by some white Brit boys. They always gave us something different. In the music of the Rolling Stones, Mick Jagger's vocal derivation from Howlin' Wolf is ever apparent; the rhythm and chord structure of Keith Richards' music is heavily reliant on straight blues formats. By contrast, the music the Beatles created with Black America's music as their inspiration took various expressions. In their covers, such as "Twist and Shout" and "Long Tall Sally," they express a raw passion, and the brutality in their interpretations matches and often far outstrips that of the originals. Just listen to Elvis Presley's version of "Hound Dog" together with Big Mama Thornton's version, and then compare McCartney's version of "Long Tall Sally" with that of Little Richard and Lennon's rendition of "Twist and Shout" with that of the Isley Brothers. Whereas Presley's "Hound Dog" is a toned-down and thereby "whitened" version of Big Mama Thornton's, McCartney's and Lennon's covers are nothing short of rock mayhem. Just how much the Beatles wanted to teach us differences can be heard in their original compositions like "All

---

[3] David Sheff and G. Barry Golson, eds., *The Playboy Interviews with John Lennon and Yoko Ono* (New York: Playboy Press, 1981), p. 78.

I've Got to Do," "This Boy," "When I Get Home," and "You Can't Do That." All of these were inspired by the soul artists Smokey Robinson and Wilson Pickett but would never be categorized as soul music. The inspiration results in—what else can we call it: Beatles music. And yet if real soul music is that which is authentically expressed from the depths of one's soul, then perhaps it *is* real "soul." As the philosopher Roger Scruton, talking about music that has moral value, expressed it:

> The long tradition of musical utterance, which enabled our parents to hum with equal facility an aria by Mozart or a melody by Nat King Cole, was a precious icon of humanity. You can hear it still in the Beatles or Buddy Holly, and to sing or move to this music is to take one step across the divide between popular and classical culture. You are beginning to think and feel *musically*—with an awareness of the voice not as a sound only, but as an expression of the soul.[4]

Like Scruton, Leo Tolstoy (1828–1910) understood what "soul" is all about in artistic expression. According to Tolstoy, we have art when someone evokes a feeling that he has experienced and expresses it in some material medium (words, lines, colors, sounds, movement) so that others are infected with the same feeling. And the value of the artistic expression is relative to its degree of infectiousness, marked by the clarity, individuality, and sincerity of the feelings communicated.[5] Certainly the Beatles' music counts as valuable art given this understanding.

Roll Over Beethoven

Like metaphysical dualism, essentialism is also an impediment to understanding what constitutes a work of art. Essentialism is the view that clear and rigid boundaries can be drawn around a kind of thing. And in aesthetics, this implies that clear and rigid boundaries can be drawn around what constitutes a work of art. But what makes a piece of music a work of art is better identified by its enriching function rather than by its structural properties. Once an essentialist view about art is combined with an

---

[4] Roger Scruton, *The Aesthetics of Music* (Oxford: Oxford University Press, 1997), p. 501.
[5] Leo Tolstoy, "What Is Art?" www.csulb.edu/~jvancamp/361r14.html

exaggerated dualism, music as art is put into a very tiny box, and all other music is thereby downgraded. The failure to hear the Beatles' music as art is as much a failure of perception as it is of understanding.

The earliest period of Beatles music was characterized by original compositions in a style that was distinctly theirs, supplemented by electrifying covers of other artists. Wittgenstein throughout his *Investigations* challenged us to question our orthodox philosophical conceptions, our pigeonholing of objects into preconceived categories. He warned us not to look for the rigid essence that unifies the meaning of a word, but to look for family resemblances or analogies instead. Similarly, the Beatles continually challenged us to question preconceived expectations regarding musical style. Right from the beginning there was something unorthodox about this group. George Martin said that when he first started working with the Beatles, he tried to figure out what the identity and who the focal member of the band should be: should it be John and the Beatles? Or Paul and the Beatles?—but he just couldn't make up his mind. That he could not, despite his presumption to the contrary, is a telling indication of how clear it was that this was an integrated group. And it was crystal clear to their fans from the beginning that this was so. It was always the four as a group: John, Paul, George, and Ringo—the fab four, the four mop-tops. In the beginning and throughout their performance career, it was always the four of them playing and singing together that was essential to their distinctive style. And although the original compositions of their early period, like "She Loves You" and "I Want to Hold Your Hand," were lyrically typical of standard teen pop themes, musically they were advanced compositions energized by a style of strong melodies, full, rich harmonies, and unique ensemble musicianship. So the Beatles, nurtured by George Martin's encouragement of their creative impulses, showed us how the typical categories of pop music do not have a unified rigid essence, but are unified by analogy.

Take one of the earliest Beatle songs. "Love Me Do" is musically repetitive with a melody that is easy to remember—on the surface a typical pop song—and its melodic and harmonic materials (employing blues notes) and instrumentation (guitars and harmonica) are drawn from what might be called folk blues. Despite the simplicity of the lyrics, the melody is quite sophisticated as it projects anticipation, yearning, humility, and confidence. This mixture of sophistication and simplicity is intuitive, no doubt, but it shows in small measure the genius of the Beatles at an early stage.

I'm Happy Just to Dance with You

Dualist preconceptions can also prejudice our appreciation of early Beatles music in other ways. Part of the experience of popular music involves what might be called the "ritualistic."[6] Environment plays an important part in this aspect, and the environment of early Beatles songs is that of the teenager and young adult: a party, a discotheque, a nightclub, a pop music concert. The Beatles are always in love and having various degrees of success with it, and they seem always to be dancing ("I Saw Her Standing There," "I'm Happy Just to Dance with You," and so on). Certainly this is characteristic of rock'n'roll, a term that signifies motion and bodily involvement. The Beatles seem to always be in motion, and nowhere is this more evident than in the scenes from *A Hard Day's Night* where the members of the group flee from frenzied fans as their rock'n'roll inspired tunes play. Through the rougher edge of these songs (with guitars naturally distorted through amplification, accented upbeats, and a "shouting" vocal style) the musicians appear to shed their inhibitions and inspire their audience to do so as well. As George Martin expressed it, "Instrumentally, the Beatles loved the loudness, the rawness of the guitar work, the heavy back beat, the thumping drums and bass, the fact that you could shout your head off when you were singing."[7] And the Beatles took this musical style to another, more passionate, visceral level. This would be a no-no for the Platonic dualist! Motion, in the tradition of metaphysical dualism, is an imperfection, an incompleteness in being. That's why philosophers conceived of God as an unmoved mover. But that music is sensual—that it appeals to the physical senses—does *not* entail that it is vulgar or lowbrow. As the philosopher of music Eduard Hanslick (1825–1904) reflected in his work in *On the Musically Beautiful* in 1854:

---

[6] Wilfred Mellers, *Twilight of the Gods: The Music of the Beatles* (New York: Schirmer, 1975), pp. 24–27.
[7] *With a Little Help from My Friends*, p. 43.

How many works by Mozart were declared in his time to be the most passionate, ardent, and audacious within the reach of musical mood-painting. At that time, people contrasted the tranquility and wholesomeness of Haydn's symphonies with the outbursts of vehement passion, bitter struggle, and piercing agony of Mozart's. Twenty or thirty years later, they made exactly the same comparison between Mozart and Beethoven.[8]

Similarly, the Beatles' music was perceived as "passionate, ardent, and audacious."

With a Little Help from My Friends

If one's criterion for art is the literal structure that is embodied in the score, then it's true that rock'n'roll and the music of the Beatles cannot measure up to the music of the classical canon. But the use of such a criterion begs the question. For the metaphysical dualist, the musical score with its precisely specified keys, notes, and dynamics is the expression of our rational nature. In the score, there is no place for improvisation based upon the artists' passions. But the music of the Beatles, like other great music in jazz, blues, and rock, cannot be judged by such a standard without draining it of its lifeblood. Some accounts of the evolution of the Beatles' music fall into this trap and read its evolution as a progression from simplistic, teen anthems to a more sophisticated expression in works such as *Rubber Soul, Revolver, Sgt. Pepper's Lonely Hearts Club Band*, and "Strawberry Fields." There is indeed a more cerebral and sophisticated expression in such works over their earlier ones, but is it better music and better art than "She Loves You" and "I Want to Hold Your Hand"? Is the closing chord of *Sgt. Pepper* in "A Day in the Life" any more dramatic, moving, and stunning than the opening chord of *A Hard Day's Night?*

Their music evolved, that is certain. At each stage in their career, they presented us with something new and daring. They first appeared not only as loud, raucous, wild rockers outperforming their idols but also as disciplined performers and original tunesmiths. And in a very short time, they had no need to rely upon their old masters. *A Hard Day's Night*, with John

---

[8] Eduard Hanslick, *On the Musically Beautiful* (Indianapolis: Hackett, 1986), pp. 6–7.

responsible for most of the songs, marked the beginning of their unshakeable confidence in their own original compositions, as it was their first album with no covers. The opening chord of "A Hard Day's Night" was the perfect opening for the album and film: none of their works began with more dramatic flair. Its crash was a musical correlate of the Beatles' crash into our consciousness. And John's contributions were such that it is not a stretch to claim that the *Hard Day's Night* album represents the most creative period in the history of pop rock by any composer before or since. Nonetheless, the identity of the band remained solid and intact. The performance of the compositions on record and on stage was still very much a fully integrated group effort. And yet if we compare the last cut of *A Hard Day's Night* ("I'll Be Back") with the last cuts on their first two albums ("Twist and Shout" and "Money"), it's clear that they were signaling a change about to come.

Revolution I

"Yesterday" from the recording *Help!* points in the direction of that change and represents a significant milestone in the development of the Beatles' music. This is Paul's composition, and (at least initially) he performed it solo, accompanying himself on acoustic guitar. The music expresses the emotion of the verse as it maintains a just barely repressed tension. This music is unlike any of the earlier Beatles songs and is further distinguished from them by the use of strings to accompany Paul on the recording. "Yesterday" is a contemplative song with a mature viewpoint that deserves its status as a standard of twentieth-century popular music, and although it is clearly identifiable as a Beatles song, there is no rigid essence that marks its identity. It clearly teaches us differences!

The Beatles deliver the above-mentioned change to a greater degree in *Rubber Soul.* Much of the album has an "unplugged" feel to it, with its reliance on acoustic guitars and piano. As such, it signals a move away from their stage lineup toward studio production based work, while indicating contempt for the commercialization of their music. With *Rubber Soul,* the Beatles showed their fans (and recording company) that they would not just keep producing Beatles records in the same style for guaranteed commercial success. Instead they would follow their own muse, wherever it would lead them. Even the album cover seems to portray this attitude shift. The Beatles no longer appear as the happy-go-lucky and respectable, albeit long-haired, charming lads—an image that Brian Epstein was instrumental in framing. Instead, they exude an air of contempt. The album's success surely galvanized the Beatles' confidence to continue exploring new musical avenues. Its success also confirmed their ability to continue to touch us with and communicate to us in the different styles of music they used to express themselves.

That the Beatles were able to move in a seemingly natural way from one mode to another, quite different mode in their repertoire of musical expression shows that they were not bound by an essentialist conception of musical expression. The standard categories and dichotomies of musical expression— music as entertainment versus music as art, pop music versus classical music, rock versus pop, blues versus soul or rock or folk or country—were categories by which the Beatles refused to be bound. For them, these categories did not have essential characteristics, and their freedom to break down the barriers between the different genres of musical expression confirms the artificial character of these categories.

Tomorrow Never Knows

With *Revolver* the shift from performing artists to recording artists was complete. The album incorporated elaborate production techniques and orchestration into many of the compositions, but still had a healthy dose of songs relatively free of such additions. Nonetheless, by the time it was finished, the Beatles were exclusively recording artists: they never performed any of the songs on *Revolver* live. Not having to be concerned with live performance allowed their musicianship to mature. This is most evident in Paul's bass work. Since he no longer had to sing and play bass at the same time, his bass became another voice in the band, not just part of the rhythm section.

Sgt. Pepper's Lonely Hearts Club Band is the centerpiece of the period that also includes "Penny Lane," "Strawberry Fields," and *Magical Mystery Tour*. From the moment of its release to the present day, *Sgt. Pepper* has received the serious attention it deserves. It's an amalgam of the many different musical influences of earlier Beatles music. But is it still rock music? Certainly the songs have lost their function as dance music, a basic element of rock'n'roll—instead, they are to be listened to and thought about. Nevertheless, there are unmistakable rock elements on the recording, as for example, in the opening theme song that juxtaposes rock with brass band music. The variety of styles and their mixtures that follow are astonishing, especially when compared to earlier recordings and to those of other popular artists. Furthermore, the Beatles and George Martin incorporated elaborate production techniques without any inhibitions, showcasing the limitless possibilities of the studio. The individual members were working more independently of each other, which produced an album of exceptional variety and depth of expression. That the Beatles were still able to hold together while asserting their individual identities is superbly exemplified by "A Day in the Life," where John and Paul approach the same theme in different ways, both lyrically and musically. Ironically, the great strength of *Sgt. Pepper* is a result of forces that would eventually lead to the dissolution of the group.

One of the most striking aspects of *Sgt. Pepper* is in the range of timbre resulting from an incredible variety of instruments. While they had used orchestral and other non-rock instruments before, they had never quite achieved the fine tailoring of sound for each song on an album as they did on *Sgt. Pepper.* The album most clearly shows the way in which the Beatles were able to extend the boundaries of their music and pop music in general without destroying its identity. Although the additions of elaborate orchestration, exotic instruments like the sitar, and electronically produced sound effects radically changed the nature of Beatles music, it is still clearly Beatles music. This is the way in which creative essences morph into new categories while maintaining their identity. Whether it is in music, the other arts, or science, creative genius discovers ways of expanding our consciousness by analogy.

As at the beginning of the Beatles' career, many songs from this period show sophistication in compositional style under a veneer of simplicity. A good example is "All You Need is Love." Its repetitive melody is organized by a complex rhythmic design (alternating four- and three-beat patterns) that expresses the mood of the pontificating lyrics. At the end of the song there is a long coda that blends quotations from "Greensleeves," possibly the most famous English popular song, and "She Loves You," possibly the most famous early Beatles song, with other melodies.

Think for Yourself

The significance of the *Sgt. Pepper* period is undeniable, but not because its stock of songs is the strongest. While it resulted in some superb pieces, such as "Strawberry Fields," "Penny Lane," and "A Day in the Life," it also contributed to the disintegration of the band of four, which up until then had been their distinctive identity. After the *Sgt. Pepper* period, the growing artistic senses of the individual members of the group began to assert themselves more forcefully. The recording known as the White Album shows this fragmentation most clearly, and the abandoned *Let It Be* became a casualty of it.

The White Album seems to show the Beatles resigning themselves to the disintegration of the group while freewheeling through multiple genres. They exhibit a wide vision of pop music expression, but it is as three individuals (John, Paul, and George) headlining on their own works with the other three Beatles as a backing group at best. The White Album is their smorgasbord for our musical appetites, containing their hardest rocker ("Helter Skelter"), their schmaltziest orchestral piece ("Goodnight"), their bluest blues ("Yer Blues"), their most bizarre and experimental composition ("Revolution #9"), and their most banal howler ("Why Don't We Do It in the Road"). It's a wide ranging *pot-pourri* of tunes where the Beatles are clearly saying, "I'll teach you differences," most obviously in the three different versions of "Revolution." And in one and the same song, "Hey Jude" (a single from the same period), Paul synthesizes two extremes of his vocal range of musical expression: the sweet balladeer of "Yesterday" with the out-of-control wailer of "Long Tall Sally" and "I'm Down."

Get Back

Although creative genius discovers ways of morphing essences into new categories, sometimes analogies break down and identity is lost. The White Album approaches and perhaps reaches this breaking point (especially in "Revolution #9"). As an antidote to the focus on recording production and the disintegration of the group, *Let It Be* is a reaffirmation of their commitment to their roots in performance based rock'n'roll. And this is much more evident in the recently released *Let It Be: Naked*. Because of its lack of sophisticated production and its return to a more standard expression of rock'n'roll, it is easy to view the album as a dip in their musical career. But Paul himself disagrees: he thought that *Let It Be* was a rather *avant garde* work.[9] And after *Sgt. Pepper*, John wanted to get back to something he called more "honest." As he expressed it: "Rock'n'roll was real . . . And the thing about rock'n'roll, good rock'n'roll, whatever 'good' means, is that it's real . . . You recognize something in it which is true, like all true art."[10] Again, it's only if one accepts the pre-suppositions of an exaggerated dualism and a questionable essentialism that *Let It Be* is a second-rate work.

The End

The Beatles' final album, *Abbey Road*, is a fitting culmination of their ensemble work, and it is their strongest collaborative effort as composers. If *Abbey Road* is their best album, it is because the contributions by George ("Something" and "Here Comes the Sun") equal or surpass the compositions of John and Paul. In order to appreciate George's genius as a songwriter, just listen to the *Concert for George*. And with *Abbey Road*, just as in the beginning, for one last time there is a real collaborative effort of the four playing and singing together.

The range of the Beatles' music is in stark relief, ranging from the gritty "I Want You," through the soulful "Oh, Darling," the gentle "Something," the playful "Octopus's Garden," to the complex "Because." Nowhere is the balance of the elements in Beatles music better illustrated than in "The End," which could serve as a concise history and summation of Beatles music as the four members of the group show us their differences. It begins in early Beatles rock style with a shouting vocal line that references the teenage dream girl and continues with a drum solo by Ringo and eventually a raucous guitar jam by the three

---

[9] Paul McCartney, *Let It Be: Naked*, liner notes.
[10] Jann Wenner, *Lennon Remembers* (Harmondsworth: Penguin, 1971), p. 101.

other Beatles. After the smoke clears, the voice returns with a philosophical epigram about love accompanied by elegant orchestration with the electric guitar taking the place of first violin. The two poles of Beatles music are represented in this song, the "low" and the "high," and the most remarkable aspect of it is how effortlessly and naturally the transition is effected. In this one song there is the expression of the two ends of the spectrum of the Beatles' musical lexicon. It starts with (as Hanslick would express it) "outbursts of vehement passion, bitter struggle, and piercing agony" and ends, by contrast, with "tranquility and wholesomeness." Appropriately, "The End" best exemplifies how the music of the Beatles cannot be categorized exclusively as either pop or art. For in the music of the Beatles, one cannot pull apart the two poles any more than one can pull apart the four of them or their respective contributions to the music.

The Beatles Compleat

What is it about the music of the Beatles that makes it art? Their music strikes a chord that still resonates today because through their creative development and extension of what was first just simple rock'n'roll, they provide us with a voice that affirms the richness of musical expression and our wholeness as human persons. Their music frees us from a primitive attachment to our passions but also from an overly intellectualized conception of what is true, beautiful, and good in human nature. In other words, those who really listen to the music of the Beatles are led by it out of the cave into the upper world, but not in the way a Platonist would have it. Contrary to Plato and the extreme dualists, we are not led out of the cave of illusion and ignorance by forsaking our desires, passions, appetites, and emotions. We are not led out of the cave dictated by rigid, artificial categories, living a life of reason and intellect separated from feelings. Even if such a separation could be achieved, such an existence would suppress our real, true human nature. We are *not* pure spirits, we are essentially embodied spirits— it's a package deal that entails that any life which is human will always be a life that includes feelings, desires, emotions, and passions: all those elements that are integral to being an embodied person. In other words, we also have to dance our way out of the cave!

As medieval philosophers would see it and the artists of the Renaissance expressed it, art is the expression of the beautiful. And since the beautiful is identical in nature and only differs in concept from the true and the good, art is also the expression of the true and the good. As John Lennon expressed it, "And the thing about rock 'n' roll, good rock 'n' roll . . . is that it's real . . . You recognize something in it which is true, like all true art." Music is *real* or *true* only to the extent that it embraces and celebrates both facets of our humanity. And only to the extent that it achieves that will it be music that is not just real, but good and beautiful as well.

The evolution of the music of the Beatles teaches us differences by showing us, in a way unequaled by any other musical artists, the capacity of the rich diversity of expression in music that nonetheless is still popular music. But that their music is unequivocally popular does not mean that it is not also art. At each stage of their brief musical history, the Beatles presented us with terrific music that was also something new and daring, challenging us to hear differently. And that's precisely what is so important about their work: they continually taught us to hear differences.[11]

---

[11] In writing this chapter, we also looked at the following: William Dowdling, *Beatlesongs* (New York: Simon and Schuster, 1989); Ian Inglis, *The Beatles, Popular Music, and Society: A Thousand Voices* (New York: St. Martin's Press, 2000); Mark Lewisohn, *The Beatles Recording Sessions: The Official Abbey Road Studio Session Notes 1962–1970* (New York: Harmony, 1988); Tim Riley, *Tell Me Why: A Beatles Commentary* (Cambridge, Massachsetts: Da Capo, 2002).

Revolvers

BEATLE ALBUM DISCOGRAHY

UK Albums

Please Please Me
(Parlophone)   MARCH 22, 1963
Side 1: I Saw Her Standing There / Misery / Anna (Go to Him) / Chains / Boys / Ask Me Why / Please Please Me **Side 2:** Love Me Do / P.S. I Love You / Baby It's You / Do You Want to Know a Secret / A Taste of Honey / There's a Place / Twist and Shout

With the Beatles
(Parlophone)   NOVEMBER 22, 1963
Side 1: It Won't Be Long / All I've Got to Do / All My Loving / Don't Bother Me / Little Child / Till There Was You / Please Mr. Postman **Side 2:** Roll Over Beethoven / Hold Me Tight / You Really Got a Hold on Me / I Wanna Be Your Man / Devil in Her Heart / Not a Second Time / Money

A Hard Day's Night
(Parlophone)   JULY 10, 1964
Side 1: A Hard Day's Night / I Should Have Known Better / If I Fell / I'm Happy Just to Dance With You / And I Love Her / Tell Me Why / Can't Buy Me Love **Side 2:** Any Time at All / I'll Cry Instead / Things We Said Today / When I Get Home / You Can't Do That / I'll Be Back

Beatles for Sale
(Parlophone)   DECEMBER 4, 1964
Side 1: No Reply / I'm a Loser / Baby's in Black / Rock and Roll Music / I'll Follow the Sun / Mr. Moonlight / Kansas City—Hey Hey Hey Hey **Side 2:** Eight Days a Week / Words of Love / Honey Don't / Every

Little Thing / I Don't Want to Spoil the Party / What You're Doing /
Everybody's Trying to Be My Baby

Help!
(Parlophone)   AUGUST 6, 1965
Side 1: Help! / The Night Before / You've Got to Hide Your Love Away
/ I Need You / Another Girl / You're Going to Lose That Girl / Ticket
to Ride **Side 2:** Act Naturally / It's Only Love / You Like Me Too Much
/ Tell Me What You See / I've Just Seen a Face / Yesterday / Dizzy Miss
Lizzy

Rubber Soul
(Parlophone)   DECEMBER 3, 1965
Side 1: Drive My Car / Norwegian Wood (This Bird Has Flown) / You
Won't See Me / Nowhere Man / Think for Yourself / The Word /
Michelle **Side 2:** What Goes On / Girl / I'm Looking Through You /
In My Life / Wait / If I Needed Someone / Run for Your Life

Revolver
(Parlophone)   AUGUST 5, 1966
Side 1: Taxman / Eleanor Rigby / I'm Only Sleeping / Love You To /
Here, There and Everywhere / Yellow Submarine / She Said, She Said
Side 2: Good Day Sunshine / And Your Bird Can Sing / For No One
/ Dr. Robert / I Want to Tell You / Got to Get You Into My Life /
Tomorrow Never Knows

A Collection of Beatles Oldies
(Parlophone)   DECEMBER 9, 1966
Side 1: She Loves You / From Me to You / We Can Work It Out / Help!
/ Michelle / Yesterday / I Feel Fine / Yellow Submarine **Side 2:** Can't
Buy Me Love / Bad Boy / Day Tripper / A Hard Day's Night / Ticket
to Ride / Paperback Writer / Eleanor Rigby / I Want to Hold Your Hand

Sgt. Pepper's Lonely Hearts Club Band
(Parlophone)   JUNE 1, 1967
Side 1: Sgt. Pepper's Lonely Hearts Club Band / With a Little Help from
My Friends / Lucy in the Sky With Diamonds / Getting Better / Fixing
a Hole / She's Leaving Home / Being For the Benefit of Mr. Kite **Side
2:** Within You, Without You / When I'm Sixty Four / Lovely Rita /
Good Morning, Good Morning / Sgt. Pepper's Lonely Hearts Club
Band (Reprise) / A Day in the Life

The Beatles' First
(Polydor [with Tony Sheridan])   SEPTEMBER, 1967
Side 1: Ain't She Sweet / Cry For a Shadow / Let's Dance / My Bonnie

/ Take Out Some Insurance on Me, Baby / What'd I Say **Side 2:** Sweet Georgia Brown / The Saints / Ruby Baby / Why / Nobody's Child / Ya Ya

The Beatles
(Apple [a.k.a. "The White Album"])   NOVEMBER 22, 1968
Side 1: Back in the U.S.S.R. / Dear Prudence / Glass Onion / Ob-La-Di, Ob-La-Da / Wild Honey Pie / The Continuing Story of Bungalow Bill / While My Guitar Gently Weeps / Happiness Is a Warm Gun **Side 2:** Martha My Dear / I'm So Tired / Blackbird / Piggies / Rocky Racoon / Don't Pass Me By / Why Don't We Do It in the Road? / I Will / Julia **Side 3**: Birthday / Yer Blues / Mother Nature's Son / Everybody's Got Something to Hide Except Me and My Monkey / Sexy Sadie / Helter Skelter / Long, Long, Long **Side 4:** Revolution 1 / Honey Pie / Savoy Truffle / Cry Baby Cry / Revolution 9 / Good Night

Yellow Submarine
(Apple)   JANUARY 17, 1969
Side 1: Yellow Submarine / Only a Northern Song / All Together Now / Hey Bulldog / It's All Too Much / All You Need Is Love **Side 2:** (Music by George Martin and Orchestra as played in the film) Pepperland / Sea of Time / Sea of Holes / Sea of Monsters / March of the Meanies / Pepperland Laid Waste / Yellow Submarine in Pepperland

Abbey Road
(Apple)   SEPTEMBER 26, 1969
Side 1: Come Together / Something / Maxwell's Silver Hammer / Oh! Darling / Octopus's Garden / I Want You (She's So Heavy) **Side 2:** Here Comes the Sun / Because / You Never Give Me Your Money / Sun King / Mean Mr. Mustard / Polythene Pam / She Came in through the Bathroom Window / Golden Slumbers / Carry That Weight / The End / Her Majesty

Let It Be
(Apple)   NOVEMBER 6, 1970
Side 1: Two of Us / Dig a Pony / Across the Universe / I Me Mine / Dig It / Let It Be / Maggie Mae **Side 2:** I've Got a Feeling / One After 909 / The Long and Winding Road / For You Blue / Get Back

The Beatles / 1962-1966
(Apple [a.k.a. "The Red Album"])   APRIL 19, 1973
Side 1: Love Me Do / Please Please Me / From Me to You / She Loves You / I Want to Hold Your Hand / All My Loving / Can't Buy Me Love

Side 2: A Hard Day's Night / And I Love Her / Eight Days a Week / I Feel Fine / Ticket to Ride / Yesterday **Side 3:** James Bond Theme (US only) / Help / You've Got to Hide Your Love Away / We Can Work It Out / Day Tripper / Drive My Car / Norwegian Wood (This Bird Has Flown) **Side 4:** Nowhere Man / Michelle / In My Life / Girl / Paperback Writer / Eleanor Rigby / Yellow Submarine

The Beatles / 1967-1970

(Apple [a.k.a. "The Blue Album"])   APRIL 19, 1973
Side 1: Strawberry Fields / Penny Lane / Sgt. Pepper's Lonely Hearts Club Band / With a Little Help from My Friends / Lucy in the Sky with Diamonds / A Day in the Life / All You Need Is Love **Side 2:** I Am the Walrus / Hello Goodbye / The Fool on the Hill / Magical Mystery Tour / Lady Madonna / Hey Jude / Revolution **Side 3:** Back in the U.S.S.R. / While My Guitar Gently Weeps / Ob-La-Di, Ob-La-Da / Get Back / Don't Let Me Down / The Ballad of John and Yoko / Old Brown Shoe **Side 4:** Here Comes the Sun / Come Together / Something / Octopus's Garden / Let It Be / Across the Universe / The Long and Winding Road

Rock 'n' Roll Music

(Parlophone)   JUNE 10, 1976
Side 1: Twist and Shout / I Saw Her Standing There / You Can't Do That / I Wanna Be Your Man / I Call Your Name / Boys / Long Tall Sally **Side 2:** Rock and Roll Music / Slow Down / Kansas City—Hey Hey Hey Hey / Money / Bad Boy / Matchbox / Roll Over Beethoven **Side 3:** Dizzy Miss Lizzy / Anytime At All / Drive My Car / Everybody's Trying to Be My Baby / The Night Before / I'm Down / Revolution **Side 4:** Back In the U.S.S.R. / Helter Skelter / Taxman / Got to Get You into My Life / Hey Bulldog / Birthday / Get Back

Magical Mystery Tour

(Parlophone)   NOVEMBER 19, 1976
Tracks same as US release (1967).

Live! At the Star-Club in Hamburg, Germany 1962

(Bellaphon)   MAY 1, 1977
Side 1: I Saw Her Standing There / Roll Over Beethoven / Hippy Hippy Shake / Sweet Little Sixteen / Lend Me Your Comb / Your Feets Too Big **Side 2:** Twist and Shout / Mr. Moonlight / A Taste of Honey / Besame Mucho / Reminiscing / Kansas City-Hey Hey Hey **Side 3:** Ain't Nothing Shakin' (Like the Leaves on a Tree) / To Know Her Is to Love Her / Little Queenie / Falling in Love Again / Ask Me Why / Be-

Bop-A-Lula / Hallelujah, I Love Her So **Side 4:** Red Sails in the Sunset / Everybody's Trying to Be My Baby / Matchbox / Talking 'Bout You / Shimmy Shake / Long Tall Sally / I Remember You

The Beatles at the Hollywood Bowl
(Parlophone) MAY 6, 1977

Side 1: Twist and Shout / She's a Woman / Dizzy Miss Lizzy / Ticket to Ride / Can't Buy Me Love / Things We Said Today / Roll Over Beethoven **Side 2:** Boys / A Hard Day's Night / Help! / All My Loving / She Loves You / Long Tall Sally

Love Songs
(Parlophone) NOVEMBER 19, 1977

Side 1: Yesterday / I'll Follow the Sun / I Need You / Girl / In My Life / Words of Love / Here, There, and Everywhere **Side 2:** Something / And I Love Her / If I Fell / I'll Be Back / Tell Me What You See / Yes It Is **Side 3:** Michelle / It's Only Love / You're Going to Lose That Girl / Every Little Thing / For No One / She's Leaving Home **Side 4:** The Long and Winding Road / This Boy / Norwegian Wood (This Bird Has Flown) / You've Got to Hide Your Love Away / I Will / P.S. I Love You

The Beatles Collection
(EMI) DECEMBER 2, 1978

Includes the following UK albums: *Please Please Me / With the Beatles / A Hard Day's Night / Beatles for Sale / Help! / Rubber Soul / Revolver / Sgt. Pepper's Lonely Hearts Club Band / The Beatles / Yellow Submarine / Abbey Road / Let It Be* **Bonus album:** *Rarities* (**Side 1:** Across the Universe [Wildlife version] / Yes It Is / This Boy / The Inner Light / I'll Get You / Thank You Girl / Komm, Gib mir Deine Hand / You Know My Name [Look Up the Number] / Sie Liebt Dich **Side 2:** Rain / She's a Woman / Matchbox / I Call Your Name / Bad Boy / Slow Down / I'm Down / Long Tall Sally)

Hey Jude
(Parlophone) MAY 11, 1979

Same as US release (1970).

The Beatles' Ballads
(Parlophone) OCTOBER 13, 1980

Side 1: Yesterday / Norwegian Wood (This Bird Has Flown) / Do You Want to Know a Secret / For No One / Michelle / Nowhere Man / You've Got to Hide Your Love Away / Across the Universe / All My Loving / Hey Jude **Side 2:** Something / The Fool On the Hill / Till There Was You / The Long and Winding Road / Here Comes the Sun

/ Blackbird / And I Love Her / She's Leaving Home / Here, There, and Everywhere / Let It Be

Reel Music
(Parlophone)   MARCH 29, 1982
Side 1: A Hard Day's Night / I Should Have Known Better / Can't Buy Me Love / And I Love Her / Help! / You've Got to Hide Your Love Away / Ticket to Ride / Magical Mystery Tour **Side 2:** I Am the Walrus / Yellow Submarine / All You Need Is Love / Let It Be / Get Back / the Long and Winding Road

20 Greatest Hits
(Parlophone)   OCTOBER 18, 1982
Side 1: Love Me Do / From Me to You / She Loves You / I Want to Hold Your Hand / Can't Buy Me Love / A Hard Day's Night / I Feel Fine / Ticket to Ride / Help! / Day Tripper / We Can Work It Out **Side 2:** Paperback Writer / Yellow Submarine / Eleanor Rigby / All You Need Is Love / Hello Goodbye / Lady Madonna / Hey Jude / Get Back / The Ballad of John and Yoko

Past Masters, Volume 1
(Parlophone)   MARCH 8, 1988
Love Me Do / From Me to You / Thank You Girl / She Loves You / I'll Get You / I Want to Hold Your Hand / This Boy / Komm, Gib Mir Deine Hand / Sie Liebt Dich / Long Tall Sally / I Call Your Name / Slow Down / Matchbox / I Feel Fine / She's a Woman / Bad Boy / Yes It Is / I'm Down

Past Masters, Volume 2
(Parlophone)   MARCH 8, 1988
Day Tripper / We Can Work It Out / Paperback Writer / Rain / Lady Madonna / The Inner Light / Hey Jude / Revolution (Single Version) / Get Back / Don't Let Me Down / The Ballad of John and Yoko / Old Brown Shoe / Across the Universe / Let It Be / You Know My Name (Look Up the Number)

Live at the BBC
(Apple)   NOVEMBER 30, 1994
Disc 1: From Us to You / I Got a Woman / Too Much Monkey Business / Keep Your Hands Off My Baby / I'll Be On My Way / Young Blood / A Shot of Rhythm and Blues / Sure to Fall (In Love With You) / Some Other Guy / Thank You Girl / Baby It's You / That's All Right (Mama) / Carol / Soldier of Love / Clarabella / I'm Gonna Sit Right Down and Cry (Over You) / Crying, Waiting, Hoping / You Really Got

a Hold On Me / To Know Her Is to Love Her / A Taste of Honey / Long Tall Sally / I Saw Her Standing There / The Honeymoon Song / Johnny B Goode / Memphis, Tennessee / Lucille / Can't Buy Me Love / Till There Was You **Disc 2:** A Hard Day's Night / I Wanna Be Your Man / Roll Over Beethoven / All My Loving / Things We Said Today / She's a Woman / Sweet Little Sixteen / Lonesome Tears in My Eyes / Nothin' Shakin' / The Hippy Hippy Shake / Glad All Over / I Just Don't Understand / So How Come (No One Loves Me) / I Feel Fine / I'm a Loser / Everybody's Trying to Be My Baby / Rock and Roll Music / Ticket to Ride / Dizzy Miss Lizzy / Kansas City / Hey! Hey! Hey! Hey! / Matchbox / I Forgot to Remember to Forget / I Got to Find My Baby / Ooh! My Soul / Don't Ever Change / Slow Down / Honey Don't / Love Me Do

Anthology 1

(Apple)   NOVEMBER 21, 1995

Disc 1: Free as a Bird / That'll Be the Day (The Quarrymen, 1958) / In Spite of All the Danger (The Quarrymen, 1958) / Hallelujah, I Love Her So / You'll Be Mine / Cayenne / My Bonnie (With Tony Sheridan, German Intro) / Aint She Sweet / Cry for a Shadow / Searchin' (Decca Audition) / Three Cool Cats (Decca Audition) / The Sheik of Araby (Decca Audition) / Like Dreamers Do (Decca Audition) / Hello Little Girl (Decca Audition) / Besame Mucho / Love Me Do (First EMI version, with Pete Best) / How Do You Do It / Please Please Me (9 / 11 / 62) / One After 909 (Sequence) (3 / 5 / 63) / One After 909 / Lend Me Your Comb (BBC) / I'll Get You (Sunday Night At the Palladium) / I Saw Here Standing There (Swedish Radio, 10 / 63) / From Me to You (Swedish Radio, 10 / 63) / Money (That's What I Want) (Swedish Radio, 10 / 63) / You Really Got a Hold on Me (Swedish Radio, 10 / 63) / Roll Over Beethoven (Swedish Radio, 10 / 63) **Disc 2:** She Loves You (1963 Royal Command Performance) / Till There Was You (1963 Royal Command Performance) / Twist and Shout (1963 Royal Command Performance) / This Boy (The Morecambe and Wise Show, 12 / 63) / I Want to Hold Your Hand (The Morecambe and Wise Show, 12 / 63) / Moonlight Bay (The Morecambe and Wise Show, 12 / 63) / Can't Buy Me Love (take 2, Paris 1 / 64) / All My Loving (Ed Sullivan) / You Can't Do That (earlier take) / And I Love Her (take 2) / A Hard Day's Night (take 1) / I Wanna Be Your Man (Around the Beatles, 1964) / Long Tall Sally (Around the Beatles, 1964) / Boys (Around the Beatles, 1964, not broadcast) / Shout (Around the Beatles, 1964) / I'll Be Back (take 2) / I'll Be Back (take 3) / You Know What to Do (6 / 94) / No Reply (Demo) / Mr. Moonlight (earlier take) / Leave My Kitten Alone / No Reply (take 2) / Eight Days a Week (Sequence) / Eight Days a Week / Kansas City / Hey Hey Hey Hey (take 2)

Anthology 2

(Apple)   MARCH 18, 1996

Disc 1: Real Love / Yes It Is (take 2) / I'm Down (take 1) / You've Got to Hide Your Love Away (take 5) / If You've Got Trouble / That Means a Lot / Yesterday (take 1) / It's Only Love (take 2) / I Feel Fine (Blackpool Night Out) / Ticket to Ride (Blackpool Night Out) / Yesterday (Blackpool Night Out) / Help! (Blackpool Night Out) / Everybody's Trying to Be My Baby (Shea Stadium) / Norwegian Wood (This Bird Has Flown) (take 1) / I'm Looking through You (first version) / 12-Bar Original / Tomorrow Never Knows (Mark I, Take 1) / Got to Get You into My Life (take 5) / And Your Bird Can Sing (take 2) / Taxman (take 11) / Eleanor Rigby (strings only) / I'm Only Sleeping (rehearsal) / I'm Only Sleeping (take 1) / Rock and Roll Music (Budokan) / She's a Woman (Budokan) **Disc 2:** Strawberry Fields Forever (demo sequence) / Strawberry Fields Forever (take 1) / Strawberry Fields Forever (take 7 and edit piece) / Penny Lane (alternate version) / A Day in the Life (take 2 and take 6 overdub) / Good Morning Good Morning (take 8) / Only a Northern Song (take 3) / Being for the Benefit of Mr. Kite! (takes 1 and 2) / Being for the Benefit of Mr. Kite! (take 7) / Lucy in the Sky with Diamonds (alternate version) / Within You Without You (instrumental) / Sgt. Pepper's Lonely Hearts Club Band (Reprise) (take 5) / You Know My Name (Look Up the Number) (long version) / I Am the Walrus (take 16) / The Fool On the Hill (demo) / Your Mother Should Know (take 27) / The Fool on the Hill (take 4) / Hello, Goodbye (take 16) / Lady Madonna (alternate version) / Across the Universe (take 2)

Anthology 3

(Apple)   OCTOBER 28, 1996

Disc 1: A Beginning / Happiness Is a Warm Gun / Helter Skelter / Mean Mr. Mustard / Polythene Pam / Glass Onion / Junk / Piggies / Honey Pie / Don't Pass Me By / Ob-La-Di, Ob-La-Da / Good Night / Cry Baby Cry / Blackbird / Sexy Sadie / While My Guitar Gently Weeps / Hey Jude / Not Guilty / Mother Nature's Son / Glass Onion / Rocky Raccoon / What's the New Mary Jane / Step Inside Love / Los Paranoias / I'm So Tired / I Will / Why Don't We Do It in the Road / Julia **Disc 2:** I've Got a Feeling / She Came in through the Bathroom Window / Dig a Pony / Two of Us / For You Blue / Teddy Boy / Rip It Up / Shake, Rattle, and Roll / Blue Suede Shoes / The Long and Winding Road / Oh! Darling / All Things Must Pass / Mailman, Bring Me No More Blue / Get Back / Old Brown Shoe / Octopus's Garden / Maxwell's Silver Hammer / Something / Come Together / Come and Get It / Ain't She Sweet / Because / Let It Be / I Me Mine / The End

Yellow Submarine Songtrack
(Apple)   SEPTEMBER 13, 1999
Side 1: Yellow Submarine / Hey Bulldog / Eleanor Rigby / Love You To / All Together Now / Lucy in the Sky with Diamonds / Think for Yourself / Sgt. Pepper's Lonely Hearts Club Band / With a Little Help from My Friends **Side 2:** Baby, You're a Rich Man / Only a Northern Song / All You Need Is Love / When I'm Sixty-Four / Nowhere Man / It's All Too Much

1
(Apple)   NOVEMBER 13, 2000
Love Me Do / From Me to You / She Loves You / I Want to Hold Your Hand / Can't Buy Me Love / A Hard Day's Night / I Feel Fine / Eight Days a Week / Ticket to Ride / Help! / Yesterday / Day Tripper / We Can Work It Out / Paperback Writer / Yellow Submarine / Eleanor Rigby / Penny Lane / All You Need Is Love / Hello Goodbye / Lady Madonna / Hey Jude / Get Back / The Ballad of John and Yoko / Something / Come Together / Let It Be / The Long and Winding Road

Let It Be... Naked
(Apple)   NOVEMBER 17, 2003
Disc 1: Get Back / Dig a Pony / For You Blue / The Long and Winding Road / Two of Us / I've Got a Feeling / One After 909 / Don't Let Me Down / I Me Mine / Across the Universe / Let It Be **Disc 2:** Fly on the Wall (The Beatles at work in the studio during January 1969)

US Albums

Introducing the Beatles
(Vee Jay)   JANUARY 10, 1963
Side 1: I Saw Her Standing There / Misery / Anna (Go to Him) / Chains / Boys / Love Me Do **Side 2:** P.S. I Love You / Baby, It's You / Do You Want to Know a Secret / A Taste of Honey / There's a Place / Twist and Shout

Meet the Beatles!
(Capitol)   JANUARY 20, 1964
Side 1: I Want to Hold Your Hand / I Saw Her Standing There / This Boy / It Won't Be Long / All I've Got to Do / All My Loving **Side 2:** Don't Bother Me / Little Child / Till There Was You / Hold Me Tight / I Wanna Be Your Man / Not a Second Time

The Beatles with Tony Sheridan and Guests

(MGM)   FEBRUARY 3,1964

My Bonnie / Cry for a Shadow / When the Saints Go Marching In / Why / (additional tracks by Tony Sheridan and the Beat Brothers; the Titans)

Introducing the Beatles

(Vee Jay)   FEBRUARY 10, 1964

Side 1: I Saw Her Standing There / Misery / Anna (Go to Him) / Chains / Boys / Ask Me Why **Side 2:** Please Please Me / Baby, It's You / Do You Want to Know a Secret / A Taste of Honey / There's a Place / Twist and Shout

Jolly What! the Beatles & Frank Ifield on Stage

(Vee Jay)   FEBRUARY 20, 1964

Please Please Me / From Me to You / Ask Me Why / Thank You Girl / (additional tracks by Frank Ifield)

The Beatles' Second Album

(Capitol)   APRIL 10, 1964

Side 1: Roll Over Beethoven / Thank You Girl / You Really Got a Hold On Me / Devil in Her Heart / Money / You Can't Do That **Side 2:** Long Tall Sally / I Call Your Name / Please Mr. Postman / I'll Get You / She Loves You

A Hard Day's Night

(United Artists)   JUNE 13, 1964

Side 1: A Hard Day's Night / Tell Me Why / I'll Cry Instead / I Should Have Known Better (Instrumental) / I'm Happy Just to Dance With You / And I Love Her (Instrumental) **Side 2:** I Should Have Known Better / If I Fell / And I Love Her / Ringo's Theme—This Boy (Instrumental) / Can't Buy Me Love / A Hard Day's Night (Instrumental)

Something New

(Capitol)   JULY 20, 1964

Side 1: I'll Cry Instead / Things We Said Today / Any Time at All / When I Get Home / Slow Down / Matchbox **Side 2:** Tell Me Why / And I Love Her / I'm Happy Just to Dance With You / If I Fell / Komm, Gib Mir Deine Hand

Songs, Pictures and Stories of the Fabulous Beatles

(Vee Jay)   JULY, 1964

Same as *Introducing the Beatles* (1964)

The Beatles Vs the Four Seasons
(Vee Jay)   AUGUST, 1964
Disc 1: Same as *Introducing the Beatles* (1964) **Disc 2:** Additional tracks by the Four Seasons

Ain't She Sweet
(Atco)   OCTOBER 5, 1964
Side 1: Ain't She Sweet / Sweet Georgia Brown (with Tony Sheridan) / Take Out Some Insurance on Me, Baby (with Tony Sheridan) / Nobody's Child (with Tony Sheridan) **Side 2:** Additional tracks by the Swallows.

The Beatles' Story
(Capitol)   NOVEMBER, 23 1964
Narrated story of the Beatles, with excerpts of interviews.

Beatles '65
(Capitol)   DECEMBER 15, 1965
Side 1: No Reply / I'm a Loser / Baby's in Black / Rock and Roll Music / I'll Follow the Sun / Mr. Moonlight **Side 2:** Honey Don't / I'll Be Back / She's a Woman / I Feel Fine / Everybody's Trying to Be My Baby

The Early Beatles
(Capitol)   MARCH 22, 1965
Side 1: Love Me Do / Twist and Shout / Anna (Go to Him) / Chains / Boys / Ask Me Why **Side 2:** Please Please Me / P.S. I Love You / Baby, It's You / A Taste of Honey / Do You Want to Know a Secret

Beatles VI
(Capitol)   JUNE 14, 1965
Side 1: Kansas City—Hey Hey Hey Hey / Eight Days a Week / You Like Me Too Much / Bad Boy / I Don't Want to Spoil the Party / Words of Love **Side 2:** What You're Doing / Yes It Is / Dizzy Miss Lizzy / Tell Me What You See / Every Little Thing

Help!
(Capitol)   AUGUST 13, 1965
Side 1: James Bond Theme (Instrumental) / Help! / The Night Before / From Me to You Fantasy (Instrumental) / You've Got to Hide Your Love Away / I Need You / In the Tyrol (Instrumental) **Side 2:** Another Girl / Another Hard Day's Night (Instrumental) / Ticket to Ride / The Bitter End / You Can't Do That (Instumental / You're Gonna Lose That Girl / The Chase (Instrumental)

Rubber Soul
(Capitol)   DECEMBER 6, 1965
Side 1: I've Just Seen a Face / Norwegian Wood (This Bird Has Flown) / You Won't See Me / Think For Yourself / The Word / Michelle **Side 2:** It's Only Love / Girl / I'm Looking through You / In My Life / Wait / Run for Your Life

"Yesterday" …And Today
(Capitol)   JUNE 20, 1965
Side 1: Drive My Car / I'm Only Sleeping / Nowhere Man / Dr. Robert / Yesterday / Act Naturally **Side 2:** And Your Bird Can Sing / If I Needed Someone / We Can Work It Out / What Goes On? / Day Tripper

Revolver
(Capitol)   AUGUST 8,1966
Side 1: Taxman / Eleanor Rigby / Love You To / Here, There, and Everywhere / Yellow Submarine / She Said, She Said **Side 2:** Good Day Sunshine / For No One / I Want to Tell You / Got to Get You into My Life / Tomorrow Never Knows

Sgt Pepper's Lonely Hearts Club Band
(Capitol)   JUNE 2, 1967
Same as UK release.

Magical Mystery Tour
(Capitol)   NOVEMBER 27, 1967
Side 1: Magical Mystery Tour / The Fool on the Hill / Flying / Blue Jay Way / Your Mother Should Know / I Am the Walrus **Side 2:** Hello, Goodbye / Strawberry Fields Forever / Penny Lane / Baby You're a Rich Man / All You Need Is Love

The Beatles
(Apple [a.k.a. "The White Album")   NOVEMBER 25, 1968
Same as UK release.

Yellow Submarine
(Apple)   JANUARY 13, 1969
Same as UK release.

Abbey Road
(Apple)   OCTOBER 1, 1969
Same as UK release.

Hey Jude
(Apple)   FEBRUARY 26, 1970
Side 1: Can't Buy Me Love / I Should Have Known Better / Paperback Writer / Rain / Lady Madonna / Revolution **Side 2:** Hey Jude / Old Brown Shoe / Don't Let Me Down / The Ballad of John and Yoko

The Beatles – In the Beginning, Circa 1960
(Polydor)   MAY 4, 1970
Ain't She Sweet / Cry For a Shadow / My Bonnie / Take Out Some Insurance on Me, Baby / Sweet Georgia Brown / The Saints / Why / Nobody's Child / (additional tracks by Tony Sheridan and the Beat Brothers)

Let It Be
(Apple)   MAY 18, 1970
Same as UK release.

The Beatles / 1962-1966
(Apple [a.k.a. "The Red Album"])   APRIL 2, 1973
Same as UK release.

The Beatles / 1967-1970
(Apple [a.k.a. "The Blue Album"])   APRIL 2, 1973
Same as UK release.

Rock 'n' Roll Music
(Capitol)   JUNE 7, 1976
Same as UK release.

The Beatles at the Hollywood Bowl
(Capitol)   MAY 4, 1977
Same as UK release.

Live! At the Star-Club in Hamburg, Germany 1962
(Lingasong)   JUNE 13, 1977
Side 1: I'm Gonna Sit Right Down and Cry (Over You) / Roll Over Beethoven / Hippy Hippy Shake / Sweet Little Sixteen / Lend Me Your Comb / Your Feets Too Big **Side 2:** Where Have You Been All My Life / Mr. Moonlight / A Taste of Honey / Besame Mucho / Till There Was You / Kansas City / Hey Hey Hey **Side 3:** Ain't Nothing Shakin' (Like the Leaves on a Tree) / To Know Her Is to Love Her / Little Queenie / Falling in Love Again / Sheila / Be-Bop-A-Lula / Hallelujah, I Love Her So **Side 4:** Red Sails in the Sunset / Everybody's Trying to Be My

Baby / Matchbox / Talkin 'Bout You / Shimmy Shake / Long Tall Sally / I Remember You

Love Songs
(Capitol)   OCTOBER 21, 1977
Same as UK release.

The Beatles Collection
(Capitol)   DECEMBER 1, 1978
Same as UK release.

Rarities
(Capitol)   MARCH 24, 1980
Side 1: Love Me Do / Misery / There's a Place / Sie Liebt Dich / And I Love Her / Help! / I'm Only Sleeping / I Am the Walrus **Side 2:** Penny Lane / Helter Skelter / Don't Pass Me By / The Inner Light / Across the Universe / You Know My Name (Look Up the Number) / Sgt. Pepper Inner Groove

Reel Music
(Capitol)   MARCH 22, 1982
Same as UK release.

20 Greatest Hits
(Capitol)   OCTOBER 11, 1982
Side 1: She Loves You / Love Me Do / I Want to Hold Your Hand / Can't Buy Me Love / A Hard Day's Night / I Feel Fine / Eight Days a Week / Ticket to Ride / Help! / Yesterday / We Can Work It Out **Side 2:** Paperback Writer / Penny Lane / All You Need Is Love / Hello Goodbye / Hey Jude / Get Back / Come Together / Let It Be / The Long and Winding Road

Past Masters Volume 1
(Capitol)   MARCH 7, 1988
Same as UK release.

Past Masters Volume 2
(Parlophone)   MARCH 8, 1988
Same as UK release.

Live at the BBC
(Apple)   DECEMBER 6, 1994
Same as UK release.

Anthology 1
(Apple)   NOVEMBER 21, 1995
Same as UK release.

Anthology 2
(Apple)   MARCH 19, 1996
Same as UK release.

Anthology 3
(Apple)   OCTOBER 29, 1996
Same as UK release.

Yellow Submarine Songtrack
(Apple)   SEPTEMBER 14, 1999
Yellow Submarine / Hey Bulldog / Eleanor Rigby / Love You To / All
Together Now / Lucy in the Sky with Diamonds / Think for Yourself /
Sgt. Pepper's Lonely Hearts Club Band / With a Little Help from My
Friends / Baby, You're a Rich Man / Only a Northern Song / All You
Need Is Love / When I'm Sixty-Four / Nowhere Man / It's All Too
Much

1
(Apple)   NOVEMBER 14, 2000
Same as UK release.

Let It Be... Naked
(Apple)   NOVEMBER 17, 2003
Same as UK release.

The Beatles Capitol Albums, Vol. 1
(Capitol)   NOVEMBER 16, 2004
Stereo and mono mixes of the Beatles' first four Capitol albums (*Meet
the Beatles, The Beatles' Second Album, Something New, Beatles '65*)

Not a Second Time

SONGS COVERED BY
THE BEATLES

NOTE: The artist listed for each song is the artist whose version of the song the Beatles covered, not necessarily the original artist. When it's not clear which version of a song the Beatles covered, the song is listed under 'Various' along with the most likely sources for the Beatles.

The information comes from Mark Lewisohn, *The Complete Beatles Chronicle* (London: Pyramid, 1992), pp. 361–65.

ARTHUR ALEXANDER

"Anna (Go to Him)" (1962)
"A Shot of Rhythm and Blues" (1962)
"Soldier of Love (Lay Down Your Arms)" (1962)
"Where Have You Been All My Life" (1962)

RITCHIE BARRETT

"Some Other Guy" (1962)

CHUCK BERRY

"Almost Grown" (1959)
"Carol" (1958)
"I Got to Find My Baby" (1960)
"I'm Talking About You" (1961)
"Johnny B. Goode " (1958)
"Little Queenie" (1959)
"Maybellene" (1955)
"Memphis, Tennessee" (1959)

"Reelin' and Rockin'" (1958)
"Rock and Roll Music" (1957)
"Roll Over Beethoven" (1956)
"Sweet Little Sixteen" (1956)
"Thirty Days" (1955)
"Too Much Monkey Business" (1956)
"Vacation Time" (1958)

PAT BOONE

"Begin The Beguine" (1957)
"Don't Forbid Me" (1957)

GARY US BONDS

"New Orleans" (1961)
"Quarter to Three" (1961)

JOE BROWN AND THE BRUVVERS

"Darktown Strutters' Ball" (1960)
"I'm Henry the Eighth I Am" (1961)
"A Picture of You" (1962)
"The Sheik of Araby" (1961)
"What a Crazy World We're Living In" (1962)

THE JOHNNY BURNETTE TRIO

"Lonesome Tears in My Eyes" (1956)

FREDDY CANNON

"Buzz Buzz a Diddle-It" (1961)

JOHNNY CASH

"All Over Again" (1958)

THE CHAMPS

"Tequila" (1958)

BRUCE CHANNEL

"Hey! Baby" (1962)

RAY CHARLES

"Don't Let the Sun Catch You Crying" (1960)

"A Fool for You" (1959)
"Hallelujah I Love Her So" (1956)
"Hit the Road Jack" (1961)
"Sticks and Stones" (1960)
"What'd I Say" (1959)

THE COASTERS

"Besame Mucho" (1960)
"Searchin'" (1957)
"Three Cool Cats" (1959)
"Thumbin' a Ride" (1961)
"Yakety Yak" (1958)
"Youngblood" (1957)

EDDIE COCHRAN

"C'mon Everybody" (1959)
"I Remember" (1959)
"Teenage Heaven" (1959)
"Three Steps to Heaven" (1960)
"Twenty Flight Rock" (1957)

BOBBY COMSTOCK

"Let's Stomp" (1963)

SAM COOKE

"Bring It Home to Me" (1962)

THE COOKIES

"Chains" (1962)

THE CRICKETS

"Don't Ever Change" (1962)

JOEY DEE AND THE STARLITERS

"Hey Let's Twist" (1962)
"Peppermint Twist" (1962)

THE DEL-VIKINGS

"Come Go with Me" (1957)

Bo Diddley

"Crackin' Up" (1959)
"Road Runner" (1960)

Marlene Dietrich

"Falling in Love Again (Can't Help It)" (1930)

Fats Domino

"Ain't That a Shame" (1955)
"Coquette" (1958)
"I Know" (1955)
"I Will Always Be in Love with You" (1960)
"I'm Gonna Be a Wheel Someday" (1959)
"I'm in Love Again" (1956)

The Donays

"(There's a) Devil in Her Heart" (1962)

Lonnie Donegan and his Skiffle Group

"Corrine, Corrina" (1960)
"The Cumberland Gap" (1957)
"Railroad Bill" (1956)
"Rock Island Line" (1954)

Ral Donner

"You Don't Know What You Got" (1961)

Lee Dorsey

"Ya Ya" (1961)

Craig Douglass

"Time" (1961)

Dr. Feelgood and the Interns

"Mr. Moonlight" (1962)

The Drifters

"Save The Last Dance For Me" (1960)
"When My Little Girl Is Smiling" (1962)

DUANE EDDY AND THE REBELS

"Movin' and Groovin'" (1959)
"Ramrod" (1958)
"Three-Thirty Blues" (1959)

RAMBLIN' JACK ELLIOTT

"San Francisco Bay Blues" (1960)

THE EVERLY BROTHERS

"Cathy's Clown" (1960)
"I Wonder if I Care as Much" (1957)
"Love of My Life" (1959)
"So How Come (No One Loves Me)" (1960)

EDDIE FONTAINE

"Nothin' Shakin' (But the Leaves on the Trees)" (1958)

BOBBY FREEMAN

"Do You Want to Dance" (1958)
"Shimmy Shimmy" (1960)
"You Don't Understand Me" (1960)

LIONEL HAMPTON AND HIS ORCHESTRA

"Hey Ba-Ba-Re-Bop" (1946)

JET HARRIS

"Diamonds" (1963, with Tony Meehan)
"Main Title Theme" (1962)

RONNIE HAWKINS

"Red Hot" (1959)

BUDDY HOLLY

"Crying, Waiting, Hoping" (1959)
"Everyday" (1957, with the Crickets)
"It's So Easy" (1958, with the Crickets)
"Mailman, Bring Me No More Blues" (1957, with the Crickets)
"Maybe Baby" (1958, with the Crickets)
"Midnight Shift" (1956, with the Crickets)

"Peggy Sue" (1957)
"Raining in My Heart" (1959)
"Reminiscing" (1962)
"That'll Be the Day" (1957, with the Crickets)
"Think It Over" (1958, with the Crickets)
"Words of Love" (1957)

FRANK IFIELD

"I Remember You" (1962)

THE ISLEY BROTHERS

"Shout" (1959)
"Twist And Shout" (1962)

THE JODIMARS

"Clarabella" (1956)

DAVY JONES

"Mighty Man" (1960)

BILL JUSTIS AND HIS ORCHESTRA

"Raunchy" (1957)

THE KALIN TWINS

"When" (1958)

JOHNNY KIDD AND THE PIRATES

"Shakin' All Over" (1960)
"Weep No More My Baby" (1960)

BEN E. KING

"Stand By Me" (1961)

BUDDY KNOX

"Open (Your Lovin' Arms)" (1962)

THE LAFAYETTES

"Nobody but You" (1962)

BRENDA LEE

"Fool Number One" (1961)

JACKIE LEE AND THE RAINDROPS

"There's No One in the Whole Wide World" (1962)

PEGGY LEE

"Till There Was You" (1961)

BOBBY LEWIS

"One Track Mind" (1961)

JERRY LEE LEWIS

"Down the Line" (1958)
"Fools Like Me" (1959)
"Great Balls of Fire" (1957)
"High School Confidential" (1958)
"It'll Be Me" (1957)
"Livin' Lovin' Wreck" (1961)
"Whole Lotta Shakin' Goin' On" (1957)

LITTLE EVA

"Keep Your Hands Off My Baby" (1963)
"The Loco-Motion" (1962)

LITTLE RICHARD

"Can't Believe You Wanna Leave" (1957)
"Good Golly Miss Molly" (1958)
"Kansas City/Hey-Hey-Hey-Hey!" (1959)
"Long Tall Sally" (1956)
"Lucille" (1957)
"Miss Ann" (1956)
"Ooh! My Soul" (1958)
"Ready Teddy" (1956)
"Rip It Up" (1956)
"Send Me Some Lovin'" (1957)
"Tutti Frutti" (1957)

VERA LYNN

"A House with Love in It" (1956)

THE MARATHONS

"Peanut Butter" (1961)

ANN MARGARET

"I Just Don't Understand" (1961)

MARINO MARINI AND HIS QUARTET

"The Honeymoon Song" (1959)

THE MARVELETTES

"Please Mister Postman" (1961)

CHAS McDEVITT SKIFFLE GROUP FEATURING NANCY WHISKEY

"Freight Train" (1957)

THE McGUIRE SISTERS

"Moonglow and the Theme From *Picnic*" (1956)

THE OLYMPICS

"(Baby) Hully Gully" (1959)
"I Wish I Could Shimmy Like My Sister Kate" (1961)
"Well . . . (Baby Please Don't Go)" (1958)

ROY ORBISON

"Dream Baby (How Long Must I Dream?)" (1962)

BUCK OWENS

"Act Naturally" (1963)

BOBBY PARKER

"Watch Your Step" (1961)

LES PAUL WITH MARY FORD

"How High the Moon" (1951)
"The World Is Waiting for the Sunrise" (1953)

CARL PERKINS

"Blue Suede Shoes" (1956)

"Boppin' the Blues" (1956)
"Everybody's Trying to Be My Baby" (1958)
"Glad All Over" (1957)
"Gone, Gone, Gone" (1959)
"Honey Don't" (1956)
"Lend Me Your Comb" (1957)
"Matchbox" (1957)
"Sure to Fall (In Love with You)" (1956)
"Tennessee" (1956)
"Your True Love" (1957)

ELVIS PRESLEY

"All Shook Up" (1957)
"Are You Lonesome Tonight" (1961)
"Baby Let's Play House" (1955)
"Blue Moon of Kentucky" (1954)
"Don't Be Cruel" (1956)
"Heartbreak Hotel" (1956)
"(Marie's the Name of) His Latest Flame" (1961)
"Hound Dog" (1956)
"I Feel So Bad" (1961)
"I Forgot to Remember to Forget" (1955)
"I'll Never Let You Go (Little Darlin')" (1958)
"I'm Gonna Sit Right Down and Cry (Over You)" (1956)
"It's Now or Never" (1960)
"Jailhouse Rock" (1958)
"Just Because" (1956)
"Lawdy Miss Clawdy" (1956)
"Love Me Tender" (1956)
"Loving You" (1957)
"Mystery Train" (1955)
"Party" (1957)
"That's All Right (Mama)" (1954)
"That's When Your Heartaches Begin" (1957)
"Tonight Is Right for Love" (1960)
"Wild in the Country" (1961)
"Wooden Heart" (1960)

JOHNNY PRESTON

"Leave My Kitten Alone" (1961)

LLOYD PRICE

"Mailman Blues" (1954)

JAMES RAY

"If You Gotta Make A Fool of Somebody" (1961)
"September Song" (1959)

CLIFF RICHARD AND THE SHADOWS

"Dream" (1961)

SMOKEY ROBINSON AND THE MIRACLES

"You Really Got a Hold on Me" (1962)

TOMMY ROE

"Sheila" (1962)

CHAN ROMERO

"The Hippy Hippy Shake" (1959)

THE ROOFTOP SINGERS

"Walk Right In" (1963)

THE SHADOWS

"Apache" (1960)

DEL SHANNON

"Runaway" (1961)

THE SHIRELLES

"Baby It's You" (1961)
"Boys" (1960)
"Love Is a Swingin' Thing" (1962)
"Mama Said" (1961)
"Will You Love Me Tomorrow?" (1961)

ARTHUR SMITH AND HIS CRACKERJACKS

"Guitar Boogie" (1946)

BARRET STRONG

"Money (That's What I Want)" (1959)

THE TEDDY BEARS

"To Know Her Is to Love Her" (1958)

JOE TURNER

"Honey Hush" (1953)
"Red Sails in the Sunset" (1959)

BOBBY VEE

"Love Love Love" (1961)
"Sharing You" (1962)
"Take Good Care of My Baby" (1961)

THE VENTURES

"Walk Don't Run" (1960)

GENE VINCENT AND HIS BLUE CAPS

"Baby Blue" (1958)
"Be-Bop-a-Lula" (1956)
"Dance in the Street" (1958)
"Hey, Good Lookin'" (1958)
"Lazy River" (1956)
"Over the Rainbow" (1959)
"Say Mama" (1959)
"Summertime" (1958)
"Time Will Bring You Everything" (1958)
"The Wayward Wind" (1958)
"Wedding Bells" (1957)
"Wild Cat" (1959)

THE VIPERS SKIFFLE GROUP

"No Other Baby" (1958)

DINAH WASHINGTON

"September In The Rain" (1961)

LENNY WELCH

"A Taste of Honey" (1962)

HANK WILLIAMS

"Honky Tonk Blues" (1952)

LARRY WILLIAMS

"Bad Boy" (1959)
"Bony Maronie" (1957)
"Dizzy Miss Lizzy" (1958)
"Peaches and Cream" (1959)
"Short Fat Fanny" (1957)
"Slow Down" (1958)

MAURICE WILLIAMS AND THE ZODIACS

"Stay" (1960)

VARIOUS

"Ain't She Sweet" (Gene Vincent and his Blue Caps [1956] and
   Duffy Power [1959])
"Baby I Don't Care (You're So Square)" (Elvis Presley [1957] and
   Buddy Holly [1958])
"Beautiful Dreamer" (composed by Stephen Foster [1862])
"España Cañi (Spanish Gypsy Dance)" (Traditional)
"Good Rockin' Tonight" (Roy Brown [1947], Wynonie Harris
   [1947] and Elvis Presley [1954])
"Harry Lime (*Third Man* Theme)" (Anton Karas [1949] and Chet
   Atkins [1960])
"Heavenly" (Conway Twitty [1959]) and Emile Ford and the
   Checkmates [1960])
"I Got a Woman" (Ray Charles [1955] and Elvis Presley [1956])
"It's a Long Way to Tipperary" (Traditional)
"Jambalaya (On the Bayou)" (Hank Williams [1952] and Jerry Lee
   Lewis [1959])
"Maggie May" (Traditional)
"Mean Woman Blues" (Jerry Lee Lewis [1957] and Elvis Presley
   [1957])
"Midnight Special (Prisoner's Song)" (Traditional and Lonnie
   Donegan and his Skiffle Group [1957])
"More than I Can Say" (The Crickets [1960] and Bobby Vee [1961])
"My Bonnie Lies Over the Ocean" (Ray Charles [1958] and Tony
   Sheridan with the Beatles [1961])
"True Love" (Bing Crosby and Grace Kelly [1956] and Elvis
   Presley [1957])
"When the Saints Go Marching In" (Jerry Lee Lewis [1958] and
   Fats Domino [1959])
"Worried Man Blues" (Lonnie Donegan and his Skiffle Group
   [1955] and The Vipers Skiffle Group [1957])

"You Win Again" (Hank Williams [1952] and Jerry Lee Lewis [1958])

"Your Feets Too Big" (Fats Waller [1939] and Chubby Checker [1961])

Evil All—It's Siluap!
Those Hidden Clues

COMPILED BY MICHAEL CAPUTO

For further fascinating commentary on the "Paul is Dead" mystery, readers may wish to consult: *The Walrus Was Paul: The Great Beatle Death Clues*, by R. Gary Patterson (New York: Simon and Schuster, 1998); http://www.iamthebeatles.com; http://www.paul-is-dead.com; and http://www.turnmeondeadman.net/index.html.

Clues in the Albums

Sgt. Pepper's Lonely Hearts Club Band (released June 1st 1967 in the U.K. and June 2nd 1967 in the U.S.A.)

- On the front of the album cover, a crowd of famous people are gathered together as if posing for a photograph, and immediately in front of them is what appears to be a freshly-dug grave.

- The red hyacinths which adorn the grave spell the band name, "Beatles." "The" has dropped out of the name, which suggests that "The Beatles" are not present. Also, the flowers placed just before the word "Beatles" can be seen as forming the numeral 3 (as if to suggest that there are now only three Beatles, not four).

- Shown on the grave are yellow hyacinths arranged in the shape of a left-handed bass guitar (the instrument played by Paul). The bass guitar (which usually has four strings) has only three strings, suggesting that the Beatles (which used to have four members) now have only three members. Furthermore, if one views the yellow hyacinths with a discerning eye, they can be seen to spell out the mysterious message, "Paul?"

- One can see, towards the left of the grave, a doll with a crack in its head, apparently alluding to the head injury which Paul suffered in the car crash that allegedly killed him.

- On the right side of the grave sits a Shirley Temple doll wearing a "Welcome the Rolling Stones" sweatshirt, implying that, with Paul's death, the Rolling Stones will supplant the Beatles as the generation's leading rock'n'roll band.

- The small model car perched on the right leg of the Shirley Temple doll looks like an Aston Martin convertible, the car that Paul was allegedly driving when he had his fatal crash. Furthermore, the model car's interior is red, which is the color of fresh blood.

- Right next to the left leg of the Shirley Temple doll, there is a left-handed driving glove stained with blood (and Paul was left-handed).

- Also on the right side of the grave, below the Shirley Temple doll, one can see another model car, this one in flames and plunging into the grave.

- Towards the right of the grave and below the image of Marilyn Monroe, there is television set with a darkened screen, representing the lack of media coverage and information regarding Paul's death.

- Standing in front of the grave is a small statue of a Hindu goddess, with arms apparently pointing at Paul and the wax figure of Paul. Some claim that this statue represents Kali the Destroyer, thus indicating that Paul has been singled out for destruction.

- Also on the album cover, Paul is depicted as being taller than the other Beatles, while in real life he was not the tallest Beatle.

- Paul's hand is placed over his heart, a religious gesture for the blessing of the dead. Also, from behind Paul, an open hand is seen being raised above Paul's head. In some societies, this gesture means that the person is dead or is about to die.

- While John, George, and Ringo hold bright brass instruments, Paul's instrument is black and made of wood. Furthermore, the left hand by which he holds his instrument displays only three fingers, indicating the number of surviving Beatles left.

- Paul's instrument is a *cor anglais* (English horn), and unlike the instruments held by the other Beatles, it is not an instrument used in a marching band. However, there is a brass tuba sitting at the feet of the wax figure of Ringo. The tuba is an instrument used in a marching band, and the tuba at Ringo's feet is presumably the tuba that Paul would be holding (to match the instruments of the other Beatles) if he were alive.

- In the group of wax figures of the Beatles, Paul is shown with his right hand on the shoulder of a saddened Ringo, apparently comforting Ringo who is grieving Paul's death.

- At the feet of the Beatles and immediately above the grave, the skin of the bass drum presents the album title. Close observation (and a small flat mirror) will reveal that the drum skin may serve as tombstone for the grave. If the edge of a small, straight-edged mirror is placed against the album cover (horizontally with the reflecting surface upwards, forming a right angle with the surface of the album cover and aligned precisely with the horizontal diameter of the bass drum's skin, so that only the upper half of the letters, "Lonely Hearts," is reflected in the mirror), then the words "Lonely Hearts" will form a peculiar image: "1 ONE I X HE ◊ DIE". The numbers (1 ONE I X) allegedly refer to the date of Paul's death. Thus, the 1 and ONE together represent the number eleven, while the I and X together form the Roman numeral IX, or nine. The message would then be either: "11 September, HE ◊ DIE" (according to the European convention for representing dates), or "November 9, HE ◊ DIE" (according to the American convention). A case can be made for reading the date according to the American convention, since November 9th, 1966, was a Wednesday, and other clues suggest that Paul was killed on a Wednesday. Another possible interpretation is that the 1, ONE, and I refer to the each of the three living Beatles, while the X refers to the missing one. "HE DIE" apparently refers to Paul's death, since the ◊ appears to be an arrow pointing directly upwards to Paul.

- On the centerfold of the album jacket, Paul's uniform is decorated with a patch bearing the letters "O.P.D.," which—according to some accounts—represent an abbreviation used by the British police for: "officially pronounced dead."

- On the back of the album cover, Paul is photographed with his back towards the viewer, while the other three Beatles are facing

forwards. Also, it appears that the other three Beatles are strategi-
cally positioned to support Paul in a standing position, since he
apparently cannot stand upright on his own.

- On the back of the album cover, each of the other Beatles (but not
  Paul) appears to be using his hands to form a letter. In order moving from left to right: George makes an "L" with his hand, Paul
  stands with his back to the viewer, John makes a "V" with his
  hands, and Ringo makes an "E" with his hands. The implication is
  that the Beatles would like to spell out the word, "LOVE," but are
  unable to do so because the real Paul (and the letter "O") are missing.

- Also on the back of the album cover, three black buttons adorn
  Paul's coat, indicating the number of real Beatles still alive.

- On the back of the album cover, the album's song lyrics are printed
  by being superimposed over the photograph of the Beatles, and
  the precise placement of specific lyrics seems to be significant. For
  example, the words "Without You" appear immediately to the right
  of Paul's head. In addition, George seems to point his finger
  directly at the first line from the song, "She's Leaving Home." This
  first line refers to the day and time of Paul's alleged death
  ("Wednesday morning at five o'clock").

- The singer (Paul) who voices the first words heard on the *Sgt.
  Pepper* album, announces that he does not want to "stop the
  show," and then promptly introduces "Billy Shears." "Billy Shears"
  is thought to stand for "William Shears Campbell," the name of the
  Paul look-alike, or impostor, who supposedly replaced Paul after
  his death.

- The album's second song, "A Little Help from My Friends," is presented as being sung by Billy Shears, and the first lines of this song
  suggest that the singer is himself a phony or an impostor, since he
  (unlike Paul) has to worry about singing out of tune.

- The song, "A Day in the Life," appears to reveal information about
  Paul's death, as it refers to a man who sustained fatal head injuries
  in a car accident, since he apparently ran a red light (having failed
  to notice that the traffic light had changed). The dead man was
  famous, as people had seen his face before. The song goes on to
  suggest that the person may have been a politician (perhaps from
  the House of Lords), but then immediately casts doubt on this

hypothesis (for nobody was sure). If one listens carefully, the line that John apparently sings about the House of Lords, is really a line about the "House of Paul."

Magical Mystery Tour (released November 27th 1967 in the U.S.A. and November 19th 1976 in the U.K.)

- The song, "I Am the Walrus," is about death or about someone who is dead; for in Scandinavian cultures, the walrus is traditionally understood to be a harbinger of death. The song's full title is printed on the inside front cover of the *Magical Mystery Tour* album: "I Am the Walrus ('No you're not!' said Little Nicola)." So even though it is John who sings "I Am the Walrus," the walrus (and death) should not be associated with John, but rather with another Beatle. The most likely candidate is Paul, who co-wrote the song with John. Throughout the song, John repeatedly sings, "I'm crying."

- On the *Magical Mystery Tour* album cover, the four Beatles are disguised in animal costumes; three of the costumes are light-colored, while one costume—that of a walrus—is black. Even though John sang "I Am the Walrus" on this album, the album cover shows one of the light-costumed Beatles wearing John's trademark gold-rimmed glasses (indicating, once again, that John is not the walrus).

- On page three of the booklet contained within the album, a still frame from the *Magical Mystery Tour* film depicts Paul sitting at a desk on top of which there is (immediately in front of him) a sign reading, "I was." In the same scene, two British flags are seen on the wall above Paul's head, crossed as they would be in a military funeral.

- On page six of the album booklet, another still frame from the *Magical Mystery Tour* film shows John standing behind a counter and selling tickets for the Magical Mystery Tour. Next to him there is a sign which reads, "The best way to go is by M&D Co." According to one popular account, the "M&D Co." was a funeral parlor. Also in this still frame, the time to "depart" is posted on a board behind John; but there is no time posted to "arrive back."

- On page eight of the album booklet, a still photograph from the movie shows several people sitting at tables in a dining hall. If one turns the photograph ninety degrees clockwise and squints to look at it, one can discern the image of a skull (the mouth of the skull is formed by the part in the blonde woman's hair).

- On page nine of the album booklet, the song title, "Fool on the Hill," appears next to a cartoon image of Paul. The second "L" in the word "hill" trails off to become a jagged shape which is superimposed on Paul's head, resembling a severe head wound.

- A group picture of the Beatles appears on pages twelve and thirteen of the album booklet. The orange-colored skin of Ringo's bass drum appears to be painted with a message in yellow: "Love the 3 Beatles." Also, one sees that Paul is not wearing shoes (but only socks) in this group picture. On the ground next to him is a pair of shoes covered with what appears to be blood.

- On page twenty-three of the album booklet, there is a still photograph from the film showing the four Beatles in white suits, all wearing carnations. John, George, and Ringo are wearing red carnations, while the color of Paul's carnation is black.

- On page twenty-four of the album booklet, a still photograph from the film shows Paul and several other people with their hands raised in the air. One of their hands appears directly above Paul's head (like the hand above his head on the *Sgt. Pepper* album cover), indicating that Paul is a dead man, or fated for death.

- According to some accounts, the strange and oft-repeated phrase, "Goo goo g'joob," comes from James Joyce's *Finnegans Wake*; in Joyce's novel, these are supposedly the last words attributed to Humpty Dumpty before his fall. The fatal injuries suffered by Humpty Dumpty parallel the fatal injuries suffered by the other "eggman," Paul, in his car accident.

- In the song, "I Am the Walrus," the phrase "Stupid bloody Tuesday" may refer to the night before Paul's fatal accident. According to this theory, Tuesday, November 8th, 1966, is a "stupid bloody Tuesday," since it is the night on which Paul stormed angrily out of the recording studio after a heated argument with the other Beatles. After leaving the recording studio, Paul got into his car and drove around for some time before getting into a fatal crash (on Wednesday morning, around five o'clock).

- During the fade-out of "I Am the Walrus", actors reciting lines from *King Lear* are heard. Some of the audible phrases include: "What, is he dead?" "Bury my body!" and "O, untimely death!"

- When the chorus of "Blue Jay Way" is played backwards, one can apparently hear the phrases, "He said 'get me out.' Paul is what is. Paul is Hare Krishna, it seems. Paul is bloody."

- As the song "Strawberry Fields Forever" fades out, one hears John's voice apparently saying, "I buried Paul." Years later, both John and Paul (or Paul's look-alike impostor) claimed that the statement was not "I buried Paul," but only "Cranberry sauce."

The Beatles (or "The White Album") (released November 22nd 1968 in the U.K. and November 25th 1968 in the U.S.A)

- In the close-up photograph found on the album's original center-fold lyric sheet, Paul is seen with small scars around his upper lip. These scars were not noticeable in photographs taken prior to this date, suggesting that it is not Paul, but Paul's impostor, in the photograph.

- The lyric sheet also includes a photograph of Paul lying in a bathtub. Paul is lying face-up, with his hair floating loosely and limply in the water, resembling a corpse.

- Also on the lyric sheet, there is a photograph of Paul standing and apparently being grabbed from behind by a pair of long, whitish, boney hands (which may be the hands of death).

- The lyric sheet also includes a photograph of Paul wearing glasses and a mustache. According to some accounts, this is not a photograph of Paul, but rather of Paul's impostor (prior to undergoing the plastic surgery which made him appear more like Paul).

- At the end of the song "I'm So Tired" and just before "Blackbird" begins, John says something unintelligible. When played backwards, John's voice seems to be saying, "Paul is dead, man. Miss him, miss him. . . ."

- The song "Don't Pass Me By" includes a line about someone who was in a car crash and lost his hair—allegedly referring to the automobile accident in which Paul sustained head injuries which killed him and caused him to lose his trademark Beatles mop-top.

- During the fade-out of "While My Guitar Gently Weeps," George seems to be moaning, "Paul, Paul."

- In the song "Revolution 9," one can hear the sound of a car crashing and a voice calling for help.

- The song "Revolution 9" features a voice repeating the words, "number nine" several times. If played backwards, the voice seems to be saying, "turn me on, dead man." Other sounds that can be heard when the song is played backward include: a blazing fire, an ambulance arriving at the scene, and a funeral choir. At one point in the song, John says the word "right" three times. If, at this point in the song, one turns the right-left balance knob all the way to the right (so that the left speaker is no longer heard), then one can hear John saying, "Paul, Paul, we called for a doctor, but you went to the dentist instead . . . because you were only a set of teeth, man. . . ."

- At the end of the song, "Cry Baby Cry," Paul's plaintive voice can be heard singing and asking the hearer to take him back where he came from.

- In the song, "Glass Onion," John quite openly provides "another clue for you all": the walrus was Paul. As noted in connection with the *Magical Mystery Tour* album, the walrus in Scandinavian cultures, is traditionally understood to be a harbinger of death.

Yellow Submarine (released January 13th 1969 in the U.S.A. and January 17th 1969 in the U.K.)

- On the front and back album covers, John's hand (like the hand on the *Sgt. Pepper* album cover) is seen raised above Paul's head, indicating that Paul is dead.

- In the tune, "Only a Northern Song," the singer acknowledges that someone "listening late at night . . . may think the band's not quite right," and also that whoever finds the harmony "a little dark and out of key" is "correct," and that "nobody's there." The implication is that the band is "not quite right" and "nobody's there," because someone (Paul) is gone.

- In "Yellow Submarine," during the song's nautical voice section, John apparently says, "Paul is dead" and "dead man, dead man."

Abbey Road (released September 26th 1969 in the U.K and October 1st 1969 in the U.S.A.)

- On the front album cover, the Beatles walk single-file in a straight line and cross the street at a crosswalk, a formation that resembles a funeral procession. As they cross, John is dressed entirely in white (representing the priest at the funeral); Ringo is dressed entirely in black (representing the undertaker); Paul is dressed in a dark suit and he is barefoot (representing the corpse); and George is dressed in the denim clothes of a manual laborer (representing the grave-digger).

- As the four Beatles cross the street, Paul is out of step with the other three. Paul is walking with his right foot in front of him, while the other three Beatles are shown with their left feet in front.

- Paul holds a cigarette in his right hand, even though he was actually left-handed.

- In the background towards the left, there is a parked Volkswagen Beetle which has a license plate bearing the letters and numerals: "LMW 28IF." The license plate apparently reminds the viewer that Paul would have been twenty-eight years old, *if* he had not been killed. And LMW may stand for "Linda McCartney Widow."

- In the background towards the right, there is a parked police vehicle, which is a morgue wagon.

- On the back of the album cover, the word "Beatles" appears on a wall. Immediately to the left is a set of eight dots which appear to form the numeral 3, thus yielding the message: "3 Beatles."

- Immediately to the right of the word "Beatles," in the play of the light and shadows on the wall, a skull can be seen.

- In the song, "Come Together," the line "One and one and one is three" indicates that there are now only three Beatles.

Let It Be (released May 18, 1970 in the U.S.A., and November 6, 1970 in the U.K)

- On the front album cover, Paul looks straight ahead and a microphone covers part of his face, while the other Beatles appear in profile or semi-profile and their faces are not obstructed.

- The backgrounds against which the other three Beatles appear on the album cover are white backgrounds, while the background against which Paul appears is red.

- When the chorus of the song "Get Back" is played backwards, one can hear a voice saying, "I need some wheels. Help me! Help me!"

Clues in the Movies

Magical Mystery Tour (released December 26th 1967 in the U.K.)

- For clues in the *Magical Mystery Tour* movie, see the list of clues from the *Magical Mystery Tour* album (above). The album was sold with a booklet which contained still photographs taken from the movie.

Yellow Submarine (released November 13th 1968 in the U.S.A. and July 17th 1968 in the U.K.)

- When the song, "All You Need Is Love," plays in the film, John seems to sing (at the end of the song): "Yes, he's dead."

- At various points in the film, different characters can be seen with their hands raised above Paul's head (like the hand above Paul's head on the front of the *Sgt. Pepper* album cover).

The Fools on the Hill

ROBERT ARP is an Assistant Professor of Philosophy at Southwest Minnesota State University, and has authored numerous articles in philosophy of mind, philosophy of biology, and modern philosophy. His book, *Scenario Visualization: An Evolutionary Account of Creative Problem Solving*, is forthcoming. He is co-editing *Contemporary Debates in Philosophy of Biology* with Francisco Ayala and *The Ashgate Companion to Contemporary Philosophy of Biology* with George Terzis. He's not very good at math, although he does realize that one and one and one is three.

MICHAEL BAUR is Associate Professor of Philosophy at Fordham University, and Adjunct Professor of Law at Fordham Law School. He has published articles and book chapters on topics including the philosophy of law, the philosophy of popular culture, epistemology, metaphysics, and ethics, and on thinkers such as Kant, Fichte, Hegel, Aquinas, Adorno, Heidegger, and Rawls. When he was younger (so much younger than today) he played a Rickenbacker 4001 bass guitar (just like Paul in *Magical Mystery Tour*) in various cover bands. He received a Ph.D. in philosophy from the University of Toronto (where he became an expert texpert), and a J.D. from Harvard Law School (where the joker laughed at him). Through his study of philosophy, he has discovered that it really does matter whether he's wrong or right, but when he's wrong he's right where he belongs (like Socrates, he knows that he does not know). He needs the love of his wife Christine at least eight days a week.

STEVEN BAUR, at the age of six, saw the Beatles' psychedelic animated adventure, *Yellow Submarine*. His doctoral degree in Musicology from UCLA roughly twenty-five years later is the eventual result of that transformational event, and the Beatles' music has followed him here, there, and everywhere in his academic career. He has taught at Occidental College in Los Angeles and has been "Back in the UCLA" as a Visiting Assistant Professor. He currently resides among the submarines, yellow and otherwise, that frequent the Sea of Green around Nova Scotia where he is Assistant Professor in the Department of Music at Dalhousie University in Halifax (where every one of us has all we need). His primary areas of research include nineteenth-century music, American music, popular music, and cultural studies in music. He has published articles on the music of Mendelssohn, Ravel, and Starr (Ringo, that is), and his work appears in the *Journal of the American Musicological Society, American Music*, and Russell Reising, ed., *Every Sound There Is: The Beatles'* Revolver *and the Transformation of Rock and Roll* (2002). He is currently working on a book (it's taken years to write, won't you take a look) investigating the role of music in defining and negotiating class relationships in late nineteenth-century America.

PEGGY J. BOWERS became a Beatles fan before she even learned to read, with a little help from her dear older brother listening to guitars gently weep. When she got older she left home to learn to think for herself about philosophy of communication, media ethics, and First Amendment law. She has published articles and book chapters on popular culture, philosophical frameworks for media ethics, and free expression in public places. She was also briefly a journalist. Her long and winding road eventually led to Clemson University, where she is Assistant Professor of Communication Studies. She often stops and thinks about the people and things that went before.

SCOTT CALEF quit the police department and got himself a steady job. He's Associate Professor and Chair of the Department of Philosophy at Ohio Wesleyan University, but he wants to be a paperback writer. He whispers words of wisdom, and has published his work in *Ancient Philosophy, Applied Ethics, Political Philosophy*, and *Metaphysics and the Philosophy of Religion*. He once received a looking glass tie for Father's Day, and got his tan from standing in the English rain.

JAMES CROOKS followed the long and winding road that leads to gainful employment as far as Bishop's University in Lennoxville, Quebec. He currently bags production in the Departments of Philosophy, Music, Liberal Arts and (occasionally) Drama. A generalist by choice and by nature, he has published articles here, there and everywhere on Nietzsche, Heidegger, Hegel, Plato, and Heraclitus. He's been working for a while now on an ethics of accommodation, the central claim of which (expressed succinctly) is that we're on our way home.

DAVID DETMER is Professor of Philosophy at Purdue University Calumet. He is the author of *Sartre Explained* (forthcoming), *Challenging Postmodernism: Philosophy and the Politics of Truth* (2003), and

Freedom as a Value: A Critique of the Ethical Theory of Jean-Paul Sartre (1988), as well as essays on a variety of philosophical topics. He denies the vicious rumor that he was the inspiration for the song "Mean Mr. Mustard."

ALEXANDER R. EODICE is Dean of the School of Arts and Science and Professor of Philosophy at Iona College. With a passion for Beatles music and professional interests in such fields as epistemology, philosophy of language and the philosophy of law, both his musical and philosophical sensibilities have been shaped by British invasions. His administrative responsibilities keep him busy eight days a week, and after a hard day's night in the office, he likes to strum his Martin guitar or bang out Beatles songs on a baby grand, and sometimes, in the evening, he's a singer with the band. He and his wife, Liz, live in New Rochelle, New York, where they have built a home sweet home with a couple of kids—Sarah and Annie—running in the yard.

RICHARD FALKENSTEIN remembers receiving the first recording he ever owned, *The Beatles' Second Album* (the U.S. release on Capitol), as a gift. He quickly learned to sing the entire album by memory. He bought *Abbey Road* as soon as it hit the record store, and after repeatedly listening to it, he taught himself to play all of its songs on the guitar. His musical career also has included some other notable achievements since these early milestones. He has performed on guitar and lute in France, Poland, the former Soviet Union, South America, and Puerto Rico, as well as in the midwestern and eastern United States and Canada. He has also made two recordings (on New World Records and Centaur) with the Buffalo Guitar Quartet. He received a Ph.D. in musicology from the State University of New York at Buffalo, and has published on topics relating to European lute music. He is currently Assistant Professor of Fine Arts in the Music Program at Canisius College in Buffalo, New York.

JACOB M. HELD is Assistant Professor of Philosophy at the University of Central Arkansas in Conway, Arkansas, where he lives with his wife and two kids. Apparently, even if you read Chairman Mao you can make it with someone, anyhow. He is co-editor of *James Bond and Philosophy: Questions Are Forever* (2006) and has published in such scholarly journals as *Journal for the British Society of Phenomenology* and *Vera Lex*. His research interests include political and social philosophy, philosophy of law, and Marx. He is currently working on issues related to the concept of recognition in Marx and Marxism. And he sincerely wants a revolution so long as he can keep his job, minivan, and house in the suburbs.

Joseph A. Hoffheimer is currently incarcerated at Oxford High School in Oxford, Mississippi and will be eligible for parole in May of 2007. Like many inmates, he's not sure what he wants to do after he gets out of the cooler. He can play several instruments, but currently just plays the clarinet with which he is first chair in the state. Joseph likes most types of music except for country (Ringo would not be proud). His favorite song by George is "While My Guitar Gently Weeps," and his favorite other Beatles song is "Norwegian Wood."

Michael H. Hoffheimer keeps a day job as Professor of Law at the University of Mississippi School of Law. He credits the Beatles for his survival to adulthood and thanks George for inspiring a passion for idealist philosophy—and an addiction to Bollywood. His books and articles are flowing out like endless rain on topics from criminal law and legal philosophy to Hegel and blues. He plays a Les Paul.

Erin Kealey went through a long, cold, lonely winter of working as a litigation paralegal after college, where Ms. K. did nothing to challenge the world. One day, years since she saw the sun, she started reading Kant's Third Critique. The ice has been slowly melting ever since, and she has received Master's degrees in Liberal Studies and Philosophy from Georgetown University and Boston College. She is currently enrolled in the Philosophy and Literature Ph.D. Program at Purdue University. She hopes to be a professor by the time she's sixty-four. Until then, her life goes on, bra . . ., and she swears her plans are not for nobody.

Rick Mayock is an Associate Professor of Philosophy at West Los Angeles College. In addition to teaching and fixing metaphysical holes, he plays guitar and writes music, and once performed in a Beatles cover duo called "The Fab Two." His songwriting influences include John Lennon, Paul McCartney, and Friedrich Nietzsche. When he is not teaching and performing in the Los Angeles area, he sometimes plays music with a little help from his friends: the West Side Blues Band, in his home town of Wilkes-Barre, where he can always get back to where he once belonged.

James B. South is Chair of the Philosophy Department at Marquette University. He edited *Buffy the Vampire Slayer and Philosophy* (2003) and co-edited *James Bond and Philosophy* (2006). He's also written essays for *Woody Allen and Philosophy* (2004) and *Superheroes and Philosophy* (2005). He primarily works in late medieval and renaissance philosophy, but makes increasingly frequent forays into popular culture. James agrees with Martin Amis that to hate the mid-period

Beatles is to hate life itself, and he can't believe that he got to quote his favorite Beatles lyric ("Beep beep m'beep beep yeah!") in a philosophy article.

JAMES S. SPIEGEL is Professor of Philosophy and Religion at Taylor University. His books include *How to Be Good in a World Gone Bad* (2004) and *The Benefits of Providence* (2005), and he has published numerous journal articles on issues in ethics, aesthetics, and philosophy of religion. He performs these scholarly tricks without a sound. When his prized possessions start to wear him down, Jim takes time for a number of things, such as writing and recording his own music. He would also like to paint his room in a colorful way, but he's old enough to know better.

JERE O'NEILL SURBER paid his way through college "doing it" in Southwestern bars with a roadhouse rock band. His long and winding road led through classics and philosophical studies at the Pennsylvania State University and the Rheinische Universität in Bonn, to a position at the University of Denver, where he's currently Professor of Philosophy and Cultural Studies. Between continuing to play a few gigs, serving as a travel guide, and captaining some sailing vessels, he's managed to write books and articles on German Idealist philosophy, poststructuralism, and cultural theory. In the last few years, he's come to share George's love for Ravi and the sitar.

PAUL A. SWIFT teaches philosophy, literature, and writing in the Cultural Studies Department at Bryant University. He is the author of *Becoming Nietzsche* (2005) and has contributed articles to the *Chronicle of Higher Education, International Studies in Philosophy*, and other publications. As a soloist and songwriter for Aardvark Spleen, he has performed numerous Beatles songs and employs music to teach critical thinking.

JOHN ZEIS, besides being Professor of Philosophy at Canisius College, has been a recreational guitarist since 1963. His musical destiny was set from the moment he saw a film clip of the Beatles on the *Jack Paar Show*, which was their first appearance on American TV. When he realized that he would never make it as a musician, he went on to study philosophy; but he still plays Beatles songs at parties for friends and family. He and his wife produced their own Fab Four (four sons) who grew up as Beatles fans and have recently twisted their Dad's arm to form a blues band with them. Although his wife is not in the band, she never fails to remind John that it was she, not he, who saw the Beatles perform in Toronto in 1966.

RONALD LEE ZIGLER realized that it really *is* all within himself during the summer of 1968. Upon making this discovery, and becoming one of the many underachieving beautiful people of his generation, he decided to become a proper educator and to teach what he had learned. He spent five months of study with Maharishi on the island of Mallorca, and followed this with four years in graduate school at the University of Cincinnati where he studied moral development and the philosophy of moral education. He subsequently made a career out of examining the common ground underlying concepts from eastern and western philosophy, and pursuing research on the mind-body problem—especially as it pertains to moral growth and development. Examples of his efforts have appeared in *Educational Theory*, the *Journal of Moral Education,* and *Journal of Beliefs and Values.* Twenty-five years after completing graduate school (by most standards, a long, long, *long* time for such an endeavor), his labors finally paid off when he was promoted, with tenure, to Associate Professor at Penn State Abington. So while he has finally become a rich man, too, he has learned that it is just not of the monetary kind.

ABCD, Can I Bring Some Philosophers to Tea?

Abbey Road (album), 14, 52, 126, 159, 199, 241
"Across the Universe" (song), 122, 123, 128, 146, 147–48
and Eastern philosophy, 148
agape, 41
alienation (Marx), 89
Allen, Woody, 129
"All I've Got to Do" (song), 232–33
"All My Loving" (song), 38
"All Together Now" (song), 18
"All You Need Is Love" (song), 18, 46, 75, 150, 239
Alpert, Richard, 19, 142
The Psychedelic Experience, 19, 140, 141
American consumerism, 73
"And Your Bird Can Sing" (song), 84, 172
annihilation of selfhood, problem of 19–20
"Another Girl" (song), 82
the Apollonian, 207
Apple Records, 92
Aristotle, 177, 208
on contemplative life, 51
on friendship, 39–40
on Friendship of Pleasure, 44
on Friendship of Virtue, 44
on happiness, 49–51
on honor, 50
on justice, 56

on love, 39
on money, 50
Nicomachean Ethics, 49, 74
on pride, 53
on vice, 53, 54
on virtue, 58–59
Asher, Jane, 38, 44
Aunt Mimi, 57
authenticity
difficulty of, 118
throwing forward in, 118
authentic meaning, 110

"Back in the USA" (song), 101
"Back in the USSR" (song), 101
bad faith, 132
"The Ballad of John and Yoko" (song), 58, 160, 161
The Beach Boys (band), 96
Beatle Burnings, 211
Beatlemania, 51, 126
and the Dionysian, 207, 208
Beatles
and altered states of consciousness, 151, 153–54, 156, 159
as anti-philosophical, 13
beginning of, 59
as breaking down musical barriers, 238, 239
as celebration of love, 184–85

class background of, 87
as collecting experiences, 204
and counterculture, 43, 97–99
and critical consciousness, 98–99,
     158
difference of, 232
as Dionysian, 205, 207
disintegration of, 240
Dylan's influence on, 97, 109
early setting of, 60
and Eastern culture and
     mysticism, 63, 139–140
and existentialism, 156
exploitation of, 90, 97
feminine sensibility of, 60
folk music's influence on, 97–98
in Hamburg, 90
as hard-working, 96–97
humor of, 209
image forming of, 95
as integrated group, 234, 237
on interpersonal communication,
     159
and LSD, 139, 144, 204
material circumstances of, 89
meta-narrative of, 176, 184
in motion, 235
and Nietzsche, comparing, 214,
     215
in 1924, 96–97
optimism of, 176–77, 184–85
pacifism of, 105
and philosophical
     postmodernism, 176
philosophical turn of, 109
playfulness of, 180
and *The Psychedelic Experience*,
     influence of, 140
as radical, 206
as recording artists, 238–39
re-invention of, 200
and tension between material
desires and creativity, 73
and value of interpersonal
     relationships, 29
wit of, 58
The Beatles (album), 100, 101
The Beatles Anthology, 37, 39
Beatles' career, negotiation of, 104

Beatles for Sale (album), 97
Beatles songs and music
in advertisements, 92
alienation in, 177–78
as art, 229, 230, 234, 242, 243
on belief, importance of, 3
call to authenticity in, 117–123
capitalist critiques in, 100
changes in, 237
community in, 34–35
compositional style of, 239
co-optation of, 104–05
as crossing categories, 242
discordancy in, 68
early, 95–96, 234
and Eastern thought, 142, 146,
     147, 148–49
emotive force in, 62
empriricism in, 5
ethical vision of interconnection
     in, 60
and ethic of care, 61, 68–69
and ethic of recognition, 70
and everydayness of philosophy,
     169–170
evolution of, 236
and Existentialism, 131–32
female icons in, 64–65
feminine sensibility in, 63, 65
and feminist philosophy, 61
and idealism, 16–17
idealistic monism in, 14, 16, 18,
     23–24
incorporating coincidence and
mistakes, 22–23
interdependency themes in, 62, 65
love as theme in, 27, 46
     maturing of, 27–28
meaning in, 14
on meaninglessness, 112
moderate skepticism in, 4, 6
money and love in, 76
narrative strategies in, 66–67
nonsense lyrics in, 13
ownership of, 91
pathos in, 64
and philosophy, 15
on pursuit of stuff, as tedious,
     84–85

self as illusion in, 182–83
as soul music, 233
and struggle against
  inauthenticity, 111–18
unity as theme in, 27
virtue and vice in, 58
The Beatles: The Rough Guide, 156
"Because" (song), 241
"Being for the Benefit of Mr. Kite"
  (song), 228
Bergson, Henri, 143, 144
Berlin, Isaiah
  on negative and positive liberty,
    33–34
Berry, Chuck, 101
Bhagavad-Gita, 144, 145, 147–48
"Blackbird" (song), 121, 131
Bloom, Allan, 230
"Blue Jay Way" (song), 134
Brahman, 143, 144, 145, 146, 148
Branch Davidians, 159
Blue Meanies, 157
brain and nervous system, as
  eliminative, 143
Broad, C.D., 143
Brown, Norman O., 152
Brown, Peter, 92
Brown, Tara, 84
Burroughs, William, 158
Bush, George W., 212

"Can't Buy Me Love" (song), 50, 76
capitalism, and self-worth, 76–71
care ethic, 60, 61, 66, 69
Carpenters (band), 94
Chandogya Upanishad, 149
Carroll, Lewis, 227
Clapton, Eric, 5, 126, 133
Cleave, Maureen, 210–11
"Come Together" (song), 66, 92,
  159
Concert for George, 241
consciousness
  altered states of, 152
    ethical question of, 160–61
  and awareness of unity, problem
    of, 21
  as intentional, 20–21

"normal," question of, 154–55,
  159
observed, 15
observing, 15
philosophical thought on, 151–52
"rational," question of, 155, 159
consumer culture, 73–74, 76–71
  and appearance, 77
  danger of, 74
  effect on human psyche, 80
  ego in, 83
  isolation in, 79
consumer-inspired conformity, as
  bad for art, 78
counterculture, 158
  counter-movement against,
    159–160
  height of, 99
  rise of, 97
critical thought, reasons for
  engaging in, 10, 11

Darwin, Charles, 209
Dasein, 110, 116
Dass, Baba Ram, 140
The Dave Clark Five, 96
Davies, Hunter, 126
"A Day in the Life" (song), 23, 68,
  85, 112, 156, 196, 239
  blurring of dream and reality, 198
  song within a song, 197–98
"Day Tripper" (song), 85
Dean, James, 133
"Dear Friend" (song), 45
"Dear Prudence" (song), 54, 118
Decade of Free Love, 37
deconstruction, 180, 181
Deleuze, Gilles, 182
  Anti-Oedipus, 183
  Dialogues, 183
  A Thousand Plateaus, 183
Delta Blues, 62
Derrida, Jacques, 176, 180, 181
Descartes, René, 151, 152, 153, 155,
  159, 161, 177, 179, 225, 231
  Meditations, 223
Descombes, Vincent, 179
dialectical materialism, 89

the Dionysian, 206–07
  and music, 207
Dionysus, 207
Dixie Chicks, 212
"Don't Bother Me" (song), 133
Doors (band), 111, 205
Dostoievsky, Fyodor, 208
"Drive My Car" (song), 50, 76, 173
dualism, 231, 235
  primacy of mental in, 224
Dylan, Bob, 3, 97, 98, 109

Eastern philosophy, 139
economic base (Marx), 88
"Eleanor Rigby" (song), 28, 68, 115,
  131, 156
Eliade, Mircea, 152
Elliott, Anthony, 66
Empedocles, 45
  on Love and Strife, 40
empiricism, 5
  limitations of, 5
"The End" (song), 14, 46, 241–42
  as bridging styles, 241–42
Engels, Friedrich, 93, 103
Epictetus, 169, 170, 172
  Discourses, 171
  on freedom, 171
epistemology, 3
Epstein, Brian, 90, 95, 238
Eros, 38
essentialism, 233
eudaimonia, 50
Everett, Betty, 96
"Everybody's Got Something to
  Hide Except for Me and My
  Monkey" (song), 58, 77
Existential *Angst*, 129, 132
Existentialism, 125, 129, 133, 155

fallacy of positive instances, 6
fallenness, elements of, 122
false consciousness, 88, 96
Farrow, Mia, 54
Farrow, Prudence, 54, 118
feminist ethic of care, 60, 61, 66, 69
"Fixing a Hole" (song), 118, 195

dark turn in, 196
  riddle of, 189–190, 191, 199, 201
Flynn, Erin, 83
Fonda, Peter, 20, 144
"The Fool on the Hill" (song), 117,
  123, 146, 166–67
  and meditation, 147
Form of Beauty, 39
Forms, 81, 82
"For You Blue" (song), 127
Foucault, Michel, 152, 179
  Madness and Civilization, 176
Frankfurt School of Critical Theory,
  155, 156–57
  and Counterculture, 157
  on instrumental reason, 157
Franklin, Aretha, 68
freedom, as state of mind, 171
Freud, Sigmund, 61, 125, 126, 152
"From Me to You" (song), 43
Fromm, Erich, 35
Frost, David, 46

Gandhi, Mohandas K., 214
Genesis (Biblical), 193
German idealism, 21
"Get Back" (song), 66
"Getting Better" (song), 52, 92, 196
Gibbard, Allan, 64
Gilligan, Carol, 60–62, 69
  critique of, 64
Ginsberg, Allen, 133
"Girl" (song), 75, 76
"Give Peace a Chance" (song), 46
"Glass Onion" (song), 13, 180, 184
"Glass Onion effect," 181
"God" (song), 11
Goethe, Wolfgang, 134
"Good Day Sunshine" (song), 63
"Good Morning, Good Morning"
  (song), 100, 111
"Goodnight" (song), 240
Gramsci, Antonio, 95
Grant, Hugh, 32
Grateful Dead (band), 152, 205
Greek tragedies, 208
Guattari, Felix, 182
  Anti-Oedipus, 183

A Thousand Plateaus, 183
gurus and leaders, as fallible, 8–9

Hamlet, 197
Hanslick, Eduard, 235–36, 242
  On the Musically Beautiful,
    235
A Hard Day's Night (album), 237
A Hard Day's Night (film), 77, 235,
  236
"A Hard Day's Night" (song), 76,
  237
  and world of work, 96
Harrison, George, 5, 8, 23, 53, 59,
  81, 82, 100, 125, 144–46, 149,
  150, 172, 182, 200, 241
  autobiography, 63
  on Beatlemania, 51
  on ego, 133
  and Existentialism, 130, 133
  family background of, 125–26
  in A Hard Day's Night, 77–78
  light imagery in, 134–35
  on problem of desire, 83
  and religion, 127
  and Sartre, comparing, 135
  on self, 134
  and sitar music, 127–28
  on "Tomorrow Never Knows,"
    144
Hegel, Georg Wilhelm Friedrich, 15,
  29, 35
  on ethical community, 30
  on freedom, 33
  on interpersonal relationships, 30,
    32
  on intersubjectivity, 30
  on love, 32–33
  on master-slave dialectic, 30–31
  as positive libertarian, 34
Heidegger, Martin, 129, 152, 153,
  176, 179
  Being and Time, 109, 110, 155
  on consciousness, 155–56
  on Dasein, 110
  on discourse, 112
  on fallenness, 113
  on finite freedom, 120–21
  on inauthenticity, 113
  on moodedness, 114
  on ownmost potential, 116
  on reticence, 118
  on thrownness, 111
  on uncanniness, 119
Help! (album), 98, 237
Help! (film), 127, 140
"Help" (song), 62, 92, 119, 220
"Helter Skelter" (song), 158, 201,
  240
Hendrix, Jimi, 205
Heraclitus, 195
"Here Comes the Sun" (song), 63,
  126, 134–35, 159, 241
"Here, There, and Everywhere"
  (song), 65, 154
Hertsgaard, Mark, 42
Hesiod
  Theogony, 38
"Hey Bulldog" (song), 22, 77
"Hey Jude" (song), 64, 69, 77, 101,
  240
"Hey Jude effect," 184
historical materialism, 88, 101
"Hold Me Tight" (song), 43
Honneth, Axel
  on spheres of recognition, 35
Horn, Paul, 9n
"Hound Dog" (song), 232
"Howl" (song), 133
Howlin' Wolf, 232
Hughes, Howard, 53
Hume, David, 161
Husserl, Edmund, 152
Huxley, Aldous, 143–44, 147, 158
  The Doors of Perception, 140, 143

"I Am the Walrus" (song), 27, 182,
  183, 184, 219, 226, 228
  and Vedanta, 149
I Ching, 23
idealistic monism, 14, 16, 17, 18
"I Feel Fine" (song), 22
"If I Needed Someone" (song), 19,
  133
"I'll Be Back" (song), 237
"I'll Cry Instead" (song), 55

"Imagine" (song), 103
"I'm a Loser" (song), 5, 220
"I'm Down" (song), 76
"I Me Mine" (song), 115, 116, 122, 134, 182
"I'm Happy Just to Dance with You" (song), 235
"I'm Only Sleeping" (song), 77, 85, 99, 154, 224
inauthenticity
   on death, 120
   in everyday existence, 110
Indian philosophy
   Vedanta branch, 142
"In My Life" (song), 66, 84, 154, 220
"The Inner Light" (song), 18, 19, 128, 134, 149
"Instant Karma" (song), 128
instrumental reason, 157
intellectual property, 91
interpersonal relationships, value of, 29
"I Saw Her Standing There" (song), 43, 235
Isley Brothers, 232
"It's All Too Much" (song), 83, 146
"I've Got a Feeling" (song), 116
"I've Just Seen a Face" (song), 117, 123
"I Want to Hold your Hand" (song), 234
"I Want to Tell You" (song), 165
   me/my mind distinction in, 168–69, 172
   as philosophical exercise, 172
"I Want You" (song), 241
"I Will" (song), 45

Jagger, Mick, 133, 232
"Jai Guru Dev," 148
James, Elmore, 127
Janov, Arthur, 9
Jefferson Airplane, 152
Jones, Jim, 159
Joyce, James
   Finnegans Wake, 227
Jung, Carl G., 19
justice, as virtue, 56

Kant, Immanuel, 41, 49, 152, 160, 166–67, 177, 180, 231
   on conscience, 168
   The Metaphysics of Morals, 167
   on practical philosophy, 167
   on space and time, 196
   What Is Ancient Philosophy?, 167
Karwowski, Michael, 44
Kesey, Ken, 152
Kierkegaard, Sᵒren, 129
King, Martin Luther, 214
King Lear (Shakespeare), 229
Kohlberg, Lawrence, 60, 61
Kozinn, Allan, 63
Ku Klux Klan, 211

Lacan, Jacques, 152
"Lady Madonna" (song), 67
Lear, Edward, 227
Leary, Timothy, 19, 98, 152, 158
   on LSD, 141
   The Psychedelic Experience, 19, 140, 141, 142, 154
Lennon, Cynthia
   A Twist of Lennon, 55
Lennon, John, 9, 41, 43, 54, 55, 56, 59, 61, 66, 73, 75, 76, 77, 81, 84, 85, 100, 128, 142, 146–49, 172, 180, 190, 198, 200, 204, 208
   apology of, 211–12
   arrest of, 159–160
   on the Beatles, 231
   on Beatles lyrics, 219
   on Beatles's popularity, 197, 210
      furor over, 211
   on Christianity, 210
   on class system, 104–05
   as dangerous force, 213
   in David Frost interview, 46
   on "A Day in the Life," 198
   death of, 175, 176
   deportation of, 104
   disbelief, of, 11
   as dreamer, 206
   and dream states, 224
   on fame and money, 51
   FBI files on, 98

fear of abandonment, 125
on God, 211
on "I Am the Walrus," 219, 228
In His Own Write, 227, 228
and inner states, 224–25
on leaders, 10
on "Lucy in the Sky with
    Diamonds," 139, 212
lyrical writing, analysis of,
    220–23, 225–27
on the Maharishi, 9, 53
and Marxism, ambivalence over,
    101–02
Marx's influence on, 103
most creative period, 237
and Nietzsche, differences
    between, 214
and nonsense lyrics, 13, 227
on not fitting in, 7
on "Nowhere Man," 179
as philosopher, 206, 213
in *Playboy* interview, 14
and political activism,
    ambivalence to, 177
on *The Psychedelic Experience*,
    140, 141
response to Peter Fonda, 20
on rock'n'roll, 241, 243
and Sartre, comparing, 130–31
"Sexy Sadie," meaning of, 53
seminal song writing of, 220
skepticism of, 8–9, 225
solipsism in, 225–26
A Spaniard in the Works, 227
subjective perspective of, 222
Lennon, Julia, 65
Lennon, Sean, 212
Leonard, Hal, 230
Let It Be (album), 111, 240, 241
"Let It Be" (song), 64, 122
Let It Be: Naked (album), 241
liberty, negative and positive, 34
Little Richard, 232
"Long, Long, Long" (song), 128
"Long Tall Sally" (song), 232
love
    and community, structural
        requirements for, 28–29
    erotic, 38, 39

as necessary, 33
philial, 39
as prescriptive, 35
Stoics on, 41
in western philosophy, 38–42
"Love Me Do" (song), 13, 234
"Love You To" (song), 128, 134
"Lucy in the Sky with Diamonds"
    (song), 117, 139, 153, 212

Magical Mystery Tour (film), 182
Maharishi Mahesh Yogi, 8, 53, 127,
    139, 147, 204
das Man, 109–110
Mann, Manfred, 96
Manson family, 158, 201
Marcuse, Herbert, 157–58
    An Essay on Liberation, 158
    and Counterculture, 157–58
Martin, George, 197, 229, 234, 235,
    239
Marx, Karl, 35, 87–88, 92, 96, 100,
    103, 208
    on class antagonism, 88–89
    on dominant ideology, 93
    on economic factors, 88
    The German Ideology, 93
    on ideas, control of, 93
    as influence on counterculture, 98
    on labor, in industrial society, 89
    on the ruling class, 93
    Theses on Feuerbach, 88
    on violent revolution, 101
Marxist theory, on popular culture,
    93–94, 102
"Maxwell's Silver Hammer" (song),
    58
maya, 128, 143, 145
"Maybe I'm Amazed" (song), 45, 46
McCartney, Linda, 39, 43, 44–45, 61
McCartney, Mary, 65
McCartney, Paul, 41, 54, 59, 61, 62,
    73, 76, 77, 89, 101, 131, 146,
    165, 184, 200, 232
    on Apple Records, 92
    bass work of, 238
    on Beatles' songs, 14, 37, 227
    "death"of, rumor of, 275–284

in "A Day in the Life," 198
family characters in his songs, 126
in "Fixing a Hole," 196
on "The Fool on the Hill," 147
in "Let It Be," 64
on *Let It Be*, 241
on "Love Me Do," 13
love songs of, 38, 45–46
    early, 42–43
on "Lucy in the Sky with
Diamonds," 139
lyrical style of, 223
on the 1920s, 39
on problem of desire, 83
on *Sgt. Pepper*, 192
McKinney, Devin, 60
"Mean Mister Mustard" (song), 52,
    79
meditation, in Yoga Philosophy, 146
mental, primacy of, 224
meta-narrative, 175
Metzner, Richard
    The Psychedelic Experience, 19,
        140, 141, 142
"Michelle" (song), 44
Mill, John Stuart, 49
Mills, Heather, 46
moderate skepticism, 4, 12
    reasons for, 6, 12
modesty, as virtue, 54
"Money" (song), 50
monism, 14
music
    as art, 233–34
    and the Dionysian, 207
"My Love" (song), 45
"My Sweet Lord" (song), 128

Nagel, Thomas, 220, 221–22
naive realism, 16
negative liberty, 34
Nietzsche, Friedrich, 152, 177
    on academic philosophers,
        227–28
    Beyond Good and Evil, 189
    Birth of Tragedy, 203, 206
    on Christianity, 197
    on columbarian, 200

on the Dionysian, 204–07
on dogmatic philosophers, 191,
    195
Ecce Homo, 200
on genuine philosophers, 205–06,
    213
on idols, 197
on metaphysics, 190
on music, 206
on philosophers, 203
on philosophy, 189, 190, 213
    and music, 203–04
on reality, as selective, 194
on religion, 208
Schopenhauer as Educator, 213
Thus Spake Zarathustra, 209
on truth, 201
on will to truth, 189, 192, 198
nirvana, 141
Nixon, Richard, 213
Noah (Biblical), 193
"No Reply" (song), 55
"Norwegian Wood" (song), 128, 132,
    140
"Nowhere Man" (song), 6, 116, 156,
    167, 179, 184, 194, 220
    and objectivity, concept of, 221
*NSYNC (band), 78
"Number Nine" (song), 81

objectivity, 221
    and subjectivity, connection
    between, 221–22
ocean consciousness, 19
"An Octopus's Garden" (song), 159,
    241
Oedipus, 201
"Oh Darling" (song), 62, 63, 241
"Only a Northern Song" (song), 53,
    78, 114
Ono, Yoko, 11, 55, 61, 101, 200

"Paint It Black" (song), 133
"Paperback Writer" (song), 19, 79
Parnet, Claire
    Dialogues, 183
"The Party" (film), 128

"Paul Is Dead" clues, 275–284
"Penny Lane" (song), 119
perceptual bias, 6
phenomenology, 141–42
philia, 39
philosophical modernism, as
    revolutionary, 177–78
philosophical postmodernism, 177,
    181, 182
    as ambivalent, 177
    pessimism of, 176, 184
    problems of, 179–180
philosophical style, types of, 169
philosophy
    and applied philosophy,
        distinction between, 166
    everydayness of, 169, 170
    meaning of word, 39
    and popular culture, 15
    as speculation, 166
Pickett, Wilson, 233
"Piggies" (song), 58, 100–01, 127, 156
Plato, 49, 81, 82, 177, 191, 195, 242
    on art, 64
    on Beauty, 43–44
    dualism of, 231
    on love, 43–44
    Symposium, 39, 82
Platonic relationship, 39
Pleasantville (film), 42
Plutarch, 169, 170
popular culture
    paradox, 104
    and philosophy, 15
popular music, pop music
    contradiction in, 94
    love in, 66
    Marxist theory on, 93–94
    negotiative aspect of, 95
    in 1924, 96
    as ritualistic, 235
positive liberty, 34
postmodernism, political mandate
    for, 183
postmodern philosophers,
    pessimism of, 176
postmodern world, 176
post-structuralism, 182, 183
"Power to the People" (song), 103

Presley, Elvis, 232
primal scream therapy, 9
private property, effect on
    relationships, 75–76
problem of incompleteness, 189,
    198
Protagoras, 191, 192
"P.S. I Love You" (song), 45

Quarry Men (band), 59, 125

"Rain" (song), 16–17, 74, 114, 171
    'I' in, 169–170
realism
    naive, 16
    as non-monistic, 17–18
    strong conception of, 221
reality, as selective, 194
Rebel Without a Cause (film), 133
"Revolution" (song), 12, 58, 92,
    101–02, 131, 150, 177, 184
"Revolution #9" (song), 101–02,
    240
"Revolution #1" (song), 66, 101–02
Revolver (album), 99, 140, 144, 153,
    154, 156, 238
Richards, Keith, 133, 232
"Riders on the Storm" (song), 111
Roberts, Julia, 32
Robinson, Smokey, 233
rock'n'roll
    as motion, 235
    roots of, 232
    and working class, 95
Rolling Stones (band), 232
Rousseau, Jean-Jacques, 67, 77
    on consumer society, 74–75
    on human nature, 80
    on inequality, 79
    on private property, 75
Royce, Josiah, 18
    The World and the Individual,
        17
Rubber Soul (album), 81, 98, 140,
    153, 156
    as change in style, 237–38
"Run for Your Life" (song), 55, 75

Sartre, Jean-Paul, 129, 154
  on bad faith, 132
  Being and Nothingness, 129
  on existence, 130
  on freedom, 131
  on history, 132
  on imagination, 130–31
Sat-Chit-Ananda, 147
"Savoy Truffle" (song), 126, 129
Schelling, Friedrich
  on consciousness and unity,
    21–22
Schopenhauer, Arthur, 206, 209
Scruton, Roger, 233
self-interest
  in Anglo–American tradition, 28
  in contemporary society, 29
Sellers, Peter, 128
Sex Pistols (band), 60, 94
"Sexy Sadie" (song), 8
  meaning of, 53
*Sgt. Pepper's Lonely Hearts Club
  Band* (album), 13, 63, 87, 99,
    140, 153, 156, 192, 196
  as amalgam of styles, 238–39
  nostalgia in, 126
  significance of, 240
Shankar, Ravi, 127, 128
"She Loves You" (song), 175, 234, 240
"She Said, She Said" (song), 20, 224,
    226
  and LSD, 144
"She's a Woman" (song), 45
"She's Leaving Home" (song), 57,
    64, 76, 84, 119
skepticism, moderate, 4, 6, 12
Small, Little Millie, 96
Socrates, 203, 212
solipsism, epistemological, 225
"Something" (song), 126, 136, 241
Sony Corporation, 91, 92
Spice Girls (band), 78
Starr, Ringo, 46, 54, 180, 198, 200,
    204n, 241
Star Trek (TV show), 179
Stoics, on love, 41
"Strawberry Fields Forever" (song),
    7, 16–17, 82, 114, 155, 172, 224,
    225

Summer of Love, 99
superstructure (Marx), 88
surplus value (Marx), 89
surrendering to the void, 143–44
synesthesia, 225

Tao Te Ching, 150
"Taxman" (song), 56, 92
"Things We Said Today" (song), 45
"Think for Yourself" (song), 134
thinking for oneself, importance of,
    10
"This Boy" (song), 233
Thornton, Big Mama, 232
Tibetan Book of the Dead, 63,
    140–41, 148
Tolstoy, Leo
  What Is Art?, 78–79
"Tomorrow Never Knows" (song),
    18, 19, 46, 82, 99, 120, 121,
    140, 142, 154, 224, 225
  and Eastern philosophy, 134
  and *Vedanta*, 143
Townsend, Pete, 126
"Twist and Shout" (song), 232, 237
"Two of Us" (song), 44, 45, 131, 132

Unheimlichkeit, 119

Vedanta, 142, 143, 144, 145, 148
vice, examples of, 52–58
virtue, 52
  examples of, 52–58
  intellectual, 51–52
  moral, 52
virtue ethics, 49

Wagner, Richard, 206
War on Drugs, 159
Warwick, Jacqueline, 68
Watts, Alan, 127
"We Can Work It Out" (song), 32,
    84
"What Is Life?" (song), 135
"When I Get Home" (song), 233

"When I'm Sixty–Four" (song), 62, 92

"While My Guitar Gently Weeps" (song), 81, 121, 122, 130, 133, 135
inspiration for, 23

White Album, 44, 54, 81, 100, 156, 159, 177, 198
fragmentation in, 240

"Why Don't We Do It in the Road?" (song), 54, 240

Wings (band), 44, 200

wit, as virtue, 57

"With a Little Help from My Friends" (song), 60

"Within You Without You" (song), 18, 32, 50, 63–64, 82, 84, 113, 121, 128, 130, 135, 145–46, 182
on illusion, 3
and *Vedanta*, 145

Wittgenstein, Ludwig, 227, 228, 231
Philosophical Investigations, 229, 234

women, relegated to private sphere, 67

Wonderwall (album), 128

"The Word" (song), 19, 46, 65, 132

"Working Class Hero" (song), 103

Yellow Submarine (film), 53, 146, 157, 158

"Yer Blues" (song), 240

"Yesterday" (song), 44, 62, 119
as milestone, 237

Yoga Philosophy, 146, 148

"You Can't Do That" (song), 55, 233

"You Know My Name" (song), 58

"You Like Me Too Much" (song), 133

"You Won't See Me" (song), 165, 168
'I' in, 170

Zarathustra, 196, 200

Zeno of Citium, 41